PENGUIN VEER

INDIA'S SECRET WAR

Ushinor Majumdar is an award-winning investigative reporter and author. He has worked as a staff writer for magazines, newspapers and websites, including *Outlook*, *Tehelka*, Confluence Media and *Hindustan Times*. His reports as a freelancer have appeared in the *Mumbai Mirror*, OCCRP and *Caravan*, among other publications, and he has been published in several languages in India and abroad. He has also consulted with the BBC and many other media outlets. He has collaborated with multiple global media outlets on cross-border investigative stories. Ushinor has taught investigative reporting as visiting faculty at a private Indian university and conducted several workshops for working journalists. He is also an executive committee member of the media non-profit Foundation for Media Professionals. He is the author of *God of Sin: The Cult, Clout and Downfall of Asaram Bapu*, published by Penguin Random House India in 2018.

ADVANCE PRAISE FOR THE BOOK

'Ushinor Majumdar's book captures India's "secret war" in graphic detail. There are interesting stories of valour and heroism of the BSF officers in what was a very challenging situation. It shows how a fledgling force can produce remarkable results under good leadership and with full political support. The book is a valuable addition to the literature on the subject'— Prakash Singh, former director general, BSF

'Majumdar has made a mark with his investigative, granular journalism. He brings a forensic expertise to this remarkable story, seldom told, of the background and on-ground operational aspects of the Border Security Force's engagement with the birth of Bangladesh. Not many realize it, but for close to a year, the BSF acted as border guards for two countries: India and Bangladesh-in-the-making. This is that story'—Sudeep Chakravarti, author of *The Bengalis*, *Red Sun*, *Highway 39*, *Plassey* and *The Eastern Gate*

'Ushinor Majumdar is a meticulous reader, and a granular researcher who relishes finding truths and has made primary sources his beat. He is moving against the current for quick, paid-for takes, preferring archives to cable news studios. He is also invariably out in the field, with officers and officials, aid workers and citizens. Wherever they live and work, Majumdar locates their stories and then has the craft to tell them in ways that are often startling and always compelling'—Adrian Levy, Emmy-winning writer and producer, and co-author of *Spy Stories* and *The Exile*

'Ushinor has done an incredible job of adding significant new information to what the world knows about the 1971 operations that led to the birth of Bangladesh, remapped South Asia and sent a resounding warning to autocrats that their oppressive methods wouldn't last forever. A must-read for anyone interested in the contemporary world'—Josy Joseph, author of *A Feast of Vultures* and *The Silent Coup*

'Journalist and author Ushinor Majumdar's war thriller book is the first critical book-length account unfolding a little-known, vast array of clandestine operations, and illuminating brilliantly the BSF's contribution in the Bangladesh liberation war. The author blends gripping historical narrative with consummate skill. The book will offer readers thrilling, captivating and unprecedented stories'—Col Guru Saday Batabyal (retd), military historian and author of *Politico-Military Strategy of the Bangladesh Liberation War, 1971*

India's Secret War

BSF AND NINE MONTHS TO THE BIRTH OF BANGLADESH

USHINOR MAJUMDAR

PENGUIN
VEER
An imprint of Penguin Random House

PENGUIN VEER

USA | Canada | UK | Ireland | Australia
New Zealand | India | South Africa | China | Singapore

Penguin Veer is part of the Penguin Random House group of companies
whose addresses can be found at global.penguinrandomhouse.com

Published by Penguin Random House India Pvt. Ltd
4th Floor, Capital Tower 1, MG Road,
Gurugram 122 002, Haryana, India

First published in Penguin Veer by Penguin Random House India 2023

ISBN 9780143460268

Typeset in Adobe Garamond Pro by MAP Systems, Bengaluru, India
Printed at Repro India Limited

www.penguin.co.in

This is a legitimate digitally printed version of the book and therefore might not
have certain extra finishing on the cover.

Contents

List of Abbreviations

Bn	Battalion
BOP	Border outpost
HQ	Headquarters
BSF	Border Security Force
EBR	East Bengal Regiment of the Pakistan Army
EPR	East Pakistan Rifles
IAF	Indian Air Force
ISI	Inter-Services Intelligence of Pakistan
PAF	Pakistan Air Force
R&AW	Research & Analysis Wing
IPS	Indian Police Service
BDF	Bangladeshi forces
G-branch	The 'General' (intelligence) branch of the BSF
DG	Director general
IG	Inspector general
DIG	Deputy inspector general
Comdt	Commandant
2IC	Second-in-charge
Dy Comdt	Deputy commandant
Asstt Comdt	Assistant commandant
SI	Sub-inspector
HC	Head constable
COAS	Chief of army staff

Gen.	General
Lt Gen.	Lieutenant general
Maj. Gen.	Major general
Brig.	Brigadier
Col	Colonel
Lt Col	Lieutenant colonel
JCO	Junior commissioned officer
POW	Prisoner of war
LMG	Light machine gun
MMG	Medium machine gun
RCL gun	Recoilless gun

Prologue

83 Battalion Headquarters
Border Security Force
Tura, Meghalaya
26 March 1971

The ringing of the field telephone woke up Deputy Commandant (Dy Comdt) Virendra Kumar Gaur of the Indian Border Security Force's 83 Battalion (Bn). The Mankachar border outpost (BOP), under his command, had called to inform that a group of East Pakistani civilians had come seeking asylum.

Surprised, Dy Comdt Gaur said, 'I cannot allow that, since there is no provision. This is the first time that such a thing has happened. I will pass on the message to the authorities in the morning and let you know their response, but do not allow anyone to come into Indian territory.'

A few minutes later, a sentry called from the Bagmara BOP with the same information, adding that the asylum seekers had reported that citizens were being killed in East Pakistan. Gaur decided to call this in to his superiors. He had just placed the receiver down when the officer at the Dalu BOP also called with the same information.

A crisis was brewing. Gaur sent an encrypted message to his reporting officer, Deputy Inspector General (DIG) Baruah, informing him of the asylum seekers. No reply. A little later, he sent another message asking if he could let the asylum seekers into the BOPs. Still no reply.

The asylum seekers were getting restless. Some of them openly expressed that they were afraid of being killed. Gaur relayed a message to the BOPs to let the asylum seekers come and stand at the boundary. Nobody would attack them there.

Someone at his headquarters woke up the DIG, who finally returned Gaur's calls. The asylum seekers had turned up at various BOPs across the DIG's jurisdiction. Finally, the DIG issued orders to put them up for the night.

Sitalkuchi Border Outpost
78 Battalion, BSF
Cooch Behar, West Bengal
26 March 1971, 2 a.m.

The company's havaldar major knocked on the door to Assistant Commandant (Asstt Comdt) Samir Kumar Mitra's hut, which served as his sleeping quarters.

'*Sa'ab, udhar sey ek subedar bhag key a gaya* [Sir, a subedar (of the EPR/East Pakistan Rifles) has come from across the border],' he told the bewildered company commander.

The EPR's junior commissioned officer (JCO) had deserted his BOP and crossed over to India, seeking asylum at the Phulbari BOP.

'Tie him up, cover his eyes and appoint a sentry to watch him. We don't know what his intentions are and why he is here. Let's wait till we get some orders,' he told the havaldar major.

Then he gave it a second thought.

'Get him on a bullock cart and bring him here to the company HQ,' he said, revising his orders.

There was no lock-up or stockade in the company headquarters, so Mitra called the officer-in-charge of the local police station and sent him there. He was to be confined there under a Border Security Force (BSF) guard. Asstt Comdt Mitra issued instructions that nobody was to interrogate the man or even speak with him. They should let him rest and await further orders.

Asstt Comdt Mitra sent a message to the Bn HQ in Siliguri. They replied saying that the EPR subedar should be sent to Siliguri the next morning.

Mahadipur BOP
74 Battalion, BSF
Malda, West Bengal
26 March 1971, 3 a.m.

Asstt Comdt B.N. Chaturvedi was woken up by loud cries. He listened and worked out that the cries came from the direction of the border. He hurried to the checkpost gate of the India–East Pakistan border and saw that a crowd was building up there. He had never seen anything like that. There were about 1000 people from East Pakistan, screaming to be let into India for safety.

'Either give us refuge in India or else shoot us,' they said.

The communication lines with his headquarters were down, and Asstt Comdt Chaturvedi had to take a call himself on what he should do. He put them up in the open area outside the BOP.

Eastern Frontier Headquarters
Calcutta, West Bengal
26 March 1971, morning

Golak Bihari Majumdar, inspector general (IG) of the BSF's Eastern Frontier, sent for the chief of communications, DIG B.N. Bhattacharya, who had earlier worked with the Calcutta Telephone Exchange.

Majumdar wanted a message sent out to the elected legislators of East Pakistan—the members of the National Assembly (MNAs) and members of the Provincial Assembly (MPAs). The message read: 'Your life is under threat. Please head to the nearest border and seek asylum at the BSF border posts. You will be looked after.'

Majumdar briefed his boss, BSF director general, Khusro Faramurz Rustamji, in New Delhi about the situation at the border. There had never been such a large-scale demand for refuge. People had turned up with scant belongings at almost every border outpost along India's border with East Pakistan. There had also never been a genocide next door. The two decided to keep the asylum seekers in camps at the border outposts as a temporary measure until Rustamji took orders from the government.

East Pakistanis fled to the border outposts when the Pakistani junta launched its pogrom with a military operation. On the first night, there was a trickle to the borders in West Bengal, Assam, Meghalaya and Tripura.

In his speech on 7 March 1971, Sheikh Mujibur Rahman (popularly known as Mujib) had called for a civil disobedience movement. Mujib was head of the Awami League, and his party had won the majority of seats in Pakistan's first general elections held in 1970. The 7 March speech was not broadcast by Pakistan Radio, but it was recorded on both video and audio, and smuggled out of the country. The speech reached millions of Bengalis in East Pakistan who joined the movement. The Pakistani authorities heard it as well, and they prepared for the 'final solution', an end to any struggle against their supremacy over all of Pakistan, including the Eastern Province. General Yahya Khan, the President of Pakistan, triggered that 'final solution' on 25 March 1971, when he failed to dissuade Mujib from establishing a democratic government in Pakistan.

* * *

On the evening of 25 March 1971, Mujib proclaimed the independence of East Pakistan, as a separate nation state from Pakistan. For twenty-five years, Pakistan had been run from and for the benefit of its western province. The East Pakistanis had tried and failed at various forms of conciliation. The proverbial last straw was the violence unleashed by the Pakistan Army that had followed the result of the 1970 general election in Pakistan, which had been preceded by several years of military dictatorship.

Mujib's party, the Awami League, swept the election and was poised to take over the governance of Pakistan. But West Pakistan did not see it that way—neither its political parties nor its military junta. After months of stalemate, the crisis erupted on 25 March 1971.

It was the day when, as promised by Pakistan's then president, Yahya Khan, the first democratically elected legislators of Pakistan were supposed to meet for their first parliamentary session. But the MNAs of Pakistan never met. Instead, it became the beginning of a pogrom by the Pakistan Army to silence Bengali dissent in East Pakistan.

The genocide started with a military campaign called Operation Searchlight, which sought to systematically target intellectuals (students, lawyers and teachers), political leaders, activists, soldiers and paramilitary personnel of East Pakistan. The targets became more arbitrary with time, the rape and violence more random, and spread across the entire eastern province of Pakistan.

The Indian government had been following the build-up. The Pakistan Army severed all channels of communication on the night the pogrom began. The first to receive word of what had happened in Pakistan was India's BSF, when East Pakistanis were fleeing their homeland to seek asylum in India. Nobody had estimated how many months they would be stuck in a limbo—braving cholera, malnutrition and an uncertain future—when they had arrived at the border gates that night.

The BSF had been founded five years before that night, and this was the first time that it was faced with a massive crisis all along the 4000-kilometre-long border with East Pakistan.

Its founding director general, Khusro Faramurz Rustamji, responded swiftly to the humanitarian crisis, as did all the BSF officers and personnel.

The Bangladesh flag flew in Dacca at the end of the 1971 Indo–Pak war on 16 December 1971. The history of the Indian armed forces' success in the war has been well documented, with granular details of its battles and operations. Historians of Bangladesh and some of the veterans who fought for their country's liberation have written the history of what led to the movement and the liberation war itself.

Scholars sought out archived documents—some that were classified for decades—and wrote what the superpowers of the world did while the elected legislators of East Pakistan were trying to establish democracy in their country for those nine months of 1971, from 26 March till the war began on 3 December. An illustration of the latter is the deep-dive book *Blood Telegram*, on the United States' role in Pakistan's genocide, by writer Gary Bass.[1] *Blood Telegram* and other books by scholars have noted that India allied with the Bangladeshis and supported their war for liberation through the BSF. Bass noted[2] that India officially never acknowledged that it supported the Bangladeshi guerrillas in the liberation war. It was definitely an important missing link in South Asian history.

This book tells an untold story of how India, through the BSF, supported the liberation war. Officers and personnel of the BSF, across its ranks, directly aided the Mukti Bahini, the Bangladeshi government-in-exile and the civilians who made cultural efforts for the liberation movement. The surviving veterans of the liberation war have a vivid memory of day-to-day life at the border posts for the nine months. The BSF has a large number of documents in its archives from 1971, inaccessible till now, which corroborate those stories and offer more. The wealth of this information is a necessary addition to the existing work on the liberation war history.

In the beginning, when hundreds of East Pakistanis came seeking refuge in India, thousands of Bengali-speaking soldiers and paramilitary personnel of Pakistan mutinied in East Pakistan, having learnt that Operation Searchlight sought to wipe them out. These were the Bengali officers and soldiers of the East Bengal Regiment (EBR) of the Pakistan Army, and officers and personnel of the border-guarding East Pakistan Rifles (EPR). Collectively, they were referred to as the Mukti Fauj or Fouj. The name was later changed to Mukti Bahini because of the Urdu origin of the word *fauj*, and much of the dissent in East Pakistan was rooted in resentment against the imposition of Urdu and the attempts to wipe out Bengali culture from East Pakistan.

The BSF launched several clandestine operations in East Pakistan from its posts in Assam, Meghalaya, Tripura and West Bengal, to aid the mutineers/Mukti Fauj. Its commando teams blew up bridges in East Pakistan in planned missions to sabotage the progress of the Pakistan Army, but the latter quashed the rebellion.

BSF intelligence operatives gathered crucial intelligence that saved lives and changed the course of the India–Pakistan war when it began. It also coordinated with members of the national and international press, helping to publish and broadcast stories of the asylum seekers under their protection. The BSF assisted the Bengali diplomats and staff of the Pakistani deputy high commission in organizing a coup. One of the most effective devices of the liberation war, outside of guns and strategy, was a clandestine radio station, which was seeded in Chittagong by staffers of Radio Chittagong.

The radio personnel escaped the Pakistan Army in Chittagong to seek help from India in Tripura. The BSF lent officers, technical staff and infrastructure to set up the radio station and ran the logistics in Tripura for two months, by which time it became an inseparable element of the resistance. Then, the BSF helped the clandestine radio station shift operations to West Bengal, where the Research and Analysis Wing (R&AW) took charge of transmitting the shows produced by radio personnel and artistes from across East Pakistan who congregated in Calcutta.

The civilian asylum seekers of East Pakistan were organized into a guerrilla force called the Mukti Bahini (freedom fighters of Bangladesh), who were embedded in BSF camps and then put up in camps next to the BSF's border outposts. The BSF fought alongside the Bengali guerrillas and also conducted its own missions deep inside East Pakistan. BSF personnel and officers ditched their identity papers, donned *lungis* and vests like the Mukti Bahini, and went deep into East Pakistan with them, sometimes travelling up to 15–20 km inside hostile territory. In those days, they forged friendships that have survived borders and time.

The elected leaders of East Pakistan, too, needed assistance. They had to be set up as a government-in-exile to rally the world for support. The inspector general of BSF's eastern frontier, Golak Bihari Majumdar, hosted the Bangladesh government-in-exile at the BSF safe houses in Calcutta, which became a hub for war correspondents and other members of the international press.

Every BSF officer who has worked with Rustamji echoes that he always emphasized the need to improvise and innovate. And the BSF, in its first trial by fire, did so. They built bunkers by stitching together what material they could get hold of; they foraged on the land while on missions deep in Pakistani territory; some learnt functional Islamic customs to pass off as Muslims in case they were caught, and so forth.

In his seminal work on the politico-military strategy that liberated Bangladesh, Col Guru Saday Batabyal (retd) has divided the fight for Bangladesh's liberation into four phases[3] before the 1971 Indo–Pak war (3–16 December 1971).

The first phase followed Mujib's Proclamation of Independence and lasted as long as the rebellion did—that is, till about early May 1971. The second phase began on 15 May, with the Indian Army assuming operational control of the borders and the training of the Mukti Bahini in guerrilla warfare. The third phase lasted through the monsoon, when the Indian Army intensified the training of the Mukti Bahini, and with the BSF, it inflicted maximum damage on the Pakistan Army.

Lt Gen. A.A.K. Niazi, chief of Pakistan Army's eastern command in 1971, later wrote[4] that the Pakistani soldiers were unable to negotiate the muddy and waterlogged terrain of East Pakistan during this third phase.

The BSF and Mukti Bahini used that to their advantage, and intensified their attacks. Lt Gen. Niazi called for more supplies and reinforcements, but the BSF and Mukti Bahini's push relegated his forces to their cantonments and scuttled their morale. The Pakistan Army resorted to the increased use of armed vigilante groups (collectively referred to as Razakars) to respond to the Mukti Bahini's raids.

In the fourth phase, the Indian Army drew up its strategy and war-gamed it while the Mukti Bahini undertook deeper missions with the BSF commandos. And, from early November onwards, the Indian Army launched set-piece attacks against Pakistan Army positions, first using the BSF and the Mukti Bahini, and then escalating the attacks to battles for key positions.

The Indo–Pak war, which lasted thirteen days, was fought on India's western and eastern frontiers, and the BSF was engaged on both, under the operational command of the Indian Army. Indian prime minister Indira Gandhi, who sanctioned its assistance to the East Pakistanis, praised its role in the war:

As the first line of our defence, the Border Security Force had to bear the immediate brunt of the enemy onslaught. The manner in which they faced the fire and the support they gave to the army played a crucial role in our ultimate success.[5]

The overall contribution made by the BSF has been recognized in the form of civilian and military honours. But its role has not been publicized because of the secret nature of the missions.

The BSF has a mandate of guarding India as the country's first line of defence. But Rustamji and the officers and personnel of the BSF went much beyond that mandate. They chose to defend humanity itself, while several countries debated whether the genocide was Pakistan's internal matter.

Perhaps it was an internal matter—for twenty-five years, only bitterness had festered in East Pakistan—until the Pakistani military junta tried to violently crush dissent. The history of East Pakistan and why it became disenchanted with the idea of Pakistan has been recorded by several historians. In our time, it is crucial to revisit that history and recall some of the events that led to the 1971 crisis.

1

The Bloody Road to Bangladesh

The differences between East and West Pakistan were evident from the time Pakistan came into being. The span of India physically separated the two wings of the Islamic country. The western wing was made from parts of colonial-era Punjab, Sind, Balochistan and the North-West Frontier Province. East Bengal, as it was then called, was built by merging parts of Assam and Tripura into East Bengal.

Before Partition, several of the prominent political leaders in East Bengal had been part of the Muslim League, one of the main actors that supported the division of British India along religious lines. However, within two years of the formation of Pakistan, the Bengali politicians found that they had different political goals from those of their Islamist colleagues in the western wing. Huseyn Shaheed Suhrawardy, the last prime minister of undivided Bengal, joined with other Bengali politicians to form the Awami Muslim League in 1949. The founding president of the Awami Muslim League was Abdul Hamid Khan Bhashani, popularly known as Maulana Bhashani. 'Bangabandhu' Sheikh Mujibur Rahman, or Mujib, was one of the many Bengali youngsters who joined the party.

While Suhrawardy and a few other Bengali leaders led Pakistan and were in top positions, it did not benefit the Bengali population of Pakistan, who felt that, despite being the majority, the welfare of East Pakistanis was low on the priority list. The lion's share of economic benefits, tax dollars and aid went to West Pakistan.

The core issue that caused a difference between the two provinces had to do with the linguistic and cultural differences between East and West Pakistan. There were several attempts by West Pakistani leaders to homogenize the language and culture of Pakistan over the years. Mohammad Ali Jinnah, the founder of Pakistan, was not an Urdu speaker but wanted to impose the language throughout the land. In 1948, during his sole visit to East Pakistan, he refused to make Bengali a federal language of Pakistan.

The inhabitants of West Pakistan themselves spoke multiple languages. In the eastern province of Pakistan, the majority spoke Bengali. There was a minority Hindi-speaking population of Muslims who had migrated from Uttar Pradesh and Bihar following Partition. Upon its creation in 1947, Pakistan had dropped Bengali from the list of national languages. The student community started a wave of protests from March 1948. Their protests were ignored by Jinnah and subsequent rulers of Pakistan, who overlooked the fact that 55 per cent of Pakistanis spoke Bengali and only 7 per cent spoke Urdu.

The conflict over language culminated into a disaster when police gunned down five protesting students in Dacca University on 21 February 1952. This spurred a mass movement called the Ekushe (literally, 'Twenty-First') movement, to honour the date when the students were martyred. The West Pakistani-dominated leadership of Pakistan reacted by changing the name of East Bengal to East Pakistan.

Despite the tensions, political leaders of East Pakistan continued to participate in the nation-building process of Pakistan, and the two wings managed to put together a constitution in 1956 that promised a parliamentary democracy. However, there were no elections; instead, in October 1958, the Pakistani military chief, General Ayub Khan, seized power from the then president, Iskander Mirza, in Pakistan's first military coup d'état. Mirza had himself suspended the constitution and seized power a few weeks before that. A Bengali-origin soldier-turned-bureaucrat, Major General Mirza was a direct descendant of Mir Jafar, who secretly allied with the British East India Company during the Battle of Plassey.

Meanwhile, Maulana Bhashani had quit the Awami League over ideological differences and launched the left-leaning National Awami Party. By that time, Mujib had risen within the Awami League and in East Pakistani politics. Gen. Ayub Khan made another constitution for Pakistan in 1962, which gave more power to his own office and to the Islamic law council.

* * *

In the same year, that is 1962, Mujib secretly reached out to India's prime minister Jawaharlal Nehru for assistance to secede from Pakistan. He sent a letter through the Indian deputy high commission in Dacca[6] and also met with Sachindra Lal Singh (who later became the CM of Tripura) in Tripura.[7] But Nehru declined to give Mujib the support he required.

The idea of secession was also rooted in the widening economic and power-sharing disparity between the two provinces of Pakistan that was compounded through the 1960s. For the time being, Bengali politicians of East Pakistan negotiated for some form of autonomy for the eastern wing, while the desire for secession simmered. With that in mind, in 1966, Mujib created the six-point agenda, formulating an autonomous federal structure. Under this programme, the federation would have power only on issues related to foreign affairs. Each wing would make their own decisions regarding all internal issues, including governance, the reserve bank and defence. This became the manifesto of the Awami League.

The Pakistani spy agency, the Inter-Services Intelligence (ISI), found out that Mujib had reached out to India in 1962. By some accounts, the spooks chased him right till the Indo-East Pakistan border when he was headed to Tripura. In 1967, the Pakistani authorities accused thirty-five East Pakistanis of sedition in the Agartala conspiracy case. The list of accused included Mujib, several prominent political leaders, military officers and civil servants. All of them pleaded not guilty to the charges. The trial began in 1968 and helped to generate a wave of public sympathy that exacerbated popular opinion against the Ayub Khan regime.

Maulana Bhashani supported Mujib and the other accused politicians and organized a mass campaign that triggered protests across East Pakistan. The protests gathered momentum through 1968. The students' organizations were active in the protests against the sedition trial. An umbrella organization of five East Pakistani students' organizations announced an eleven-point agenda that they had created based on Mujib's six-point agenda. The student body called for protest meetings that ended in violent clashes with the authorities, resulting in the death toll of sixty-one over the course of the year.

Within a month of the students' protests, the Pakistani authorities withdrew the charges against the accused in the Agartala conspiracy case on 22 February 1969. Meanwhile, Ayub Khan's presidency was on the brink of collapse because of his massive unpopularity in West Pakistan. There were riots and protests in West Pakistan, and political party workers etched derogatory graffiti about Ayub Khan. Some believe that it was the first time in the history of Pakistan that abusive terms were used about a leader in a public space.

Ayub Khan had lost his clout over the military, without which he was unable to declare martial law. He was faced with a catch-22 situation. He needed martial law to quash dissent against his presidency. But, if he called for martial law, Gen. Yahya Khan, the commander-in-chief of the Pakistan Army, would seize power.

On 25 March 1969, Ayub Khan resigned and handed over power to Gen. Yahya Khan. This was exactly two years before the launch of the genocide of East Pakistanis under Operation Searchlight.

Gen. Yahya Khan assumed the presidency with promises of ushering in a parliamentary democracy in the country. Initially, he went the extra mile to build a relationship with Mujib. Later in 1969, Mujib travelled to London, where he met with Bengali expatriates and, at a meeting, used the name 'Bangladesh' (or Bangla Desh) for the first time to refer to East Pakistan.

In October 1970, Gen. Yahya Khan announced a general election to the national and provincial assemblies of Pakistan. In January, he withdrew martial law, which enabled political activity in all of Pakistan. Mujib launched the Awami League campaign with the declaration that the election was going to be a referendum on the six-point agenda and, consequently, the autonomy of East Pakistan.

The National Assembly of Pakistan was to comprise 313 seats, distributed across the East and the West, based on proportional representation of the population. East Pakistan, with its higher population, was allotted 162 seats and West Pakistan 138 seats. The elected leaders had to draft and enact a constitution within six months of convening the National Assembly. Gen. Yahya Khan reserved the right to reject such a constitution if it didn't meet with his interpretation of Islamic doctrines.

This rider was a blow to the politics of the Awami League, which abstained from mentioning Islamist laws in its political manifesto. Throughout the nine-month-long campaign, Mujib mostly stayed away from campaigning in West Pakistan, except for a single trip in June 1970. He focused his energy and that of the Awami League on securing the full support of the Bengalis. The assessments of the media, and of the Awami League itself, showed that the party was going to sweep the elections.

The seasonal floods in East Pakistan during the monsoon of 1970 pushed the date of the election to December. But the most devastating tragedy came later that year in the form of Cyclone Bhola, which made landfall on 12 November 1970. It ripped through most of the southern district of East Pakistan and crashed a twenty-foot tidal wave on the islands in the south. According to a conservative estimate, Cyclone Bhola affected close to 5 million people and killed at least a quarter of a million.

Yahya Khan's government failed to respond swiftly to the devastation caused by the cyclone. The Pakistani authorities realized the magnitude only after being spurred by coverage in the international press and by the relief work from abroad. India's prime minister, Indira Gandhi, pledged $1.3 million (1970 USD valuation) and sent relief trucks to East Pakistan. Yahya Khan refused India's offer to move relief materials by air and use military aircraft for rescue operations. The political leaders in East Pakistan were quick to capitalize on the delayed and poor reaction of the West Pakistani authorities.

Just before the election, Maulana Bhashani announced that the National Awami Party wouldn't contest, paving a clear route for the Awami League to sweep the polls. Yahya Khan tried to delay the election because of Cyclone Bhola, but neither Mujib nor Zulfikar Ali Bhutto (then leader of the Pakistan People's Party [PPP]) in West Pakistan agreed with that. It was the first direct democratic exercise in Pakistan.

As expected, the Awami League swept the election, and won 160 of the 162 seats and seven seats reserved for women candidates in East Pakistan. The Bhutto-led Pakistan People's Party won eighty-one of the 138 seats and five seats reserved for women in West Pakistan. The right-wing Islamist political parties—including the Muslim league, its splinters and the Jamaat—won a combined total of thirty-seven seats.

This result gave the Awami League the democratic authority to form the government and made Mujib the democratically elected leader of all of Pakistan. This also meant that hypothetically, the Awami League had the power to frame the next constitution for the country. Mujib was quick to announce that the people of East Pakistan had spoken in favour of his party's six-point agenda.

Yahya Khan went to Dacca to meet with Mujib in December. On his way back, he told the press that Mujib was 'the future prime minister [of Pakistan]'. However, Bhutto made a public comment discounting the importance of the Awami League's majority seats, indicating that the government of Pakistan would be run from its western wing.

On 3 January 1971, Mujib held the first public rally with all his party's elected members of the National Assembly (MNA) and members of the Provincial Assembly (MPA). He reassured the people that he would uphold the six-point agenda. Soon after, Bhutto travelled all the way to Dacca to convince Mujib that he needed the PPP's support to form an effective government and would also have to dilute the six-point agenda. Bhutto said he would support autonomy only if he was given a cabinet berth. Mujib, whose party had already won the majority, called Bhutto's bluff, and the latter left East Pakistan empty-handed.

* * *

Two men hijacked an Indian commercial aircraft on 30 January 1971, flew it to Lahore and announced that they were members of the separatist National Liberation Front (precursor to the

Jammu Kashmir Liberation Front). They demanded the release
of their comrades held in Indian jails. Bhutto hugged them and
posed for pictures with them. India asked for the aircraft to be
returned, and Mujib supported that demand. The hijackers set
the aeroplane on fire, and the pilots, cabin crew and twenty-eight
passengers were returned. India responded by banning the flight
of Pakistani military aircraft over its airspace, extending the ban
to civilian aircraft four days later. That imposed a literal cost on
the Pakistanis. The air route connecting the two wings would now
require flying around the entire Indian peninsula, with a refuelling
stop in Ceylon.

Meanwhile, Mujib kept up talks with Yahya Khan for the
transfer of power to the elected leaders, so that the government
and the constituent assembly could be formed. Yahya Khan called
for a meeting of the National Assembly in Dacca on 3 March. But
Bhutto asserted that he would boycott the session.

Bhutto and Yahya Khan went into a huddle at the former's
farmhouse in West Pakistan, emerging with an announcement
that the session was postponed. This led to violent protests in
Dacca. The anti-West Pakistan sentiment grew in the eastern
wing, and the flag of Bangladesh's liberation movement—against
a green background, with the map of Bangladesh in gold across
a red sun—appeared for the first time during a students' rally at
Dacca University.

On 3 March 1971, Mujib announced that the Bengalis
controlled East Pakistan. The West Pakistani politicians blamed
Bhutto, who had been well and truly cornered, for the breakdown.
He emerged with a selfish solution: divide the National Assembly
for each wing of Pakistan. His motive was to rule West Pakistan.

Gen. Yahya Khan sent across one of his generals as East
Pakistan's martial law administrator. Lt Gen. Tikka Khan was
known as the Butcher of Balochistan—a moniker he had earned
for brutally quashing a rebellion in Balochistan. The chief justice

of East Pakistan refused to acknowledge him as the governor and declined from administering an oath of allegiance. The Bengali staff of the governor's official residence stayed away in an act of defiance.

A mood of non-cooperation swept through East Pakistan, formalized and popularized by Mujib's speech of 3 March 1971 in which he openly called for civil disobedience till power was transferred to the elected legislators.

Given the reluctance of the West Pakistanis to transfer power to Mujib and the Awami League, several of Mujib's political colleagues among others had put a lot of pressure on him to take a radical decision. Mujib announced another rally on 7 March, and many expected him to make a formal declaration of secession from Pakistan during the public event.

The day before, on 6 March, Yahya Khan broadcast a public address and announced that the National Assembly would meet on 25 March. It toned down Mujib. On 7 March, despite the expectations, Mujib advised patience while prescribing a firm display of civil disobedience.

From the racecourse in Dacca, he warned:

Ebaarer shongram, muktir shongram.
Ebarer shongram, shadhinotar shongram.

(The struggle is now for liberation.
The struggle is now for independence.)

The Pakistani authorities cut the radio feed and stopped the broadcast. The speech signed the death warrant of Pakistan with its two wings. It had far-reaching effects and was a flashpoint that galvanized the East Pakistani Bengalis to join the brewing movement to liberate Bangladesh from Pakistan.

Mujib was not unaware of the consequences of his speech and the arrival of the Butcher of Balochistan. He sent Tajuddin

Ahmed, the general secretary of the Awami League and MNA, to secretly meet with the Indian diplomatic head in Dacca and ask for assistance.[8] On 17 March, India gave[9] a positive response of assistance in case of a breakdown.

On 15 March, Yahya Khan landed in a deserted Dacca, the streets emptied and the shops shuttered by citizens as a mark of protest against the delay in transfer of power. After a week of negotiations with Mujib, Yahya Khan also invited Bhutto to Dacca. The PPP supremo was put up in a high-security building, away from the streets where people had already begun to display the flag of Bangladesh.

The fissure between the two political parties was sharp and deep, and Yahya Khan could do nothing about it. On 23 March, Pakistan's Republic Day, Mujib held up the Bangladesh flag publicly for the first time and also attached one to the bonnet of his car.

Moved by Mujib's 7 March speech, Bengali radio producers had dropped the name Pakistan from their broadcasts. Radio East Pakistan in Chittagong announced programmes as Radio Chittagong. Radio Dacca played Rabindranath Tagore's 'Amar Sonar Bangla' (My Golden Bengal), which had become an anthem of the Bengali movement in East Pakistan. March 23, 1971, became Resistance Day, and cries of 'Joy Bangla' (Victory to Bengal) resounded across the cities of East Pakistan.

That day, unbeknown to the East Pakistanis, the Pakistani junta set plans into motion for the final solution to the hurdles created by the Bengalis. These plans—Operation Searchlight—had been designed on the instructions of Gen. Yahya Khan soon after his arrival in Dacca.

The stalemate between Mujib, Yahya and Bhutto could not be broken. Bhutto and Yahya Khan conceded that they had not been able to shake the Awami League's resolve. The talks ended on 25 March, which was two days after Resistance Day.

That evening, Bhutto and other Pakistani political leaders returned to Islamabad. Gen. Yahya Khan sneaked out of Dacca on a military plane. Lt Gen. Tikka Khan gave the green signal for Operation Searchlight to Maj. Gen. Rao Farman Ali and Maj. Gen. Khadim Hussain, the architects of the genocide.

The Pakistani authorities later challenged the unilateral Indian embargo on Pakistani flights over Indian airspace before the International Civil Aviation Organization Council. An appeal against the proceedings would also be argued before the International Court of Justice. In the meantime, through 1971, Pakistani flights remained banned from Indian airspace.

Michael Thomas Nicholson, war correspondent of the UK-based ITN TV, read about the political crisis in East Pakistan[10] and headed to Karachi along with his cameraperson. From there, they tried to board the daily shuttle flight to Dacca. But they were turned away at the Pakistan International Airways (PIA) office in Karachi, several days in a row, with the reason that the flight was full.

Nicholson found it odd because there were never so many people flying to Dacca from Karachi on the large Boeing aircraft used by PIA. And there was no official embargo on travelling to Dacca at the time. Nicholson took a trip to the Karachi airport to see if the flights were indeed full. He arrived well in time for the flight and found the airport empty except for airport staff.

The Boeings were parked in their respective bays, with their engine cowlings off and doors open. On the way back to his hotel in the city, Nicholson saw lorries from the army barracks carrying soldiers dressed as civilians.

Pakistan had military planes, including C-130s. But the troop movement was so massive that they had booked out all the seats on commercial airlines. The soldiers flew in civilian clothing, carrying their weapons.

* * *

The Pakistan Army rolled out tanks, armoured vehicles, jeeps and trucks along with soldiers who marched into pre-decided venues and launched Operation Searchlight. The Pakistan Army moved into Dacca University, at the heart of many of East Pakistan's political and cultural movements, and attacked both the teachers' quarters and the students' hostels, where they rounded up people whose names were on their list and shot them. Later, they killed larger groups of students.

They blasted the Kali Temple at the Dacca Racecourse, and captured Dacca Radio and Dacca Television. Foreign reporters were packed into planes and flown out of Dacca. Pakistan Army soldiers set ablaze the offices of Bengali-language newspapers that had carried anti-Pakistan articles.

A group of soldiers moved to the headquarters of the East Pakistan Rifles (EPR) in Pilkhana, Dacca, and shot down anybody they could find. The EPR personnel, border guards of Pakistan's eastern wing, included only Bengalis. The coordinated movement of the Pakistan Army, with its lists of targets, had been prepared in advance and was rolled out around midnight between 25 and 26 March 1971.

Around 1 a.m. on 26 March, Mujib declared the independence of Bangladesh through a message to Chittagong, to be transmitted using the EPR wireless:

> This may be my last message: from today Bangladesh is independent.
>
> I call upon the people of Bangladesh, wherever you might be and with whatever you have, to resist the army occupation to the last. Your fight must go on until the last soldier of the Pakistan occupation army is expelled from the soil of Bangladesh and final victory is achieved.

Soon afterwards, a unit of Pakistan Army soldiers surrounded Mujib's house and began to fire at it. The plan was to assassinate him and announce that separatist extremists in East Pakistan had killed him. Mujib had taken cover and during a lull in the firing, he called out to the commander of the unit to stop firing since his family was with him. The Pakistan Army soldiers arrested him ad took him away.

The same coordinated army movement was made in other cities of East Pakistan, targeting political persons, students, academics, policemen, civil servants and EPR personnel, among others. There was no pattern. Some people were shot where they were found, some were taken away from their houses—they neither returned nor were their corpses ever discovered.

The pogrom spilled on to every corner of East Pakistan and continued throughout the liberation war—its momentum reduced only when the guerrilla operations increased. The soldiers raped women of all ages without mercy. They mutilated the breasts of the women with their service knives.[11]

The East Bengal Regiment (EBR) of the Pakistan Army had both Bengali and non-Bengali officers. A number of the Bengali officers across the country had been given the strange order to deposit their weapons in the armoury before Operation Searchlight. They were hunted out and some were killed in their barracks.

Some Bengali officers of the EBR escaped and, with the Bengali soldiers under their command, began the first insurgency inside East Pakistan. The EPR personnel posted at the borders revolted too, and pockets of insurgency lined the India–East Pakistan border. This first group of decentralized insurgents was called the Mukti Fauj. The name was later changed to Mukti Bahini because of the Urdu origin of the word *fauj*. Using an Urdu word contradicted the Bhasha Andolan and the fight for a Bengali nation.

The Awami League legislators went into hiding, donned disguises and began to emerge at the India–East Pakistan borders.

So did thousands of citizens who fled the pogrom. By the end of the year, the genocide, rape, civil war and their economic consequences turned the thousands into 10 million East Pakistani refugees in India. Lt Gen. Tikka Khan had added another title to his list of monikers: the Butcher of Bengal.

The top offices of the Indian government were carefully following the developments in East Pakistan while Gen. Yahya Khan was trying to broker a compromise with Mujib in Bhutto's (and West Pakistan's) favour.

Indira Gandhi and her top advisers went into a huddle on 26 March, after newsflashes of Mujib's declaration of Independence.

The first Indians to experience and understand what was happening in East Pakistan were the 'bordermen', the officers and personnel of the BSF, India's first line of defence.

2

The First Plan

Srinagar Border Outpost
92 Battalion, BSF
Tripura
26 March 1971, morning

Asstt Comdt Parimal Kumar Ghosh was at the Srinagar BOP that morning. The border was unfenced, and the western perimeter of the BOP was just a few metres from the international boundary. Hardly 250 metres from that perimeter wall, across a paddy field, was the Chittagong–Dacca Trunk Road.

Asstt Comdt Ghosh saw a Pakistan Army column moving north from Chittagong in the direction of Comilla. He headed to the observation post with Inspector Ram Kumar and Sub-Inspector Thapa. The convoy moved slowly, led by a flag car, signifying that it had at least a brigadier's car. It meant that the unit was at least a brigade.

Among the rows of trucks carrying personnel, they spotted a battery of artillery. A little later, the Pakistan Army battalion stopped for several minutes. Then the convoy resumed its onward march. At the time, the three of them, watching from the observation post, didn't understand the reason for the pause.

Anticipating some problem in Chittagong, Asstt Comdt Ghosh filed a sitrep (situation report) about the movement and passed the message to 92 Bn HQ in Agartala.

* * *

Capt. P.K. Ghosh had completed his service with the Indian Army's Emergency Commission in 1970. In August the same year, he joined the BSF, after which he was posted to South Tripura with the 92 Bn as an assistant commandant and given charge of Foxtrot Company.

He had charge of the BOPs at Amlighat, Srinagar, Samarendraganj and Nalua, covering close to 50 km of the India–East Pakistan border in south Tripura. The adjacent area in East Pakistan was then its Noakhali district and the Chittagong Hill Tracts (CHT).

The border had been quite peaceful since Asstt Comdt Ghosh had taken over in August 1970. The East Pakistan Rifles personnel were Bengalis, and so were most of the BSF personnel in Tripura as well as Asstt Comdt Ghosh. The EPR head constable who led the East Pakistani BOP at Chhagalnaiya was a Bengali named Nooruddin. He often came up to the border to speak with Asstt Comdt Ghosh, and the two shared a cordial relationship.

Asstt Comdt Ghosh had heard Mujib's 7 March speech on the radio and was moved by it. But Mujib's words were also cautionary, forewarning people of the turmoil that was to ensue. Not far away from where Asstt Comdt Ghosh was at the time of the speech, Major Ziaur Rahman had also heard the speech from his location in Chittagong, and it inspired him to prepare to rebel.

Ebaarer shongram, muktir shongram
Ebarer shongram, shadhinotar shongram.

Following the 7 March speech, Asstt Comdt Ghosh ensured that all his officers also kept in touch with their counterparts across the border. He wanted to keep tabs on the developments. The commanding officer of the local EPR HQ was a West Pakistani, and Nooruddin didn't trust him.

Asstt Comdt Ghosh sought Nooruddin out to inquire about the developments inside East Pakistan. Nooruddin wanted to know if the BSF had any idea of what India was planning to do to help the Bengalis in case of a crackdown.

'Sir, you are like our commandant. Please tell me what we should do,' Nooruddin had said during one of their meetings.[12] He didn't appear to have faith in his West Pakistani commander.

'I can't tell you what you should do, but keep your ears to the ground. Keep your arms close at all times. If you suspect any foul play, don't hesitate to act first,' Asstt Comdt Ghosh had replied.

In Dacca, the mayhem was one-sided. But in Chittagong,[13] the Bengali army officers revolted. They laid siege to the city till the Pakistan Air Force bombed them and the Pakistan Army called for reinforcements.

* * *

A few hours after Asstt Comdt Ghosh filed his sitrep about the movement of the Pakistan Army brigade, Nooruddin appeared with two civilians in tow. The men were introduced as Obaidullah Mazumdar, MNA for Noakhali-1 in East Pakistan, and Amir Hussein, an Awami League party leader from Comilla.

The two men said that the Pakistan Army had launched a pogrom against Bengalis across East Pakistan. In Chittagong, the Bengali officers of the Pakistan Army had revolted against the genocidal campaign. There was heavy fighting in Chittagong, and they needed India's support immediately. Asstt Comdt Ghosh told them it was not in his power to do anything but he would inform his superior.

Constable Nooruddin said that a Pakistani brigade had passed by that morning and stationed a section[14] of soldiers to guard the Subhapur road bridge.

Subhapur town was on the main Chittagong–Dacca Trunk Road, and the road bridge was important for the Pakistan Army's transport of supplies and personnel. The residents of Subhapur had heard of the genocidal campaign across East Pakistan and how the Pakistan Army was resorting to murder and rape without restraint. Nooruddin said that the women in Subhapur were feeling unsafe, because of the Pakistan Army soldiers guarding the bridge. He requested Asstt Comdt Ghosh to deploy the men under the latter's command, to get rid of the Pakistan Army soldiers at the bridge.

'I cannot leave my post or cross the border without instructions from the Indian government,' Asstt Comdt Ghosh said. 'But I can make some tactical suggestions that may help you defend against the soldiers.'

He chalked out a tactical plan on a piece of paper whereby the EPR personnel could trap the Pakistan Army. They would not be able to move from their positions to go to the village or fetch drinking water from the river. Depriving them of access to water and food would weaken their morale.

The two politicians and the EPR constable requested that, if he was unable to send the BSF personnel, Asstt Comdt Ghosh could at least come along with them to Subhapur. He could help them with tactical directions at the spot.

Neither Inspector Ram Kumar nor SI Thapa, who were at this meeting, spoke Bengali, but they could make out the nature of this request. They both advised Asstt Comdt Ghosh that he shouldn't cross the border.

Asstt Comdt Ghosh was in a dilemma. His two subordinate officers were giving him sound advice. Yet, it did not sit well with his conscience. The words of Swami Vivekananda rang through his mind:

> '*Otho, jaago, oshohaye loker pashe darao, shahajyo koro* [Awaken and stand with the helpless].'

A few decades earlier, the same words had set Subhas Chandra Bose and many other Bengalis on the path of actively seeking freedom from British rule. And on that day in 1971, Swami Vivekananda's words made Asstt Comdt Ghosh ask himself if he should sit around idly while defenceless people were in need of help. Even if he lost his life or his job, his intervention may help save a few lives.

Asstt Comdt Ghosh had been born in Fazilhat in Tangail district of East Pakistan, from where his family had fled in the early 1950s due to communal tensions. East Bengal was his home too. At that moment, his attachment with his roots kicked in, and he felt that these people in the darkest hour of their lives, the people of East Bengal, were his people.

Asstt Comdt Ghosh made up his mind. He changed out of his uniform into civvies and stowed away his weapon. He needed an East Pakistani identity in case the Pakistan Army or its loyalists caught him across the border. MNA Obaidullah Mazumdar came up with one. Mazumdar christened Ghosh as Professor Ali, a teacher in Patiya College in Chittagong district. Mazumdar himself was the principal of the college and he could vouch for Professor Ali's credentials, if questioned.

With his new credentials, Asstt Comdt Ghosh crossed the international boundary and stepped into East Pakistan. They walked for a while and then took rickshaws to the Subhapur bridge. Seeing the men with Constable Nooruddin, the villagers of Subhapur gathered within minutes. The assembled villagers began raising slogans of 'Joy Bangla'. The Pakistani soldiers who were close by heard the cry for freedom and responded with a burst of light-machine-gun fire in their direction.

'As an elected member, I authorize you to take any action you deem fit,' Mazumdar told Asstt Comdt Ghosh.

Constable Nooruddin and six of his EPR colleagues were present there. The EPR constables had .303 rifles and about fifty rounds each—a total of 300 rounds in all. Nooruddin had a Sten gun and some magazines. This was the first group of freedom fighters of Bangladesh, and Asstt Comdt Ghosh suggested that they should be administered an oath of allegiance.

He asked them to gather a fistful of East Pakistani soil in one hand and their weapons in the other, and swear allegiance to the liberation of Bangladesh. The oath was a simple one—that the freedom fighters would protect the interests and honour of their motherland, and serve its people faithfully.

The swearing-in done, Asstt Comdt Ghosh divided them into two groups—three each for the right and left flanks of the road. They had to approach the bridge from the north and take up positions that were concealed from the field of view of the Pakistan Army soldiers. Their sole objective was to prevent the Pakistan Army soldiers from moving from their post by the bridge.

'*Oder bhatey martey hobe, oder panitey martey hobe* [We have to make sure that they have access to neither food nor water till they are forced to crawl out],' Asstt Comdt Ghosh told the EPR constables.

He had banked on two factors. The section of Pakistani soldiers had come out from a column on the move; so their rations and water were limited. Second, his own experience said that the Pakistan Army soldiers were trigger-happy. They used more bullets than was necessary.

He told the EPR constables that they should conserve their ammunition till they spotted the Pakistani soldiers.

Once the enemy was spotted, they should fire only one round at a time, alternating between each flank. This would deceive the Pakistani soldiers to believe that the rebel EPR team was larger and instigate them into firing. That would finish the trigger-happy Pakistani soldiers' ammunition quickly, and, with slim chances of replenishment of supplies, they would probably surrender.

The EPR constables assumed the appointed positions after taking the instructions. Wishing them success, Asstt Comdt Ghosh returned to Chhagalnaiya and crossed back into India to the Srinagar BOP.

In his office, he filed a sitrep on the events in Subhapur but did not mention that he had crossed the border and gone into East Pakistan. Lieutenant Colonel A.K. Ghosh, commandant, 92 Bn, was happy with the report and, by return message, told Asstt Comdt Ghosh to keep in touch with the EPR personnel and to keep apprising the headquarters of any further developments.

March 26 was a blood-soaked day in the history of the Bangladesh liberation war, and it was also a day of many firsts. For the first time:

- a group of armed Bengalis, considered inferior by their non-Bengali countrymen, had taken an oath to defend and liberate their nation;
- Awami League leaders had organized a small band of defectors into a resistance group;
- a BSF officer had carried out a clandestine mission in East Pakistan.

It was a small move to claim an unknown bridge on a road in a corner of East Pakistan. It seemed insignificant in the face of the developments that would take place across South Asia or the world over the subsequent nine months of the year. But it would trigger a chain of reactions, creating ripples that would be felt far away.

The next morning, Lt Col A.K. Ghosh arrived at the Srinagar BOP early in the morning to have breakfast. A big man with closely cropped hair, the commandant seemed his usual jovial self upon seeing Asstt Comdt Ghosh. He wanted details of what was going on in Subhapur.

Tea was served, and breakfast was on its way to the table. Asstt Comdt Ghosh was relieved that the commandant had come. Though he hadn't included it in his message the evening before, he had made up his mind to brief his commanding officer (CO) that he had crossed the border and helped the East Pakistanis.

When the constables were out of earshot, he told Lt Col Ghosh that he had crossed the border and helped in setting up the EPR personnel at the Subhapur bridge.

Lt Col Ghosh immediately blew a fuse. He slammed his palm down on the table, upsetting the tray and spilling the tea. 'How dare you cross the international border without any permission?'

A lull fell on the camp.

After a pause, Lt Col Ghosh said, 'Do you know you can be court-martialled for this?'

He got up and stormed off towards his jeep. Asstt Comdt Ghosh stood up to salute his superior officer but the commandant, in his fury, neither acknowledged the salute nor returned it. He left with the threat of a court martial and a subsequent, almost certain, likelihood of a dismissal hanging in the air.

3

Professor Ali

A host of emotions gripped Asstt Comdt P.K. Ghosh as soon as his superior officer, Lt Col A.K. Ghosh, left the Srinagar BOP. On the one hand, he felt he had done the right thing and had no regrets. Yet, the threat of court martial and a dishonourable discharge was a serious one.

Inspector Ram Kumar came up to Asstt Comdt Ghosh and said, '*Sir, aapne jo kiya, theek kiya tha. Logo ki jaane bach gayee* [Sir, you did the right thing, you have saved lives].'

Asstt Comdt Ghosh was moved by the kind words and patted the inspector on his back as a gesture of gratitude. The entire BOP had heard the slap on the table and the dressing-down Ghosh had received from the commandant. A dark cloud enveloped the BOP for the rest of the day.

Meanwhile, across the border, the EPR constables kept vigil through the night. They slept in shifts on the two flanks of the approach road to the bridge. When they needed to answer nature's call or have meals, they crawled backwards on their bellies till they were out of Pakistan Army soldiers' sight.

Asstt Comdt Ghosh's plan turned out to be sound. The section of Pakistani soldiers at the Subhapur bridge ran out of water. They first sent three of the soldiers out of their shelter to fetch water. To get to the water, the three soldiers had to break cover and access the river by walking through an open area. The EPR constables spotted them the minute they broke cover. Constable Nooruddin signalled them to wait. He gesticulated to two of his men to mark a soldier each. He marked the third and told another three of his men to also take aim as a back-up. In case the first three missed the Pakistan Army soldiers, the second team would be there to take them out.

Shots rang out. The EPR men shot dead the three soldiers. The corpses lay by the bank of the river the entire day. The other Pakistan Army soldiers couldn't recover them. If they tried, the EPR constables were waiting to take them out as well. In frustration, they fired in bursts from their automatic weapons at where the EPR men were hidden. The EPR constables didn't respond, careful to not give away their exact location.

By the night of 27 March, the Pakistan Army soldiers guarding the Subhapur bridge found themselves in a fix. They had run out of food and water, and their brigade had not replenished their supplies. They couldn't break cover and go to the village for supplies, since they knew there were armed men waiting for them.

Demoralized, some of the Pakistan Army soldiers tried to escape that night. Either they were deserting their position or they wanted to hike to the nearest Pakistan Army camp for help. The townsfolk were keeping vigil outside Subhapur at night. They caught the fleeing Pakistani soldiers and killed them.

On the morning of 28 March, a Sunday, the rest of the Pakistan Army soldiers came out of hiding, holding their weapons above their heads—the universal gesture of surrender. Constable Nooruddin and the others captured and killed them. They had no provision to take prisoners.

The Subhapur bridge had been liberated; it was a tiny oasis in a nation that had been thrown into complete chaos by genocide and civil war. Asstt Comdt Ghosh's tactical plan had worked well. Nooruddin headed to the Indian camp and requested

On 29 March, news spread that an Indian defence officer had met with the rebels. Once the consignment of the mortar and shells was delivered, it seemed that India was going to back the liberation war. Asstt Comdt Ghosh had made it clear that he had gone in his personal capacity as a Bengali in solidarity with the 'East Bengalis'. But Major Zia saw his reaching out as a gesture from India, and he passed on the message to the other Bengali officers fighting the Pakistan Army.

4

Mission Sanction

Khusro F. Rustamji was the only inspector general of a state who opposed the formation of a centralized border police in May 1965. He was chief of the Madhya Pradesh Police, and this was a conference of home ministers and police chiefs of all the states in India.

Prime Minster Lal Bahadur Shastri, who was chairing the meeting, didn't acknowledge Rustamji's objection. Two months later, Rustamji was sitting in a new office in New Delhi as the founding director general (DG) of the BSF. Not just the founder, he was also the only 'borderman', as he called himself.

He built the force from scratch, absorbing the border police units of the states. He knew his way about New Delhi, having served in the Intelligence Bureau for six years, ending his deputation to the central agency as a deputy director. But that didn't make things any easier for him. He had to navigate red tape and opposition in some quarters to raise the force. He started a recruitment process to create a service cadre, and brought in a number of retired and serving officers from the Indian armed forces to lead the new force.

The government was about to release emergency commissioned officers (ECOs), who had been commissioned to the Indian Army in 1962. These officers had seen action during the 1965

India–Pakistan war, and Rustamji took in about 600 of the ECOs as officers and instructors to lead fresh recruits and fifty-two battalions of border guards absorbed from the state police units.

In 1971, the BSF was a young force. Its armoury and infrastructure were not comparable to those of any of the three armed forces, but Rustamji had learnt to improvise and advised all his officers to innovate.

Rustamji had been closely watching the crisis unfolding in East Pakistan. And when he heard of the genocide, he wanted the Indian government to act immediately. Rustamji had grown impatient with the government every day since the news of the genocide, till he got a green signal. It finally came on 28 March at a high-powered meeting in New Delhi and was endorsed the next day by the chief of the army staff, General Sam Manekshaw.

The plan was to move the senior officers and instructors at the BSF Academy in Tekanpur, Madhya Pradesh, to the borders and control operations from there. As soon as he got the confirmation, Rustamji called up the senior officers at the academy with the following directions:

> Brig B.C. Pande with his 104 Commando Bn to proceed to Tripura to help the Bangladesh liberation forces.
>
> Col Rampal Singh with his 103 Commando Bn at Cooch Behar, West Bengal.
>
> Col Megh Singh with his 18 Commando Bn at Bongaon, West Bengal.
>
> Brig Michael S. Chatterjee with his commando staff from Hazaribagh at Balurghat, West Bengal.

The Indian parliament passed a unanimous resolution on 31 March 1971:

> This House records its profound conviction that the historic upsurge of the 75 million people of Bangladesh will triumph.

The House wishes to assure them that their struggle will receive the wholehearted sympathy and support of the people of India.

The same day, Prime Minister Gandhi told Rustamji, 'Do what you like, but don't get caught.'[15]

* * *

The heads of the security agencies, including the R&AW chief, R.N. Kao, made plans for the BSF's initial operations. They decided that the BSF would help the Bengali military and paramilitary officers and personnel across the border to sustain their ongoing battles against the Pakistan Army. In several places, the EBR was fighting the Pakistan Army. The EPR had taken control of the border posts. The BSF commandos would also conduct secret missions in East Pakistan to support them.

One of the immediate missions was to sabotage the Pakistan Army by choking its supply lines. The most important supply route was from the Chittagong port to Dacca and to other major cities which had large garrisons. The Bengali soldiers were still fighting in Chittagong, but the Pakistanis could overwhelm them with numbers. A BSF demolition crew could sabotage roads, railway lines and bridges to cut off the rest of East Pakistan from Chittagong.

* * *

In Tekanpur, Madhya Pradesh, Brigadier Pande sat with his deputies all through the morning of 31 March to identify the best men to work with him in Tripura and plan their operations. He had picked three commanders to lead teams of five soldiers each. The sabotage teams were to operate from the headquarters of the battalions stationed in Tripura.

Asstt Comdt Lila Ram Rana, a senior instructor at the Tekanpur Academy, was away in Gwalior that morning. When he returned on his scooter the sentry at the gate stopped Rana and told him that somebody at the office was looking for him. They had made announcements over the PA system.

'*Aapko kothi pe bulaya hai* [Please head to the main building].'

The 'kothi' was once a palace, or at least a lake house, used by the erstwhile royal family of Gwalior, the Scindias. Rustamji had negotiated a deal for the BSF to acquire the sprawling estate, including the lake and the palace, for Rs 6 lakh in 1966 to start the BSF academy.[16]

Brig. Pande was sitting with other senior officers in the kothi, and instructors of Asstt Comdt Rana's rank were also there.

'You know what is happening in East Pakistan. Please get ready, you have to go there. We will go to Delhi first, where the DG will brief you,' Brig. Pande told Asstt Comdt Rana. He then read out a list of names of fourteen others who would accompany him.

Asstt Comdt Rana nodded, and went off to tell the others and to pack his bag. They took the next flight to New Delhi and, upon landing, headed straight to the North Block, where they waited in the BSF control room till Rustamji called for the three team commanders to brief them on their mission.

Along with Asstt Comdt Rana, the three other instructors from the BSF Academy were assistant commandants Ashoke Kumar, P.K. Sharma and Bharat Bhushan. They returned to Tekanpur and headed to the BSF supply store to see what they could get. They got hold of tents, jungle boots, 9 mm pistols, ammunition and as many explosives as they could carry. There was a fresh supply of PEK explosives and some TNT bars; more would be procured in Tripura.

The R&AW lent two of its An-12 planes from its aviation unit (Aviation Research Centre/ARC) for the operation, and two of its operatives went along with the team. They left early on 30 March. Asstt Comdt Rana's plane landed but the second one couldn't due to some technical snag. Packed with explosives, the plane headed back westwards and landed at the Bagdogra airport in West Bengal and arrived in Agartala the next day.

At the time when the Tekanpur commandos were settling into the BSF headquarters in Agartala, two weary travellers turned up close to the India–East Pakistan border. They had walked for three days to get there.

* * *

Tajuddin Ahmed, general secretary of the Awami League, and Amirul Islam, a Dacca-based barrister—both elected members of the Pakistan National Assembly—hid as soon as they heard of the crackdown on the night of 25 March. The Pakistan Army was out for blood, picking targets off a list. And the Awami League leaders were high-priority targets. They spent two nights at Lalmatia in Dacca, not far from Mujib's residence in Dhanmondi.

Amirul Islam was convinced that they would get help in his native Kushtia district. The two disguised themselves and headed west, towards Kushtia, on 27 March. He had prepared a contingency plan to reach out to an Awami League leader in Jhenaidah in case things took a turn for the worse. The time had come, and the plan was activated.

It took them three days, walking and riding on bullock carts, to get to the western edge of Kushtia district. When they got close to the border, Amirul Islam met with Bengali civil servants at a pre-arranged place on 29 March.

Tawfiq Elahi Chowdhury, sub-divisional officer of Meherpur, and Mahbubuddin Ahmed, sub-divisional police officer of Jhenaidah, were already in touch with the BSF officers of 76 Bn at the Banpur–Gede border. Tawfiq Chowdhury had publicly declared his allegiance to the Bangladesh government on 28 March.

Along with Ahmed, he was coordinating the liberation movement in that part of Kushtia district. Major Abu Osman Chowdhury, an officer of the EPR, was leading the Bengali troops there. Tawfiq Elahi Chowdhury had already hinted to the BSF commanding officer that two senior leaders of the liberation movement were on their way from Dacca.

On 30 March, Tawfiq Chowdhury sat down with his guests in a forest close to the Indian border and sent word to the BSF officers of 76 Bn on their behalf: Two senior members of the Awami League, who were part of Mujib's inner circle, were close to the border. They would like to meet with the Indian prime minister if welcomed as state guests.

The 76 Bn officer sent an encrypted signal to IG Golak Majumdar as soon as he got the message from Tawfiq Elahi Chowdhury. Majumdar picked up the hotline to his boss in New Delhi, shot off directions to the commanding officer of 76 Bn and headed out from his office. Rustamji rushed to the airport and boarded the BSF plane to Calcutta.

The BSF commander at the Banpur–Gede BOP in Nadia district of West Bengal sent a section of BSF men to receive the politicians and welcome them to India as guests and potential representatives of state. The official welcome by a senior officer could wait. The security of the two Awami League leaders was more important.

Two hours later, Golak Majumdar's jeep screeched to a halt, and he came out bearing refreshments for the two Awami League leaders, who were famished and tired from their arduous journey across East Pakistan.

Dumdum Airport was on the northern outskirts of Calcutta, and on the way back to Majumdar's office, the jeep took them to the airport first. They drove right up to the tarmac, where the BSF aircraft carrying Rustamji landed soon afterwards. They were all shepherded into a black Ambassador and driven to the city.

Majumdar had made arrangements to put them up at Assam Bhavan on Russell Street, a stone's throw from the BSF's Eastern Frontier office building on Lord Sinha Road. It was past 1 a.m. on 31 March when they arrived at Assam Bhavan. At that hour, there was nowhere to buy food or clothes for the two guests.

Rustamji always kept a kit handy in case of urgent travels. He pulled out spare sets of pyjamas from the kit for the guests. But organizing food was still a hurdle.

Majumdar's friend and Kolkata-based art collector Nihar Ranjan Chakravarty is ninety-nine years old at the time of writing this book. But he has a clear memory and can easily recollect the events of the night.

Chakravarty used to live on Russell Street at the time. Majumdar asked him for food. He sent over eggs while he went to wake up his cooks and get a meal prepared. Rustamji pulled out a camping stove and pan from his kit, and Majumdar got to work making omelettes for all of them. Then, Chakravarty arrived with the best dinner he could have rustled up in that time.

The next day, Chakravarty was sent to New Market to buy ready-made clothes for their guests. Rustamji wanted the best suits for them, because they were to meet the Indian prime minister as representatives of another country. While Chakravarty went shopping, Tajuddin and Amirul Islam told Rustamji and Majumdar of the developments since the election. The multiple rounds of talks, the wavering of Yahya Khan, the pushy attempts by Bhutto, the stalemate and, finally, the massacre. Rustamji had passed on the message to Indira Gandhi's office about their guests and was waiting for word on the date of the meeting. Meanwhile, Tajuddin was keen to meet with Maj. Abu Osman Chowdhury, who was leading the freedom fighters in Kushtia district, as well as get an idea of the military help India could provide.

5

A Helpful Neighbour

On the morning of 1 April 1971, IG Golak Majumdar, Tajuddin and the BSF intelligence chief, IG P.R. Rajgopal, headed to the India–East Pakistan border near Krishnanagar. Across the border, the territory was held by the Mukti Fauj, led by Maj. Abu Osman Chowdhury, who commanded the Kushtia–Jessore sector, and Dr Ashab-ul-Haq, an elected member of the Provincial Assembly of East Pakistan, for Kushtia. The operations in that sector were being controlled from Chuadanga in East Pakistan.

On 27 March, Maj. Osman had organized 700 men, comprising EBR and EPR personnel, and civilians who had been recruited by Dr Haq. They attacked a company of the Pakistan Army's Baloch regiment in the Kushtia cantonment. Around seventy of the Pakistani soldiers survived the attack and fled towards Jessore in a convoy of trucks and jeeps. But the Bengali freedom fighters had already rigged the vehicles with explosives. Around 30 km from Kushtia, Maj. Osman's men fired upon the trucks and blew them up. The survivors were hunted down by armed Bengali villagers, and the freedom fighters could save only a lieutenant of the Pakistan Army. He was taken POW and held in Chuadanga.

Maj. Osman met with Tajuddin and the two BSF officers at the Gede BOP of the BSF's 72 Bn on 1 April. Maj. Osman asked the two senior BSF officers for help with arms and ammunition. They promised to provide a limited supply. The next day, the BSF sent one of its officers, Col A. Chakravarty, with a team of commandos in a truck. All of the men were dressed in civvies and fully armed, ready for clandestine warfare as Mukti Joddhas (freedom fighters).

Majumdar returned to Calcutta with Tajuddin and Amirul Islam after the meeting. On the same evening, that is, 1 April, Rajgopal and Majumdar escorted them to New Delhi to meet with the Indian prime minister. According to one account, the R&AW had verified Tajuddin's credentials with a close confidant of Mujib's in Calcutta, Chittaranjan Suttar. He was an Awami League leader and had spent time in prison with Mujib after his arrest. Suttar had been told by Mujib that Tajuddin was to lead the liberation movement in his absence.

Tajuddin and Amirul Islam spent two days meeting with officials, diplomats and some East Pakistani intellectuals, before they met with Mrs Gandhi on 4 April.[17] (Some sources date the meeting to 3 April 1971).

India and Pakistan had not come to the brink of war since 1965, but there had been a steady worsening of relations between the two neighbours, with Kashmir being the biggest source of dispute. Pakistan spoke tough, emboldened by its alliance with China and the US. The threat of a Chinese attack on India hung in the air. Using a pretext of troop build-up close to its borders, China could launch an offensive to help its ally Pakistan.

The US was one of the most powerful countries in the world and had the support of other Western powers, including the NATO constituents. It was engaged in different parts of Asia, in competition with the USSR, for influence and control. In 1971, the Cold War was at its peak. The US was in the thick of the Vietnam War, and President Richard Nixon wanted to reach out to China. His national security adviser, Henry Kissinger, had promised to open a direct channel to China through Pakistan.

Against that backdrop, all eyes panned to South Asia as news of the Pakistani genocide on the Bengalis spread across the world. The bureaucrats were divided on what and how much help India should provide to its neighbours. The Indian Army needed time to organize itself for war. DG Rustamji insisted that at least his force should not hold back.

Mrs Gandhi met with Tajuddin, Amirul Islam and others at her office. The tone of the meeting had been set by the Indian parliamentary resolution assuring them of Indian sympathy and support for the struggle.

Tajuddin later told senior journalist Manash Ghosh that the Indian prime minister had treated Tajuddin as an equal and been candid about her support for their efforts. Mrs Gandhi's adviser, P.N. Haksar, confirmed this to Ghosh later. According to Ghosh, Tajuddin asked for unfettered movement of Bengali freedom fighters through the India–East Pakistan border, and use of Indian territory to plan missions and train the freedom fighters. He also asked for supplies of arms and ammunition for the liberation war.

Amirul Islam, too, wrote about the meeting. Tajuddin had asked for arms, ammunition and other supplies that were needed to wage the liberation war inside East Pakistan, to which Mrs Gandhi had readily agreed. In a later interview, Amirul Islam said that the Awami League leader and lawyer Serajul Haque had been present at the Prime Minister's Office (PMO) at the time. Through a keyhole, Serajul Haque, also known to the Indian authorities as a close personal friend of Mujib's, had confirmed the identities of Tajuddin and the others before they were allowed into the meeting.

Tajuddin told Mrs Gandhi that he was meeting her as a representative of a provisional government, picked by Mujib as a contingency in the event of his absence. According to Ghosh, Mrs Gandhi asked Tajuddin to form a government in order to legitimize the liberation movement on a global level too. The war, she said, had to be fought on different fronts, and a sworn-in government of elected legislators would create a deep impression on the rest of the world. She also asked Rustamji to extend full cooperation and support to the Mukti Joddhas. Mrs Gandhi had already given the same direction earlier, during closed-door meetings of the government, that the R&AW would strategize and the BSF would be the implementing agency.[18]

The positive tone of the meeting with Mrs Gandhi reassured Tajuddin. He met a few times with Rustamji in New Delhi, in whom he had found a supporter of the Bangladesh liberation war. He wanted to set up a government-in-exile and needed Rustamji's help.

The BSF flew down to New Delhi some senior elected leaders of East Pakistan from the places in India where they had taken refuge. This included Syed Nazrul Islam, who had appeared at Dalu border checkpost in Meghalaya. There was Col M.A.G. Osmani, who had retired from the Pakistan Army; Captain Mansoor Ali, MPA for Pabna; Khondokar Moshtaq Ahmed, MNA for Comilla; and Kamruzzaman, MNA for Jessore. Maulana Bhashani, the founding president of the Awami League, also joined them from Assam, where he had fled through the India–East Pakistan border in Meghalaya.

A democratic government needed a codified constitution. The BSF law officer, Col N.S. Bains, helped Amirul Islam, a barrister, prepare a draft that was vetted by another barrister from Calcutta, Subrata Roy Choudhury. It was approved, after due changes, sometime between 6 and 7 April.[19] This became the constitution of the 'provisional government of Bangladesh' and came to be known as the Proclamation of Independence. It served as the constitution of Bangladesh for the duration of the liberation war.

The name 'Bangla Desh' was chosen by the leaders, after some alternatives had been considered and rejected, in New Delhi. Rustamji later wrote that at a meeting held to decide the name, the East Pakistani leaders had mulled over names like East Bengal,

Banga Bhumi (Land of Bengal), Banga (Bengal) and Swadhin Bangla (Independent Bengal). It was Tajuddin who pointed out that Mujib had suggested the name Bangla Desh (the Nation of Bengalis), and all of them decided to go with it. (The one-word variant, Bangladesh, came later).

A flag of Bangladesh already existed, created by a group of students in Dhaka University in June 1970. The students were part of the Swadhin Bangla Biplobi Parishad (Free Bengal Revolutionary Council), led by Serajul Alam Khan. Also called the Swadhin Bangla Nucleus, this group was established in 1961 by Mujib, and other similar student movements had later taken shape across East Pakistan.

The background of the flag was green, with a red sun in its centre. This part is similar to the present-day flag of Bangladesh. But the flag used during the liberation war had a map of East Pakistan, filled in gold, on top of the red sun. The golden silhouette of East Pakistan's map signified 'Sonar Bangla' (Golden Bengal). It was a reference to the song that had united Bengalis in East Pakistan. This very song, written by Rabindranath Tagore, which the Bengalis had used during their protests, was chosen as the national anthem of Bangladesh.

The imposition of Urdu by West Pakistan involved the stamping out of any affinity that the Bengali Muslims had for their own language and culture. The Bengalis in East Pakistan were fond of Rabindra Sangeet (the songs of Tagore) and Nazrul Geeti (the songs of Kazi Nazrul Islam). In 1967, Pakistani authorities banned the broadcast of Rabindra Sangeet over the radio.

A report from Rawalpindi, published on 24 June 1967 in the *Pakistan Observer*, noted:

Khawaja Shahabuddin, Minister for Information and Broadcasting, told the National Assembly today that songs by Poet Rabindra Nath Tagore, which he termed as 'against Pakistan's cultural

values', was banned from future broadcasts, and the use of other
songs was to be reduced.

Shahabuddin had said this, in response to a question in the
Pakistani parliament. At the same session, he had said that they
had not banned the use of Nazrul Geeti. The Bengali Muslims
took this as another affront to their mother tongue.

The move to ban Rabindra Sangeet came two decades after
the authorities in West Pakistan had removed Bengali from the list
of national languages, triggering the *bhasha andolan*. At the time
of Partition, nearly 56 per cent of the population was Bengali,
and they opposed the imposition of Urdu, meant to cement the
Islamic identity of the country. They wanted to preserve their
distinct cultural identity of being Bengalis.

With the constitution, flag and anthem ready, Tajuddin and
the other legislators wanted the exiled government to take oaths
of office in a swearing-in ceremony. Rustamji suggested that it
should take place in East Pakistan. This was roughly between
7 and 8 April 1971.

At that time in East Pakistan, the Bengali officers and
personnel of the EPR and EBR had liberated some areas within
East Pakistan, several of which were close to the borders. The
glaring exception was Abdul Kader Siddiqi and his 'Kader Bahini',
which had picketed 'liberated zones' in Tangail district, which was
not close to any border.

Considering security and other factors, Rustamji suggested
choosing a place across the border adjacent to West Bengal.
Majumdar was tasked with finding a place that was accessible
from Calcutta, from where they could take members of the
international press.

One possible venue was Rajshahi district, which borders
Malda and Mushirdabad districts in West Bengal. The other
was Chuadanga district, which borders Nadia district in
West Bengal. The situation in Rajshahi district was not ideal.

Two companies of the BSF's 74 Bn had attacked the Pakistan Army and cornered its soldiers in the Rajshahi cantonment. Dacca had sent reinforcements, and there was intense firing and shelling at the border every day.

Majumdar suggested Chuadanga as the best possible place for the swearing-in ceremony. It was far from any major cantonment of the Pakistan Army, and the BSF had control over it. Rustamji approved the plan, and Majumdar began to make the preparations. The exact place that was selected was a mango grove on the eastern fringe of Meherpur town, in a locality called Baidyanath Tala.[20]

* * *

Tajuddin returned to Calcutta on 9 April, on a mission to secure the support of the elected leaders of East Pakistan. The provisional government had to pick its leaders and cabinet members.

The Pakistani authorities had arrested Mujib on 25 March, after he'd made the Proclamation of Independence, and transported him to a jail in West Pakistan. The provisional government chose him as the president of Bangla Desh. The seniormost person after Mujib was Nazrul Islam, who was chosen as the vice president of Bangla Desh and its acting president in the absence of Mujib. Tajuddin would be the prime minister. These decisions needed the support of the Awami League leaders, elected lawmakers and the influential heads of other political parties of East Pakistan, such as Maulana Bhashani.

After his meeting with the Indian prime minister and the arrangements for the formalization of the provisional government, Tajuddin returned to Calcutta. There, Majumdar had planned to put up the political leaders at a private hotel. He was making long-term arrangements to accommodate East Pakistani political leaders in a safe house from where they could operate.

The BSF owned a few buildings in and around Calcutta. The best location was two buildings away from the Eastern Frontier

HQ, which housed Majumdar's office. The headquarters were on Lord Sinha Road, a few metres from its junction with Theatre Road. Around the corner is 8 Theatre Road. This property, a large bungalow with a spacious yard and garden, was in the BSF's possession.

This tiny neighbourhood is possibly one of the invisible lines demarcating south and central Calcutta. The house on 8 Theatre Road was a landmark, steeped in history. The freedom fighter and spiritual guru Sri Aurobindo was born in this house, when it was numbered 4 Theatre Road. The premises were later handed over to the Aurobindo Society.

It turned out to be a convenient location to house the provisional government and was being prepared so that they could shift in. For the time being, they were in a private hotel across the road, where the BSF kept rooms on hold for visiting officials.

While the swearing-in ceremony and their office was being readied, Tajuddin set about meeting with as many of the elected representatives and other political leaders of East Pakistan as was possible. Many of them had fled the genocide and were already in Calcutta. Some of the political and youth leaders did not support Tajuddin's decision to meet with Mrs Gandhi. They also did not think that Tajuddin should lead the Bangladeshi government. They preferred a revolutionary council to direct the liberation war. However, Tajuddin was convinced by the Indian government's argument that a liberation required the support of the United Nations (UN). The member countries of the UN could be persuaded if a democratically elected government held the reins of the liberation effort.

Other Awami League leaders had emerged in border states of eastern India—Assam, Meghalaya and Tripura. Tajuddin used the BSF's help to get to some of those places and meet with the politicians as well as the military leaders. The BSF provided a

Dakota plane to fly him to Meghalaya, and to other places in West Bengal, Assam and Tripura.

In the second week of April 1971, Tajuddin headed to Agartala and met with the local Awami League leaders who were working out of the refugee camps. He also met with the military leaders who were working out of Tripura, where the Mukti Bahini had had some success.

Col Osmani had retired from the Pakistan Army and had been a successful candidate of the 1970 general election in Pakistan. He had won from a constituency in Sylhet, now in northern Bangladesh. On the night of Operation Searchlight, he was in Mujib's house in Dacca. After it became known that Mujib had decided to remain in his house and face arrest, Col Osmani hid elsewhere in Dacca for four days. Then, he travelled in disguise to northern East Pakistan and crossed into Tripura. He held meetings with the EBR officers and suggested that they capture territories. The officers were in favour of a political government being established to call the shots of the liberation movement.

It was shortly after this that Tajuddin arrived in Agartala and met with Col Osmani and the other leaders. There, he also met with Khondokar Moshtaq Ahmed, the Awami League leader and legislator. On this trip, Tajuddin was able to build a consensus on the composition of the government-in-exile. Khondokar got the foreign ministry post in the cabinet in exchange for his support. The Awami League leaders reached a consensus on the creation and composition of the provisional government they were to form. The provisional constitution of Bangla Desh, drafted in New Delhi, was adopted on 10 April and came into effect prospectively on 26 March, the day Mujib had made the Proclamation of Independence.

The same day as the meeting of the Awami League legislators, that is, 10 April, Tajuddin recorded a speech with the staff of the

Swadhin Bangla Betaar Kendra, a pro-liberation clandestine radio station, on 11 April. It was picked up by other radio stations and broadcast elsewhere. Indian newspapers reported the speech the next day, and the international press, camped in Calcutta, picked it up too.

Tajuddin's 11 April speech, delivered in Bengali on behalf of the provisional Bangla Deshi government, was the first public address by a political leader to the people of East Pakistan since the genocide had been launched on 25 March. It was a clarion call to the Bengalis of East Pakistan to pick up arms for the liberation of Bangla Desh and an outline of the future.

Tajuddin opened the address by saluting the freedom fighters who continued to fight and those who had sacrificed their lives for the liberation of Bangla Desh ever since the crackdown by the Yahya Khan regime. He described the movement as a form of 'epic resistance' that was winning the admiration of the world. Tajuddin said that before they had responded to the genocide, the Bengalis were considered a people who immersed themselves in art and culture—violence and fighting had been alien to them. But the same people had admirably responded to the unfolding genocide as warriors. He asked more of them to join the liberation effort and to use their tools as weapons to fight off the Pakistan Army.

Tajuddin outlined the sectoral leadership of the Mukti Fauj under the Bengali officers of the Pakistan Army who had revolted. He said those military officers had liberated many places in Bangla Desh and had sequestered the Pakistan Army into their cantonments at Dinajpur, Bogra, Pabna and Rangpur. Tajuddin acknowledged that Major Zia was the first to announce the existence of a provisional government of Bangla Desh.[21] He said that the government had been set up in a liberated zone, with a regional branch administering the eastern zone from Sylhet–Comilla.

He invited humanitarian agencies to get directly in touch with the government to provide aid to the citizens of Bangla Desh. He asked for support in the form of arms to repel the Pakistani military from East Pakistan.

Tajuddin pointed out that some countries (indicating the US and China) had given arms to Pakistan so that it could protect its people, but the Pakistani military was using the arms to kill and maim the very people they were supposed to protect. He asked the countries supplying weapons to Pakistan to suspend further deliveries.

He asked Bengalis settled abroad to mobilize funds and supply weapons for the liberation effort. He also made the same appeal to other countries. 'To the extent that Yahya's mercenaries remain insensitive to world opinion and continue with their planned genocide of Bengalis, we appeal for arms from all countries who value freedom and have fought aggression in their own time,' he said.

The Bangla Desh government wanted aid but without any strings attached. 'Whilst there is still talk in some countries of this being an internal affair of Pakistan, it is becoming evident that the massacre of 75 million people and the attempt to suppress their struggle for freedom is now an international issue of major dimensions which threatens the conscience as much as the peace of the region.'

The provisional government released a press statement on 13 April:

A six-member war cabinet headed by Bangabandhu Sheikh Mujibur Rahman was formed today. It was announced that Syed Nazrul Islam as vice-president and the Awami League party General Secretary Tajuddin Ahmad as prime minister, would guide and coordinate the war of liberation. According to the announcement, other members of the government are Khandaker Mushtaque Ahmed, Capt Mansoor Ali A.H.M. Kamaruzzaman.

There were four days left before the swearing-in ceremony. The Awami League leaders and the designated war cabinet headed back to Calcutta to prepare to take their oaths and settle in. Like everything else preceding it, this too was a hush-hush affair.

6

Mujibnagar

Many of the BSF's officers from New Delhi flew down to Calcutta to help with the swearing-in ceremony. The threat from the Pakistani armed forces was both over land and by air.

There were no military installations in Baidyanath Tala. The only civilian area that had been strafed and bombed by the Pakistan Air Force (PAF) was the radio station in Chittagong. The thick cover of the mango grove was considered adequate protection from eyes in the sky. Besides, the Mukti Fauj and 76 Bn held the neighbouring areas in East Pakistan. An Indian Army unit was also close by.

For the event, there would also be operatives of the R&AW and the IB present, though incognito. The planning took place in Fort William, the headquarters of the Indian Army's Eastern Command. The Indian Army had stationed[22] a brigade close by. One of the officers posted to that brigade was Captain (later Brigadier) R.P. Singh, who later became a trainer at the first war course for sixty-one officers of the Bangladesh forces near Siliguri in West Bengal. Mujib's son, Sheikh Kamal, was one of those sixty-one officers who completed the course on 9 October 1971.

The commandant was instructed to move an entire company near Gede in addition to the one already present there. The Indian Army unit was close by at the border, but only officers attended the event along with military intelligence operatives. All the troop movements took place before dawn on 17 April.

In the days leading up to the event, Majumdar was terribly busy. He was present at all meetings and took decisions during the planning, which were classified as secret. Yet, on several evenings before the event, Majumdar disappeared with his close friend Nihar Ranjan Chakravarty, dressed in civvies. Nobody knew the reason why the Eastern Frontier's IG would go missing when a crucial event, which he seemed personally invested in pulling off, was just around the corner.

But the global headlines in a few days made it all clear. While the troops of the Indian Army and the BSF were buffing up the border protection, the public relations officers of the BSF, Samar Basu, and of the Indian Army's Eastern Command, Col B.P. Rikhye, had a cumbersome task. They needed to organize and ferry reporters of the Indian and foreign press camped in Calcutta. This had to be done surreptitiously and without letting the reporters know why they were being summoned.

Basu had a list of all the Indian and foreign reporters and their addresses, totalling eighty-two names.[23] The two divided the list and, on 16 April, set about informing the reporters that they should get to the Press Club of Calcutta by 4 a.m. on 17 April. There was to be an announcement regarding the Bangladesh liberation movement, but nobody was told what its content was and who was to make it.

The task of ferrying such a large press contingent was going to be difficult. There weren't many private vehicles available. The BSF didn't want to directly contract vehicles, as that might have pricked up the ears of foreign spies. Getting hold of cars from other government agencies involved red tape and might lead to a news leak. Majumdar feared that there were several CIA and ISI spies in the city. So he entrusted the task to his friend Chakravarty while diplomats in Calcutta tried to find out what the announcement was about.

Chakravarty was well networked and reached out to his businessman friends to rent cars. No single car rental agency had so many vehicles available. Chakravarty spent all of 16 April getting hold of close to fifty private vehicles that were to ferry the foreign and Indian reporters to Baidyanath Tala in Meherpur.

Early the next morning, both the BSF and Indian Army public relations officers were there to receive the reporters outside the Press Club of Calcutta. Chakravarty arrived with his fleet of around fifty vehicles comprising jeeps, cars and buses. He had personally checked each vehicle and its roadworthiness. The eighty-two journalists were packed into the vehicles before 4 a.m.

Rustamji arrived with Golok Majumdar, P.R. Rajgopal and the elected legislators of East Pakistan in a separate convoy of cars. The convoy of VIPs led the cavalcade. The drivers of the vehicles carrying the journalists did not know the route or the destination. Before he gave the direction to move out, Rustamji took a brief pause. In his memoirs, he has described[24] this fleeting moment:

> The tremble may well have been out of the excitement of the opportunity given to me for associating myself with an event which eventually would have a far-reaching effect on international affairs in general, and on the history of nations of the subcontinent in particular.

Journalist Manash Ghosh, who was part of the press contingent, wrote that only when they had crossed Kalyani did he realize that they were on the way to the India–East Pakistan border—a trip he had made quite a few times recently. The objective was still a mystery.

* * *

The BSF company, in civvies, were guarding the periphery of the mango grove. There was imminent danger that the location could be strafed by Pakistani aircraft. Early that morning, to protect the venue, BSF troops had stacked sandbags on the ground on the edge of the mango grove, and built machine-gun nests that would protect against attacks by ground or air.

A BSF team was specifically deployed to prepare the venue. Along with EPR personnel, they put together a low dais using wooden planks procured from Gede village, and it was decorated using garlands of flowers. They borrowed a dozen chairs and placed them on the dais, and installed a microphone and a battery-operated PA system with aluminium-cone speakers. All of this was done in an hour, after the cars had passed a specific checkpoint two hours from the swearing-in venue.

The convoy of cars carrying the East Pakistani legislators and press contingent from Calcutta snaked into the Baidyanath Tala mango grove before noon on 17 April. Indian Air Force planes began air patrols along the border at 1 p.m. Their mission was to keep any PAF fighters out. Policemen from East Pakistan, the EPR and the civilian guard were present to give a guard of honour to East Pakistani legislators. Their uniforms were not in the best shape, but their morale was high.

Majumdar got hold of a tabla and harmonium from Meherpur, to accompany a group of singers brought from Krishnanagar town, who were asked to sing 'Amar Sonar Bangla'—it was the first official rendition of the Rabindra Sangeet tune as the national anthem of Bangla Desh. The BSF men had erected a bamboo pole and raised the wrapped flag of Bangla Desh on it, with the pull ropes attached to it. The flag had been arranged by Golak Majumdar with the help of tailors from the New Market area of Calcutta.

The elected legislators climbed the dais and took their seats. The Indian authorities stayed away from both the dais and the microphone on it. Majumdar and Rajgopal, who were the seniormost Indian officials present, returned to the Indian side of the border as the event was about to start. Rustamji, too, left and returned to Calcutta. But the venue was far from empty. Counting the journalists, politicians, the BSF personnel, the spooks of many agencies and residents of Indian and East Pakistani villages, the estimated crowd was 15,000.

Yusuf Ali, the Dinajpur MNA, first took the microphone and read out the text of the Proclamation of Independence, which became the operational constitution of Bangla Desh:

PROCLAMATION OF INDEPENDENCE[25]
Mujibnagar, Bangla Desh
Dated 10th day of April 1971.
Whereas free elections were held in Bangla Desh from 7 December 1970 to 17 January 1971, to elect representatives for the purpose of framing a Constitution,
AND
Whereas at these elections the people of Bangla Desh elected 167 out of 169 representatives belonging to the Awami League,
AND
Whereas General Yahya Khan summoned the elected representatives of the people to meet on 3 March 1971, for the purpose of framing a Constitution,
AND
Whereas the Assembly so summoned was arbitrarily and illegally postponed for indefinite period,
AND
Whereas instead of fulfilling their promise and while still conferring with the representatives of the people of Bangladesh, Pakistan authorities declared an unjust and treacherous war,
AND

Whereas in the facts and circumstances of such treacherous conduct Bangabandhu Sheikh Mujibur Rahman, the undisputed leader of the 75 million people of Bangladesh, in due fulfillment of the legitimate right of self-determination of the people of Bangladesh, duly made a declaration of independence at Dacca on 26 March 1971, and urged the people of Bangla Desh to defend the honour and integrity of Bangla Desh,

AND

Whereas in the conduct of a ruthless and savage war the Pakistani authorities committed and are still continuously committing numerous acts of genocide and unprecedented tortures, amongst others on the civilian and unarmed people of Bangladesh,

AND

Whereas the Pakistan Government by levying an unjust war and committing genocide and by other repressive measures made it impossible for the elected representatives of the people of Bangla Desh to meet and frame a Constitution, and give to themselves a Government,

AND

Whereas the people of Bangla Desh by their heroism, bravery and revolutionary fervour have established effective control over the territories of Bangla Desh,

We the elected representatives of the people of Bangla Desh, as honour bound by the mandate given to us by the people of Bangla Desh whose will is supreme duly constituted ourselves into a Constituent Assembly, and

having held mutual consultations, and

in order to ensure for the people of Bangla Desh equality, human dignity and social justice,

declare and constitute Bangla Desh to be sovereign People's Republic and thereby confirm the declaration of independence already made by Bangabandhu Sheikh Mujibur Rahman, and

do hereby affirm and resolve that till such time as a Constitution is framed, Bangabandhu Sheikh Mujibur Rahman shall be the

President of the Republic and that Syed Nazrul Islam shall be the Vice President of the Republic, and

that the President shall be the Supreme Commander of all the Armed Forces of the Republic,

shall exercise all the Executive and Legislative powers of the Republic including the power to grant pardon,

shall have the power to appoint a Prime Minister and such other Ministers as he considers necessary,

shall have the power to levy taxes and expend monies,

shall have the power to summon and adjourn the Constituent Assembly, and

do all other things that may be necessary to give to the people of Bangla Desh an orderly and just Government,

We the elected representatives of the people of Bangla Desh do further resolve that in the event of there being no President or the President being unable to enter upon his office or being unable to exercise his powers and duties, due to any reason whatsoever, the Vice-President shall have and exercise all the powers, duties and responsibilities herein conferred on the President,

We further resolve that we undertake to observe and give effect to all duties and obligations that devolve upon us as a member of the family of nations and under the Charter of United Nations,

We further resolve that this proclamation of independence shall be deemed to have come into effect from 26th day of March 1971.

We further resolve that in order to give effect to this instrument we appoint Prof. Yusuf Ali our duly Constituted Potentiary and to give to the President and the Vice-President oaths of office.

Professor Yusuf Ali

Duly Constituted Potentiary

By and under the authority of the Constituent Assembly of Bangla Desh

* * *

Golak Majumdar reported to Rustamji that it was a very emotional moment when the flag was unfurled to the rendition of 'Amar Sonar Bangla' in the background.

The Constituent Assembly of Bangla Desh appointed Sheikh Mujibur Rahman as its president and Syed Nazrul as the vice-president, which made him the acting president in Mujib's absence. Professor Yusuf Ali administered the oaths of office to the legislators. After they were sworn in as members of the Mujibnagar government, Nazrul Islam, the acting president of Bangla Desh, appointed Tajuddin as the prime minister and the following six legislators as members of his war cabinet:

Finance minister: Mansur Ali
Home minister: A.H.M. Qamaruzzaman
Information and broadcast: Abdul Mannan
Foreign minister: Khondokar Moshtaq Ahmed
Planning commission: Nurul Islam
Defence minister: Col (retd) M.A.G. Osmani (and commander-in-chief of Mukti Bahini)

The Proclamation itself renamed Baidyanath Tala as Mujibnagar. The government came to be known as the Mujibnagar government, but that was the only time the entire war cabinet was physically present there during the Bangladesh liberation war.

The Mujibnagar government moved to the office at 8 Theatre Road, Calcutta, provided by the BSF. Tajuddin lived in a room behind his office, and the ministers worked out of the bungalow on Theatre Road but lived in another BSF-owned colonial-era building on Ballygunge Circular Road, which became the venue for several historic events in the liberation war.

As soon as the event was over, Golak Majumdar jumped into his jeep to head back to Calcutta, where Rustamji was waiting for him. The two had cooked up something big. It was the perfect icing on the cake of the swearing-in of the Mujibnagar government.

7

The Diplomatic Switch

A Few Days before the Swearing-in

Golak Majumdar and Rustamji were at the Eastern Frontier HQ in Calcutta, working out the details of the swearing-in. Things seemed to be falling into place, despite the high level of secrecy that they had to maintain.

Something seemed to be bothering the BSF director general. Rustamji picked up the telephone and dialled the PMO. He had access to the PM's hotline. While Tajuddin had been in Delhi meeting with the prime minister, two Pakistani diplomats of Bengali origin had defected to Bangla Desh. Some other Bengali diplomats of Pakistan did the same elsewhere in the world later.

K.M. Shehabuddin, the second secretary of the Pakistani diplomatic mission to India, and Amjadul Haque, the assistant press attaché, made their decision right upon hearing of the genocide and the arrest of Mujib. With the support of their families, they reached out to a bureaucrat at the Indian Ministry of External Affairs on 28 March. They publicly severed their ties with Pakistan at a press conference in New Delhi on 6 April and met with the Indian PM on 9 April. They were given asylum in India, and, later in the year, the two were shifted to an office in New Delhi that was assigned to the Mujibnagar government.

Rustamji had a similar idea but on a much grander scale. He proposed to Mrs Gandhi that they should offer support to the entire Bengali-majority staff of the Pakistani deputy high commission in Calcutta to defect to Bangla Desh along with the building itself. A mass defection![26]

Majumdar heard the prime minister sternly rebuke Rustamji, forbidding him to carry out this plan. The tiniest of errors could lead to the most terrible of consequences, she warned.

Majumdar was curious. He glanced quizzically at his boss, who ushered him outside. The two men strode out in their uniforms into the hot April summer of Calcutta. They left the BSF office, headed up to Theatre Road, turned west to Chowringhee and then walked over to Calcutta Maidan, a sprawling park of several acres, home to the city's sporting clubs and other institutions.

Out of earshot of the office staff, Rustamji confided his plan to Majumdar. About 2 km east was the Pakistani deputy high commission. Most of the staff was Bengali, as was their head. There were logistical issues, but perhaps Majumdar could talk to the Bengali deputy high commissioner of Pakistan.

Golak Majumdar was not one to shy away from a difficult task. He enlisted the help of his friend Nihar Ranjan Chakravarty once again, but without giving him too many details. Chakravarty arranged a meeting at a discreet place.[27]

Majumdar passed on notes to M. Hossain Ali, the Pakistani deputy high commissioner, asking to meet him. Because of the Naxal insurgency, most of Calcutta's residents wound up for the day quite early in the evening. Police officers had high security cover, but Majumdar ditched his guards, donned civvies and headed out for the first meeting at Blue Fox restaurant on Park Street.

Using his influence with the owner, Chakravarty had arranged to empty the premises, so that Majumdar and Hossain Ali could meet at ease. Majumdar told him about Rustamji's proposal to support a defection. The Pakistani diplomatic mission in Calcutta had sixty-five Bengali diplomats. The provisional government had been formed, and if Hossain Ali and the entire staff and the building were to defect to Bangla Desh, the BSF would support them.

The non-Bengali Pakistani diplomatic staff at the New Delhi mission had misbehaved with K.M. Shehabuddin and Amjadul Haque and their families after they had got wind of their defection. They had reportedly thrown out the belongings of the Bengalis from their residential quarters on the street.

Hossain Ali was the seniormost Pakistani diplomat in India after the Pakistani high commissioner in New Delhi. He had succeeded another Bengali, Abdul Fateh, just a few months earlier to that post. But the Pakistani authorities feared a backlash from the Bengali officials, and they issued marching orders to Hossain Ali, calling him back to Pakistan.

As the head of that diplomatic office, Hossain Ali had to consider the safety and comfort of the other sixty-four staff members and their families and dependents back home. How were they to survive without the pay?

Golak Majumdar heard out all the problems and said he would look for solutions. He persuaded Hossain Ali to meet with him again. The next day, Majumdar spoke with the secretary for banking in the Indian finance ministry to look for a solution. The banking secretary knew what to do. He held the reins to the Pakistani money in India. He could freeze those accounts and seize them, which could be used to pay the diplomatic staff their salaries.

They picked 18 April, the day after the swearing-in, as the date for the mass defection. The details were discussed with Hossain Ali over a few more meetings. To be careful, Majumdar changed the venue each time. He used Gaylords restaurant at Lytton Hotel in Calcutta's backpacker district in Sudder Street. He also sent some officers from his staff for some of the meetings so that the diplomat wasn't spotted meeting with a senior BSF official. The clincher was when Tajuddin met with Hossain Ali at Gaylords.[28]

After he returned from the swearing-in ceremony of the Mujibnagar government, Majumdar went for a final meeting with Hossain Ali at the Blue Fox restaurant. The BSF was ready, he told Hossain Ali.

Colonel Megh Singh of the BSF Academy in Tekanpur sent a few of his toughest commandos, who would give security cover to the diplomatic mission during the switch. Chakravarty had made not one but two flags of Bangla Desh for the swearing-in ceremony. He handed one to Hossain Ali, for hoisting on the flagpole at the Pakistani mission. A signboard had also been prepared. The BSF's bigwigs would be in attendance outside the mission for support: Director General K.F. Rustamji; IG, Ops, Maj. Gen. Narinder Singh; IG, Intelligence (G branch), P.R. Rajgopal; and IG, Eastern Frontier, Golak Bihari Majumdar.

After the meeting, Majumdar told his colleagues that Hossain Ali was still unsure. They went over the plan a few times late into the night.

18 April was a Sunday. That morning, Majumdar's daughter, Jayanti Ghosh, saw him leave the house in a kurta pajama, which he had probably worn to bed the previous night. Since the East Pakistan crisis, he had been going to office every day, in uniform. Majumdar didn't pause to explain.

It was a cool, calm morning. The skies were overcast, possibly with an approaching *kalboishakhi* (nor'wester) storm. He headed to Circus Avenue (now Suhrawardy Avenue) and sat down next to a cobbler, right next to the diplomatic mission, pretending to get his shoes fixed. Circus Avenue has buildings on one side of the road, and across the road from the diplomatic mission is the Park Circus Maidan. Some of the BSF officers were walking on the footpath adjacent to the park. One was inside the park. None of them could spot or recognize Majumdar, who saw Rustamji pass him by a few times. Finally, he beckoned to one of his constables and told him to convey to the DG that he was present outside the Pakistani deputy high commission.

Around 10 a.m., the storm hit Calcutta. The wind beat the trees in the Park Circus Maidan with massive force and dislodged the flagpole, with the Pakistan flag, atop the deputy high commission. Hossain Ali and his staff arrived after the storm had subsided. One of them picked up the pole and switched the flags, and the flag of Bangla Desh was hoisted atop the mission past noon on 18 April 1971. BSF personnel replaced the Pakistani diplomatic mission's board with signage that said:

'Office of the High Commissioner, Gana Prajatantric Bangla Desh'

(People's Republic of Bangla Desh)

* * *

Pakistan no longer had a diplomatic mission in Calcutta. After five days, they passed an order to wind up the deputy high commission in Calcutta. It was an order in writing only; there wasn't any winding up to do. The consular office had switched flags. Pakistan's only diplomatic reaction was to ask India to shut its diplomatic mission in Dacca—India's deputy high commission in East Pakistan, which had played its own part in the events leading up to 1971. They were given a deadline of three days to leave the country.

M. Hossain Ali's defection inspired other Bengali-origin Pakistani diplomats to defect. In his own office, the other diplomatic staff included third secretary Kazi Nazrul Islam, assistant press attaché Maksud Ali and first secretary Rafiqul Islam Chowdhury.

The next defection of a Pakistan diplomat came a week later, on 25 April 1971—the vice consul of the Pakistani consulate in

New York, Mahmood Ali. This diplomat was one of the first to protest against the genocide and was suspended by the Pakistani diplomatic service for hoisting a flag of Bangla Desh in New York. He did not have access to any help, but his wife took up a job to support their family.

Abdul Maal Abdul Muhith was a Bengali civil servant of Pakistan posted as the economic counsellor with the Pakistani embassy in Washington, DC, and the first to walk out of it on 30 June. The Pakistani official to publicly defect in the West was Mohiuddin Ahmed, who, on 1 August 1971, announced at a public meeting his decision to support Bangla Desh.

The seniormost Bengali diplomat to defect was Abul Fateh, Pakistan's ambassador to Iraq, on 15 August 1971. With the help of the Indian diplomatic staff there, he managed to flee the country and turned up in London, where he announced his allegiance to Bangla Desh.

The office of the high commissioner of the People's Republic of Bangla Desh in Park Circus, Calcutta, became the main diplomatic mission for the Mujibnagar government, whose office was barely 2 km from that building. The only other physical building given to the defected diplomats of Pakistan was in New Delhi. K.M. Shehabuddin, the second secretary of the Pakistani diplomatic mission to India who had defected to Bangla Desh, inaugurated the mission office located at the Shanti Niketan residential colony in New Delhi by hoisting the flag of Bangla Desh.

Many more Bengali diplomats of Pakistan also switched their allegiance. This greatly aided the diplomatic efforts of both India and the Mujibnagar government. Till the war broke out in December, no country recognized Bangla Desh as a separate nation, but the diplomatic efforts created a great impact.

* * *

India had to secure the support of UN member states so that it could launch the war to liberate East Pakistan. The most crucial meeting was between India and the US in the month of October, where the prime minister refused to toe the line of the American president, Richard Nixon, and his powerful national security adviser, Henry Kissinger.

The two of them were well aware that East Pakistan would no longer remain in the grasp of their ally Pakistan. But they wanted to hold off the inevitable for as long as possible. There was a lot of pressure on them from within their own country, brought to bear by the cultural activism by Bengali artistes.

The Concert for Bangla Desh, perhaps the most popular example of that activism, was organized by the sitar virtuoso Pandit Ravi Shankar and his friend and former member of the Beatles, George Harrison, on 1 August. Shankar had approached Harrison to help raise $25,000 for the refugee camps for East Pakistani asylum seekers in India. The event—two shows on the same day—was a success and raised around $10 million, of which $2 million was sent that same year through UNICEF. Much of the funds raised came from the sales of records released by the artistes: the single 'Bangla Desh' by Harrison and 'Joi Bangla' by Shankar.

The music concert also featured sarod player Ustad Ali Akbar Khan and tabla player Ustad Alla Rakha, the doyens of Indian classical music, and American music icons Eric Clapton and Bob Dylan. Both Pt Ravi Shankar and Ustad Ali Akbar Khan had roots in East Bengal. The concerts were attended by a number of African journalists and created a global buzz. Documentaries on Cyclone Bhola and the genocide in East Pakistan shown during the event had a great effect.

The news of the genocide, of the flight of millions of Bengalis from East Pakistan, of the deaths by cholera and of the revolution created quite a stir in the West. For the American public, the information that the genocide was sponsored by guns and ammunitions supplied by their government came as a shock. Support for East Pakistanis poured in from all over the world, and several other cultural figures also contributed to raise awareness about the genocide and civil war. A few weeks after the Concert for Bangla Desh, US senator Edward Kennedy visited the refugee camps in Tripura and West Bengal.

Another noteworthy cultural contribution was by the American beat poet Allen Ginsberg, who travelled to India in September 1971 and wrote the famous poem 'September in Jessore Road'. Ginsberg was travelling to Calcutta eight years after his last visit to India. He was a guest of the Bengali poet Sunil Ganguly, and the two of them went down Jessore Road, stopping at refugee camps on the way and speaking with asylum seekers headed west to Calcutta from the Petrapole–Benapole border. Bob Dylan, who had performed at the Concert for Bangla Desh, recorded the poem with Ginsberg.

> *Millions of souls nineteen seventy one*
> *homeless on Jessore Road under grey sun*
> *A million are dead, the million who can*
> *Walk toward Calcutta from East Pakistan*
>
> *Taxi September along Jessore Road*
> *Oxcart skeletons drag charcoal load*
> *past watery fields thru rain flood ruts*
> *Dung cakes on treetrunks, plastic-roof huts*

In his poem, Ginsberg described the despair and tragedy that he saw unfolding on the way to and at the border. The context was unmistakable. The US of 1971 was fighting wars in Asia, and the refugees of East Pakistan had fled the genocide orchestrated by the American ally in South Asia, Pakistan. Most of Pakistan's weaponry was supplied by the US, and the Bangla Desh government pointed out multiple times that the weapons supplied to defend Pakistan were used against its own citizens.

The BSF facilitated as much cultural and news media coverage as it could at the borders. Like Ginsberg, many people would travel right down to the borders to meet with the asylum seekers. At the same time that Ginsberg visited Calcutta, the BSF PRO Samar Basu also organized a trip for a features team of the All India Radio to the India–East Pakistan border.

The star of the radio team was the legendary radio artiste and Padma Shri awardee Melville de Mellow. In September 1971, he travelled close to Raiganj in northern West Bengal and recorded an interview with one Sylvia O'Connor about the aid work she was doing at the refugee camps, tending to the women and children in the camps and to the wounded freedom fighters. Little known to anyone at the time was that Sylvia O'Connor was living there with her husband, who was the commanding officer of 70 Bn of the BSF. She would go on to win an international award for her aid work in the refugee camps. Her husband, Lt Col Noel Gregory O'Connor, was awarded with a Vir Chakra for his role in leading the BSF during the Battle of Bantara in November 1971.

8

Demolition Crew

Asstt Comdt Lila Ram Rana took out his pouch of Capstan tobacco and plucked out the stick of cigarette papers in it. Extracting a single leaf from the stick, he deftly spread a fat pinch of moist tobacco shreds on it to make a stout roll. He held a match to it and puffed to make sure it was well lit before taking a deeper drag. With his free hand, he picked up the fuse and signalled to Naik Prakash Chand to be ready. He squinted as he brought the cigarette and the fuse towards each other slowly.

This had to work. But not faster than the three minutes he had accounted for when measuring the fuse.

* * *

On the afternoon of 31 March 1971, the commando team from the BSF Academy at Tekanpur picked the first target. Asstt Comdt G.S. Pradhan, quartermaster of BSF's 92 Bn at Bagafa, recommended that they blow up the Subhapur road bridge over the Feni River.

Previously, floods had damaged the bridge twenty-four times over the years, and it had been repaired after each flood. It was an important installation on the Chittagong–Dacca trunk road. Pradhan told them that the company commander in charge of the border there had decommissioned the road bridge by cutting one of the girders with a gas cutter.

The Tekanpur commandos, led by assistant commandants Lila Ram Rana, Ashoke Kumar, P.K. Sharma and Bharat Bhushan, had been charged by Rustamji to run the clandestine missions from Tripura under Brig. B.C. Pande's command. They could ensure that the bridge stayed decommissioned if they blew up the other pillar.

Asstt Comdt Rana got to work, preparing the explosive charges. He packed empty ammunition boxes with TNT slabs and wrapped them with plastic explosive Kirkee (PEK), sticking detonators into the middle of the yellow, malleable material. He connected Cordtex (electric) fuse wires to the detonator and sealed the boxes. After he had demonstrated preparing the first explosive charge, the other commandos from the BSF Academy in Tekanpur and those of 92 Bn began building the others. When the charges were ready, Asstt Comdt Rana had them wrapped in sufficient lengths of rope so that they could be tied to the pillar.

Meanwhile, Lt Col A.K. Ghosh informed Asstt Comdt Ghosh that the commando team had arrived at Bagafa for the demolition missions. The first target was to completely decommission the Subhapur road bridge. Since it was a covert op, the commandos would have to be in and out of the spot very quickly.

Asstt Comdt Ghosh had made the previous trips on his own. The way to the trunk road was a short hike over a paddy field in East Pakistan, just outside the Srinagar BOP. A 200-metre hike over the paddy field had taken him to the Chittagong–Dacca trunk road, and from there he had taken rickshaws or bicycles. The Tekanpur commandos had to be able to move quickly.

The paddy field of 200 metres was a hurdle. The soil was too soft for the jeeps to quickly get across. The solution was to make a motorable road for the jeeps carrying the commandos.

Asstt Comdt Ghosh didn't want to set off alarms by calling the East Pakistanis for help in making the road. He informed the Awami League leaders of what he was doing and employed a platoon of BSF constables to dig up dry soil on the evening of 31 March. They carried it to the paddy field next to the Srinagar BOP, and made a thick and stable layer on top of the silt, wide enough for a jeep to drive through. They patted the soil down to smoothen it.

The East Pakistanis were kept in the dark about this, as were the BSF jawans, except those who had helped build the road. The entire operation was a secret.

Back at Bagafa, the PEK had left yellow stains on everyone's hands. It was difficult to wash the stains away with soap and water. They had dinner in the 92 Bn mess, and the PEK added a bitter taste to their food.

After dinner, around 10 p.m., the entire team of eighteen commandos headed out for their first-ever black-op mission in East Pakistan. They changed into half-sleeved shirts or jerseys, and wore half pants and their 'jungle boots'. Everyone carried 9 mm pistols and ammunition—basic handguns that could help them escape a confrontation.

The Pakistan Army was staying put in their cantonments, and there was no threat of a night patrol from Comilla, since the Mukti Fauj—the Bengali rebels of the EBR—was active in that area. The Mukti Fauj was also fighting the Pakistan Army on the north and east of Chittagong, so movement from the south was unlikely.

When it got dark on the evening of 31 March, Asstt Comdt Ghosh had sent a platoon each to the north and south approach roads of the Subhapur bridge to secure the area.

A two-hour drive, in jeeps with dimmed lights, from Bagafa took the commandos to Srinagar. Here, Asstt Comdt Ghosh joined them in his jeep, which guided them across the road on the paddy field and took them to Subhapur. They skirted the town and parked away from the bridge, close to where Asstt Comdt Ghosh's platoon stood guard. They walked down the embankment to the riverbed.

Another officer of 92 Bn, Asstt Comdt C.P. Arora accompanied the Tekanpur commandos. He had a background in engineering and suggested that since one girder had already been demolished, they should blow up the other one. That would destroy the Subhapur road bridge completely.

Everyone pitched in to set up the charges. The commandos trod over the muck and then waded through the waist-deep water, holding the ammo-box charges over their heads. It was pitch black. They didn't even use a torch, to avoid detection. They fastened the boxes of charges to the pillar of the bridge, the base of which stuck out in the dry season. By the time they were done, it was 2 a.m. on 1 April 1971.

One of the officers walked downstream and identified a mound of earth behind which they could take shelter during the explosion. Next, they had to take a call on who would inaugurate the first clandestine mission by blowing up the fuse. While the others did not have much experience with charges, that was what Asstt Comdt Rana taught at the BSF Academy and had also learnt during his own commando training as an officer of the Indian Army.

He picked Naik Prakash Chand to assist him, who measured the distance from the fuse to the safe spot behind the mound of earth, using his wristwatch to count the minutes. He repeated this a few times and then walked back toward Asstt Comdt Rana and said, 'Three minutes.'

Asstt Comdt Rana nodded, measured the length of the fuse coil he needed and cut it from the spool.

'*Slippery hai. Daudna nahin hai* [It's slippery, don't run]. First one minute we will crawl and then we will run,' Asstt Comdt Rana told Naik Prakash Chand.

Lighting the fuse with a match needed two people, and sometimes it was difficult to spot the spark. Asstt Comdt Rana pulled out his tobacco pouch to roll a cigarette, the embers from which would do the honours.

* * *

The burning end of the cigarette ignited the gunpowder in the fuse and made it sparkle merrily, shrinking deeper into its coil and advancing towards the Subhapur bridge. The adrenaline kicked in.

Clad in standard-issue jungle boots, Asstt Comdt Rana and Naik Chand walked slowly and carefully over the riverbed's muck for a full minute, careful not to slip. A slip, a fall or loss of balance could be fatal for both. If one of them fell, the other was code-bound to stop and help.

The jungle boots came in useful, the soles gripped the mud as the boots dug into the soft clay. Asstt Comdt Rana and Naik Chand took a full minute to make it to firm ground, a bend in the riverbed, and then sprinted to the safe spot. They jumped across the mound of earth, put their backs to it and crouched, with knees drawn to their chests. Eight minutes went past. Asstt Comdt Rana had made a ten-minute fuse just to be safe.

BOOM!

The earth shook. The birds chattered in alarm and flew off from the nearby trees. They waited awhile. Asstt Comdt Rana checked himself to see if everything was intact and if there were splinters sticking out of any part of his body. Everyone else got up, dusted themselves and started to move out.

The explosives had been packed correctly, Asstt Comdt Rana thought to himself. They peered over the mound and edged out of the bunker, away from the bridge. Everyone agreed they should not check right away if the bridge had been blown up. The jeeps were a few minutes' walk away. It was possible that a Pakistan Army patrol was nearby and had heard the sound. Asstt Comdt Ghosh said he would check in the morning and inform everyone else.

All of them crouched out of the bunker in single file and headed back to the jeeps. The adrenaline spike subsided on the way back, but they remained alert till they got past the border and into Indian territory.

* * *

The demolition of the Subhapur road bridge, verified by Asstt Comdt P.K. Ghosh the next morning, was the first planned clandestine mission that any Indian agency would carry out across the border in 1971. It was the first such mission for Rana with the BSF too.

Asstt Comdt Lila Ram Rana was a former officer of the Indian Army. His father had served with the British Indian Army, fighting with the Gurkha Regiment, and opted for India after Partition. Rana had been born at the cantonment hospital in Abbottabad (now in Pakistan) in British India while his father was posted there as a soldier.

Later, Rana studied at King George's School (now Rashtriya Military School) in Belgaum, Karnataka, where the curriculum encouraged a career in the army. He cleared all the subjects in his class-ten boards, except for maths, which he passed only four years later, while posted in Srinagar as a jawan. On the field, though, he could correct mortar fire, calculate exactly how much explosive he required and the length of the fuse needed for his team to stay alive.

Rana then enlisted with the Emergency Commissioned Officers (ECO) service in 1963 and went through intensive training with the army. He shone in commando training, and when the India–Pakistan war broke out in 1965, he was at the front line with an artillery unit.

Following the first mission on 1 April 1971, the entire team of commandos from the BSF Academy in Tekanpur set out again with the prepared charges a day or two later. Brig. Pande had chalked out a plan for them. He had identified a number of railway bridges they could blow up. The EBR officers had helped by getting hold of a train for them—a diesel engine tugging a first-class and a general coach. They drove north from Agartala, crossed the border to East Pakistan at Teliapara tea garden, where an EPR JCO joined them as a guide, and drove southwest to Brahmanbaria. The captain at the local police station had arranged for the train here.

The train took them to a small town to the west. On the way, they slowed down while crossing a station. The villagers saw the EPR JCO with them and realized he was with the Mukti Fauj. They scrambled behind the train and shouted in Bengali for it to stop. The train came to a halt.

The villagers had dismantled a track from the railway line to immobilize Pakistan Army movement. They got the track back to its right place, retrieved the nuts and bolts, and put it back again. The train resumed its journey after that.

The commandos got to their destination, which was between two stations. They walked forward to the railway bridge and blew it up with the prepared charges. The villagers had seen the team and come to see the explosion. Once the commandos were done, the villagers said that that there was a road bridge close by which was used by Pakistan Army trucks. 'Close by' turned out to be an 11-km hike through paddy fields and a short boat ride across a lake.

The villagers had already used their tools to dig up the surface of the bridge's road surface. They had to blow up the pillar and topple it. There was a pond next to the bridge, which made the bridge indispensable for the Pakistan Army to get to the other side. The commandos were not carrying any more prepared charges, but there were enough spare explosives and bomb-making paraphernalia in the train. They carried the material to the bridge, made the charges and blew it up.

By the time they made the 11-km hike back to the train, it was quite late. The villagers prepared a meal of fish and rice for the commandos, and laid out beds.

In the morning, they saw that the driver had left the engine running all night long. He was scared that if he shut it and it didn't turn back on, they would be stuck there for a long time.

They returned to Brahmanbaria and headed west to Ashuganj. Past the Ashuganj railway station is a British-era railway bridge over the Meghna River, built in 1937, but they left it intact. They moved further ahead to Ramnagar and blew up the railway bridge there which connected Brahmanbaria to Dacca via Ashuganj.

The Ramnagar bridge was the last one that the commandos blew up as a joint mission. After that they began operating in teams of six, led by an officer each. The number of targets kept increasing.

* * *

Before the Tekanpur commandos launched their covert op from Tripura, Asstt Comdt Ghosh had met Major Zia to supply a mortar and shells on 29 March. Over the next few days, Major Zia's forces of the Mukti Fauj began to withdraw further from Chittagong. Major Zia kept travelling between Tripura and the battle zones in Chittagong. It was convenient for him to be based in the Srinagar BOP, which was a median between Agartala, Bagafa on the one side and Chittagong district on the other.

On his first visit to the Srinagar BOP, Major Zia thanked Asstt Comdt Ghosh and the Indian government for their help. He had heard of the demolition of the Subhapur bridge and the first attack on the Pakistani section which had defended the Subhapur bridge. He knew of the moniker that Awami League legislator Obaidullah Mazumdar had given Asstt Comdt Ghosh and decided it no longer fit his role. 'You can no longer be called Professor Ali,' Major Zia declared. 'Nobody will believe that a professor has pulled off these covert ops. From this moment onwards, you will be known as Captain Ali.' Through the liberation war, 'Captain Ali' became a code name that the Mukti Bahini would also use to refer to Asstt Comdt Ghosh; and Major Zia used it in his handwritten notes to Asstt Comdt Ghosh.

Colonel Osmani and Lt Col A.K. Ghosh also conducted several meetings at the Srinagar BOP, where they discussed strategy. In one such meeting, they discussed how to hold off the Pakistan Army advance as long as possible. The Pakistan Army was now cut off in that part of East Pakistan. To the north of Subhapur were the Comilla and Brahmanbaria cantonments. To the west was Dacca. The demolition of the Subhapur bridge had severed the connection between Chittagong and these other cantonments. This cut off reinforcements and supplies from West Pakistan by road. But there was still a train line moving them.

The Pakistan Army was using the railway line from Chittagong port to move the bulk of their supplies. A week earlier, the Subhapur bridge had been demolished for good by the commandos. But the transport of supplies continued, using the railway line that connected Chittagong to Comilla and Dacca. From Comilla, the supplies went to north and north-east East Pakistan, the areas east of the Meghna. From Dacca, the supplies went to Jessore and all the way up to the Rangpur and Rajshahi divisions, as well as Tangail and Mymensingh.

The map showed that the train line crossed the Feni River over the Dhumghat bridge, a few kilometres west of the Subhapur bridge. The Pakistan Army was fighting the Mukti Fauj far from this bridge at the time.

Around that time, Rustamji was in Tripura, and at a meeting, Asstt Comdt Ghosh proposed that the Tekanpur commandos blow up the Dhumghat rail bridge. Duly approved by Brig. Pande, the mission was fixed for 6 April.

On 6 April, assistant commandants P.K. Sharma, Leela Ram Rana and the other commandos went with an advance party to conduct a recce of the bridge. The plan was to work out how to blow up the bridge. It was decided that Asstt Comdt Ghosh would accompany the men who had prepared the charges. They would blow up the bridge as per the plan made by the advance party and make a quick job of it.

A few villagers were around when the BSF men arrived in civvies and started inspecting the bridge. The locals called for others from Dhumghat, who arrived brandishing farm tools as weapons and surrounded the advance party.

'Where is Captain Ali?' they asked.

'On his way.'

'Then don't move till he is here.'

The commandos didn't know what to do. If they made any false moves, they might end up becoming victims of a mob attack. The commando team had spoken to the locals in Hindi. Confused by that, the locals began to think if it was actually a commando team of the Pakistani forces, who had also spoken to them in Hindi.

Asstt Comdt Ghosh arrived with the rest of the team and the explosives. He heard them out and gathered all the villagers at one spot. Head Constable Bimal Chandra Dutta, one of the commandos, heard some of the villagers say that they didn't want the bridge to be blown up. It was also a means of transport for them, and the local station provided livelihoods to some of them. Some loudly said that this was the national property of Pakistan and nobody could damage it.

'Why do you think we are doing this? I know it will cause some inconvenience, but the greater peril to you is from the Pakistan Army. They will use these roads and railway lines to fuel their troops with weapons and ammunition that they will use against you,' Asstt Comdt Ghosh explained.

He had never been an articulate public speaker, but the words came straight from his heart on that day. His explanation had turned into a speech and the budding mob into an assembly of keen listeners.

'I am Captain Ali of Bangladesh. These people are here to help me,' he said.

Major Zia had popularized the name Captain Ali by that time, and the local freedom fighters knew it. Asstt Comdt Ghosh dropped the names of EBR officers—Major Zia, Major Khaled Mosharraf—in case it helped pacify the crowd and show them that the mission had the sanction of Bengali officers.

Neither the pseudonym Captain Ali nor the names of the Mukti Fauj officers changed the mind of the majority of the crowd. But they appeared a little pacified and seemed less likely to turn into a mob. Some in the crowd also said that the team could go ahead. A few of the commandos, including Asstt Comdt P.K. Sharma, were shaken by the confrontation. Asstt Comdt Rana suggested they let it go for that day and come back again.

'Since some of you seem unconvinced, we will not carry it out today. All of you take some time to think it over and if you still feel we shouldn't, we will not blow up this bridge,' said Asstt Comdt Ghosh, addressing the gathered crowd.

The team collected their gear to head back to the Srinagar BOP. Asstt Comdt Ghosh scribbled a brief note to Dr Obaidullah Majumdar. The Awami League leader had earlier been briefed about the operation, so Asstt Comdt Ghosh had to inform him about the confrontation with the villagers, after which the commandos left.

The next day, Asstt Comdt Ghosh was the first to return and gauge the mood of the villagers. He saw that the majority of them remained convinced that the bridge should remain intact; others were reticent. Hundreds of locals were sitting on and around the bridge. He cancelled the plan again.

Major Zia heard of the local resistance to the operation and was quite angry. The Bengali soldiers were holding off the Pakistan Army and losing men to the fight every day. He suspected that pro-Pakistani elements within the village were stoking resistance against the insurgency. Major Zia volunteered to personally lead the mission.

The explosives were prepared and delivered to him. On 8 April, Major Zia approached the bridge from the southern bank of the river with a Mukti Bahini team, led by a barrister from Chittagong, Nurul Afsar.

The BSF team went from the northern bank. Asstt Comdt Ghosh was unavailable, but assistant commandants P.K. Sharma and Leela Ram Rana were there. It was a massive bridge, and required the right mix of pressure and cutting charges.

Major Zia didn't wait to inform any of the villagers. He stood guard with the Mukti Bahini and, before the charges were set off, ensured that nobody was around. The explosions rocked Dhumghat and cracked open the pillars of the bridge, keeling the deck to one side and into the river.

* * *

A few days later, assistant commandants Rana and Ashok Kumar went to Comilla to conduct a recce of a bridge they had to blow up. They crossed the border on foot through Sonamura and got into Comilla, from where they took a cycle rickshaw to take them towards the bridge. On the way, they saw thousands of East Pakistanis walking on foot to the border to seek asylum in India. Close to the bridge, they got off the cycle rickshaw, asked the operator to wait and walked the rest of the way.

Once they had conducted the recce, they went back to the cycle rickshaw and set off for Comilla. A while later, they spotted a Pakistan Army armoured vehicle 200 yards away. The rickshaw operator had understood by then that his passengers were Indians. He stopped, and all of them jumped off and pushed the cycle rickshaw quickly into a field, off the elevated road. They jumped into the field and hid behind the bushes. The armoured vehicle drove up slowly and went past them.

The three heaved a collective sigh of relief and pushed the rickshaw back on the road. Back in Comilla, they melded with the crowd of refugees and crossed into India.

The demolition team blew up around twenty-nine road and railway bridges in East Pakistan in less than six weeks. The BSF's records show that this list includes:

- Subhapur bridge over the Feni on the Chittagong–Comilla line
- Ujanisar road bridge over the Titas on the Pakistan National Highway linking Comilla with Sylhet
- Gangasagar railway bridge between Chittagong and Comilla
- Ramnagar railway bridge on the Comilla–Dhaka railway line
- Dhumghat railway bridge over the Feni, linking Chittagong with Naokhali and Comilla
- Bijaipur road bridge
- Mian Bazar road bridge on Kakri Nullah
- Shahbazpur road bridge on the Titas
- Chauddagram road bridge
- Gunabati rail bridge on the Feni
- Goadanagar road bridge

These missions were carried out uneventfully, except a few. In one case, an officer of the EBR had identified a road bridge that needed to be demolished. He approached Brig. Pande, and Asstt Comdt Rana was asked to go with his team.

The riverbed was sandy there, so he thought they could use the charges to uproot the pillars from their foundations. Asstt Comdt Rana asked his men to dig a four-foot hole into the ground at the base of the pillar. He dropped the charges into the pits and attached a fuse, long enough to reach the riverbank. They climbed out of the riverbed and lit the fuse.

The EBR officer was waiting in a rest house that was right next to the road bridge. After they had lit the fuse and started running towards the rest house, Asstt Comdt Rana saw that the EBR officer was standing behind a window that had glass panes. He shouted at him to move from there.

Luckily, the EBR officer acted swiftly. He ducked and, within seconds, the explosion rocked the ground, shattered the glass panes and sent a million little glass projectiles to where the EBR officer had been standing.

This was a near casualty. But in a couple of cases, there were two actual casualties. On 1 May, the team was at a road bridge. A batchmate of Asstt Comdt Rana from the Indian Army, J.P. Agnihotri, who had also joined the BSF, had accompanied him to see the process of demolition.

It was a road bridge, but the riverbed was particularly slushy. Asstt Comdt Rana prepared the bombs and went down to fix 'cutting charges' on the pillars. Inspector Agnihotri also wanted to go down to the riverbed, but Asstt Comdt Rana tried to dissuade him.

'*Main dekhna chahta hoon kaise lagaata hai tu* [I want to see how you do it].'

'*Tu mota hai, bhaag nahin payega* [No, you are heavy, you will not be able to run],' Asstt Comdt Rana replied.

Asstt Comdt Rana tried his best to argue with Inspector Agnihotri. But the latter didn't listen, and Asstt Comdt Rana finally relented because time was running short. Asstt Comdt Rana lit the fuse, after which they both ran, Inspector Agnihotri heaving behind Rana.

They went back to the cantonment after the explosion. Asstt Comdt Rana was just preparing to take a nap when a constable came running and said that the inspector lay dead in the veranda.

They had made it out safe from the demolition, after which Asstt Comdt Rana had returned in the jeep and Inspector Agnihotri in a truck. There was no reason to suspect anything was wrong. But back at the cantonment, Inspector Agnihotri had had a heart attack, collapsed and passed away. He was pronounced dead by a doctor at the hospital where they took his body.

During a separate operation, a BSF constable from Manipur had laid the charges, lit the fuse and started running away from the bridge he was to demolish. An East Pakistani Ansar (Ansars were a paramilitary force deployed with the EPR) who was with the demolition crew thought that Pakistan Army soldiers had arrived on the scene. The Ansar shot in the direction of the BSF commando running from the bomb and killed him.

The demolition operations required calm and steady nerves, and those without training couldn't pull them off. Asstt Comdt Rana saw that up close at his last demolition mission. He had been tasked with blowing up the King George VI bridge on the Meghna River that connected Ashuganj with Bhairab Bazaar. They went by road to Ashuganj from Agartala. There were Ansars with them as guides, helping to carry the equipment and charges.

At Ashuganj, they elected to get off at the railway station and walk on the railway tracks to the bridge. They were on the platform of the railway station when the Ansar walking closest to Asstt Comdt Rana fired two rounds in the air.

Asstt Comdt Rana reached out and slapped him across the face. 'Why did you fire your weapon?' he asked.

The man looked shocked and held his palm across his smarting cheek. 'Sir, I thought there may be Pathans.'

'Where? Where do you see Pathans?' asked Asstt Comdt Rana, furious.

The demolition crew was afraid that Pakistan Army sentries may have heard the shots and come to investigate the source. That would force the demolition crew to abort the mission.

They hurried to the King George VI bridge to complete their task. They had to rush it.

Because there was a risk of Pakistan Army soldiers arriving at any moment, they didn't wait to check the impact of the explosion. They just lit the fuse and ran. The next day, they heard that the bomb had only tilted the bridge and not destroyed it.

Brig. Pande called the three officers leading the Tekanpur commandos to his office in Agartala the next day. The Indian Army was taking over operational command of the BSF. He decided that it was time for the commando team to return to the BSF Academy in Tekanpur. They gathered their things and boarded a helicopter, which flew them to Calcutta. They were going to take a train to Jhansi for a connection to Gwalior.

9

Prisoner of Covert War

'Do what you like, but don't get caught.' These were, according to Rustamji himself, the words with which PM Gandhi signed off on the BSF providing support to the Bangladesh liberation war in March 1971.

Rustamji passed on these words of caution to the BSF personnel as they began their commando operations. The commando teams operating inside East Pakistan had different objectives in different sectors. They were also a mixed lot: experienced soldiers along with young, exuberant rookies who were seeing action for the first time.

Rustamji had raised the BSF by absorbing the emergency commissioned officers (ECOs) discharged by the Indian Army,[29] armed forces' veterans on the verge of retirement, some Indian Army officers who were deputed and personnel from the border units of the state police. The next step for Rustamji was to recruit young officers. These young men were to serve alongside the experienced officers and learn from them, so that one day they would be able to lead the BSF.

Brig. B.C. Pande suggested recruiting from the National Cadet Corps (NCC), which trained youngsters in survival and combat in difficult situations. Their training included crash courses with the army, where instructors also initiated them into weapons

training with air rifles and World War II models of the 303 Lee–
Enfield rifles. Rustamji liked the idea and got the home ministry
to sign off on giving senior NCC cadets, who had completed their
graduation, a direct entry into the BSF as junior officers.

In 1965, few people outside New Delhi knew of the BSF.
Youngsters keen on serving as soldiers made a beeline for the three
armed forces. Those interested in policing attempted the state
services or IPS to become officers. So, Rustamji had pamphlets
printed and distributed all over the country, especially in colleges,
announcing vacancies in the new border protection force.

The recruitment campaign was a hit among NCC cadets.
Several NCC cadets in and around Calcutta, who later became
officers in the BSF, had responded to these pamphlets too.

In the summer of 1967, Roopak Ranjan Mitra had just
finished his classes at Motijheel College in the Dum Dum area
of North Calcutta when he found a BSF recruitment pamphlet.
It lay torn and crumpled by the side of the road, and the words
'DIRECT ENTRY' had caught his eye.

After Partition, Mitra's family had remained at their ancestral
home in East Pakistan's Jessore district. But when communal
tensions resurfaced in 1951, they decided to migrate to Calcutta a
year later. They travelled east on Jessore Road and, as many others
like them had, took up residence at a house in Dum Dum, at the
eastern end of the road.

An affluent trader had built Jessore Road to connect Jessore
city to Kalighat in Calcutta. It was also an important trade route,
and later became an important link between Dacca in East Bengal
and Calcutta in West Bengal. This was the road that the American
beatnik poet Allen Ginsberg had immortalized in his poem
'September on Jessore Road'.

Mitra's father had a job as a sanitary inspector for the Dum
Dum municipality, and without any capital for business or
family wealth to lean back on, Mitra wanted to land a job in

government service. He liked sports and outdoor activities, and the NCC programme fulfilled this need. He made it past the seniormost 'C' cadet training, which made the BSF recruiters immediately offer him the PCDE (Platoon Commander Direct Entry) when he passed the recruitment test with flying colours.

Mitra's was the first batch of 120 PCDE recruits for the BSF, and that bonded them with each other for life. There were recruits from all around the country, with similar backgrounds and interests. There were others from West Bengal, such as Sukdev Choudhuri (who was with 70 Bn and 77 Bn during the liberation war), and some even had similar background as Mitra's. P.K. Halder was one such person.

Sometime in the 1950s, Halder's family, too, had left their home in Barishal. This was when he was a young boy. The communal tension between Hindus and Muslims forced them to flee East Pakistan. They made it to Khulna city, on foot or on bullock carts, and boarded a train to the Sealdah station in Calcutta. Hundreds of people paid the fare of Rs 4 and settled with their belongings in the crowded general-class coaches. Arriving in India, they entered their names in the register of refugees and either went to relatives' houses in West Bengal, rented houses or stayed at the designated refugee camps. When Halder's family arrived in Calcutta, they headed to Belghoria, just outside the city. The houses there had all been let out, so they stayed at a refugee camp till they were allotted land.

As with Mitra, Halder had also enlisted with the NCC while at school and continued in college as well. On the way to his final exams for graduation, Halder bumped into a BSF officer. He had never heard of the BSF and didn't know what service it was.

Most people hadn't. Once, on a train in West Bengal, Asstt Comdt N.S. Choudhary was asked by a traveller if BSF stood for 'Birla Security Force'. The Birlas owned the Hindustan Motors factory (famous for manufacturing Ambassador motor cars) near

Calcutta, and the passenger had assumed that they had raised their private security team.

When Halder spotted the emblem on the BSF officer's uniform, he didn't make the same mistake. He engaged with the BSF officer and learnt that the border guarding force was recruiting young men like him. Soon after, Halder chanced upon an advertisement for recruitment to the BSF in Barrackpore and took it to be a providential sequence of events.

Halder's father was against this—he didn't want Halder to become a policeman. Halder decided that he would still go and confided in his mother the day he went for the recruitment. He made it through the trials and then headed for the Tekanpur Academy. His father bid him a reluctant goodbye, not happy with his son's choice.

A few of the recruits dropped out, but the rest completed the training and were made platoon commanders (PCs) with the rank of sub-inspector. Both P.C. Mitra and P.C. Halder were posted at different BOPs of 72 Bn. They ended up at the India–East Pakistan border, close to the Petrapole–Benapole checkpost on Jessore Road.

Commander Harendra Kumar Mukherjee, commanding officer of 72 Bn, was fond of the young Roopak Ranjan Mitra for his pluck and innovative streak. When the Bengalis fled persecution in East Pakistan in March 1971, Mukherjee rearranged the platoons of his battalion and placed some of his best men in Mitra's platoon. He gave them charge of the border posts just north of the Petrapole–Benapole border.

* * *

When covert operations began along the border, Dy Comdt K.B. Singh set up a Mukti Bahini camp next to Mitra's platoon HQ and put the young Bengali platoon commander in charge of coordinating the first set of missions from that border.

Singh told the men that India could not officially join the liberation war, so the BSF men would have to take precautions. The raiding personnel could not wear uniforms or the standard-issue jungle boots, nor could they carry any Indian-made weapons. The EPR had raided armouries, and these weapons, which bore the markings of the Pakistani forces, were shared among the raiding parties.

Mitra decided that these precautions were not enough. What if they were caught across the border and tortured? So, he had the East Pakistanis train the raiding BSF personnel in their dialect and also teach them local customs. Everyone practised greeting each other with 'assalamwaleikum' and 'waaleikumassalam' salutations. Some of them also learnt verses from the Koran and practised how to read the namaz during prayers, along with the names of the five different prayers of a day. The Hindu BSF men changed their names too—Mitra became Talib Hussein. They practised addressing each other with those names even in the camps to get used to them.

On the days of the raids, Mitra organized the men around sunset and had them dress in vests and *lungis*, with *gamchhas* slung over their shoulder. 7.62-mm pistols and ammunition were tucked out of sight into waistbands. As a first move, Dy Comdt Singh told them to keep the Pakistani soldiers confined to their barracks and cantonments at nights. The only way to prevent movements and patrols in the night was ambushing them along the roads and highways. This gave the fighters better access to East Pakistan and also allowed the civilians fleeing persecution a safe passage to India.

Mitra and his men would get close to the highways and wait for hours. They often found Pakistan Army patrols or troop movements initially. The patrols were smaller and easier to surprise. After a few successful ambushes, the Pakistan Army stopped night patrols, and the Pakistan Army officers stopped travelling at night, barring a few exceptions.

The larger troop movements were a different story, and raiding those needed some advance information and better planning. The joint team of the Mukti Bahini and BSF began to watch for patterns, and also worked with villagers for intelligence on troop movements. During a recce mission in April, Mitra and his team spotted a Pakistan Army patrol close by and fired at it.

Mitra and his group—a mix of BSF and Mukti Bahini— were straddling a highway, with most of the men on its eastern side, which had a thinner tree cover. Mitra and the rest were on the western side, and they provided cover fire for the others to retreat. When those on the eastern side had retreated towards the India–East Pakistan border, the Pakistani soldiers fired at the western side. The volley of fire from the Pakistan Army scattered the fighters who were with Mitra. Oblivious, Mitra continued to engage the Pakistan Army patrol. When he could retreat from the road, Mitra found himself alone. His training made him think it was best to wait it out in the forest till daybreak.

Mitra spent the night awake and roaming the forest but trying to stay as close to the highway as possible. There were no sustenance supplies since it was supposed to be a short mission, and the reconnaissance party was supposed to return to the BSF camp before nightfall. It had not rained for quite some time, but he found a narrow creek from which he drank water. When he saw first light, Mitra ditched his pistol and 7.62-calibre ammunition in the forest, and began to head southwards to the border. A crowing cockerel indicated he was close to a village, and Mitra headed towards the sound of the bird.

Past a clump of trees and an empty field, Mitra turned towards a road which he assumed would lead him to the safety of the border. As he got on the road, men in bottle-green uniforms saw him as soon as he spotted them. It was a patrol of five Pakistan Army soldiers, and they immediately pointed their rifles at Mitra. Mitra raised his hands in alarm and started to stammer. Three of the Pakistani soldiers ran past him to check if there were any others. The night in the forest had taken a toll on his clothes—low-lying branches in the forest had ripped Mitra's half-sleeved shirt, and his pants were soiled by the earth from where he had sat. The sweat-stained and grimy vest was visible because the heat had forced him to leave his shirt unbuttoned. His dishevelled appearance prevented the Pakistani soldiers from suspecting that Mitra was an Indian soldier, leave alone an officer.

But the soldiers were suspicious of this young man who had suddenly appeared from the forest. Many youngsters had fled East Pakistan, joined the Mukti Bahini and were disrupting the Pakistan Army. So they searched him but found nothing, neither papers nor weapons. Mitra tried playing dumb, but their leader was not convinced. He kicked Mitra squarely on his thigh. The platoon commander fell to the ground and lay still, pretending to be hurt. The soldier prodded him with the muzzle of his rifle and told him to stand up. Mitra stood up slowly, as if with great difficulty, and started to limp, pretending that the blow had hurt his leg.

The soldiers took Mitra with them, and he was convinced that they were going to torture or shoot him. But he kept up the pretence of the injury with a pronounced limp. It earned him a few more prods with the rifle muzzle, but gentler ones.

At the village, the soldiers took him to their base—the local school, which had been sandbagged to make bunkers for sentries. Mitra was able to make out that it was a base for a Pakistan Army platoon, since most of them were in bottle-green uniforms and a few in khaki. Some civilian women were cooking breakfast while the Pakistani soldiers lounged around.

The Pakistani platoon commander asked Mitra, '*Tu jangal mein kya kar raha tha* [What were you doing in the forest]?'

'*Ustaad, mein pata nahin* [Sir, I don't know] . . .'

Mitra played dumb and pretended to know only a smattering of Hindi. He broke into Bengali as well as verses from the Koran. A few more questions satisfied the platoon commander that Mitra was not a threat. A jawan handed him a broom to clean up the yard followed by other chores. Mitra spent the rest of the morning attending to the chores but observed the camp's routine.

A soldier rang a gong every hour that helped him to keep track of the time. Around 1 p.m., the women served lunch to the soldiers, and, when they were done, the soldiers looked in Mitra's direction and discussed something among themselves.

One of them walked up to him. '*Khana khayega* [Do you want to eat]?' he asked, using the universal gesture that describes eating.

'*Je*, ustaad.'

He was served an aluminium bowl full of fat, coarse-grained rice, dal and a red-and-green slop that tasted like a mash of vegetables. After lunch, most of the soldiers rested. Mitra was happy to sleep after the sleepless night in the forest. The four o'clock gong woke him up, and he was given some more chores. Later, there was a call for *azan*, and he too joined in to offer the Maghrib namaz. Mitra was worried that they might pack him off to a larger base as a POW or ship him to a jail in Dhaka, escape from which was near impossible. He had no papers and no way to talk himself out of it. The best way out was to try and escape from this camp. But even if he escaped, Mitra did not know where he was and how he might get back to Indian territory.

Later, a young boy came from the village bearing the evening supply of country liquor. The JCO's share—the largest—was extracted first, and one of the women who had cooked lunch took it to the JCO, who was sitting in the headmaster's room.

One of the other JCOs began chatting with Mitra using a mix of Hindi and hand gestures.

'Are you from a nearby village?

'Je, ustaad.'

'Can you get us some women?'

'Give me a few days. I can do it.'

'*Tu kaam ka banda hai* [You are a useful person].'

The soldiers seemed to have found some use for him.

Another gong, another hour: 8 p.m. The yard cleared a little, and nobody hung around guarding Mitra. The school's perimeter had been fenced using bamboo stems with sharpened ends, and the sole gate was guarded by a sentry. But the fence wasn't reinforced with barbed wire.

Mitra got up, walked to the fence not far from the gate, scaled it and briskly walked to the east. A little farther, he circled around, maintaining a safe distance from the school and the village, and headed southwards. All he knew was that the direction he was headed in was where the border and the safety of his base were. He had watched the sun earlier and had a sense of which way south was. Mitra took a brisk, adrenaline-filled walk in that direction till he hit a forest. A few hundred metres later, he stopped, sat down and took his first sigh of relief.

But it was not yet over. He had an entire night to pass and then make his way to the border at dawn again. This time, he was not going to get on a road where he could be blindsided and detained again. He resumed walking till he heard dogs howling in the distance, which meant there was a village close by. He walked towards the sound of the dogs till he saw the lights of the village sparkling in the distance. He halted there for the night.

This forest seemed wilder and the ground worse than the one where he had spent the previous night, and he had to slap away mosquitoes all night. A crowing cockerel alerted Mitra to dawn, and he cautiously looked out from the bushes and saw that the area was empty. He headed to the village, avoiding the road, and found himself in a mango orchard.

There, a man who was just about to squat for his morning ablutions spotted Mitra and asked him who he was and where he was headed. Mitra said that he was an Indian and had strayed across the border while returning from one village to the other, and was now lost. Could he help Mitra get back?

The man was sympathetic and helped Mitra correct his course. A forty-five-minute hike took Mitra to another village. The etchings on the houses told him that it was populated by Hindus, and he heaved a sigh of relief: he was back in India.

The first man he met here took Mitra to the village headman, who could not believe that the unkempt young man in torn and dirty clothes was any kind of officer. But they fed him and escorted him back to the battalion headquarters in Bongaon.

Dy Comdt Singh welcomed him with a few words and told him to be back at his station the next day. Back at his platoon's camp, he was welcomed like a hero. They had feared that the soldiers had shot him dead. But he was alive and had escaped the Pakistanis, which became an inspiring story across the battalion's posts. The Pakistani soldiers had not even realized that they had captured a platoon commander of an Indian force who was responsible for disrupting their nightly patrols.

And a day later, 'Talib Hussein' was back leading raids in East Pakistan. It lasted for less than a month. Mitra was promoted to the rank of inspector, transferred to 73 Bn, which was headquartered at Kadamtala, next to Siliguri in north Bengal, where the entire security apparatus of India was strengthening its forces.

Mitra's batchmate, Halder remained with 72 Bn for the entirety of the Bangladesh liberation war. His role and what he witnessed is described in a later chapter.

10

Clear, Hold, Blow Up

The demolition of the Subhapur road bridge and the Dhumghat rail bridge in April were key to stopping the supply chain of the Pakistan Army. The Mukti Fauj was holding up the Pakistan Army advance from Chittagong. Meanwhile, Asstt Comdt Ghosh and Major Zia decided that they would fortify the demolished Subhapur bridge and hold it.

The combined forces of the BSF and the Mukti Bahini took positions on the northern bank of the Feni around the blown-up Subhapur bridge. That kept the river between them and the approach from the south, where Chittagong was. That was the likely direction from which the Pakistan Army would attack. There were two platoons of the BSF, drawn from the border outpost in Srinagar. And the same number of freedom fighters, half of whom were civilians, recruited from the refugee camps.

The refugees had come in waves, and some were set up in Srinagar village. Nurul Afsar, the young barrister from Chittagong who was in the refugee camp at Srinagar, was one of the first to volunteer for the Mukti Bahini. With Dr Amir Hussain, the first Awami League leader to meet with Asstt Comdt Ghosh since the crisis began, Afsar went to the refugee camps to recruit volunteers. Quite a few youngsters enlisted.

Lt Col A.K. Ghosh had a training camp set up for the volunteers at the higher secondary school complex in Srinagar. He sent down some of his trainers from the battalion HQ to staff the camp. Subordinate officers and BSF constables from the BSF post at Srinagar and others nearby also pitched in with the training.

The defence of the Subhapur bridge was both a strategically important and a symbolic objective for the Mukti Bahini. There was little time to train the civilian volunteers, but the BSF personnel did the best they could.

The first thing was to explain to the trainees what the weapon was and then how to use it: loading, aiming and firing the bolt-action rifles. They were heavy to carry, so the men were made to get used to always carrying unloaded weapons around, including during drills. Then came practising at a makeshift range next to the BOP. BSF head constable Bimal Chandra Roy set up targets in a bamboo grove at the border, outside the Srinagar BOP. He marked a few targets but first told the trainees to fire in the general direction of the bamboo stems, to get them used to the weapons and the recoil. Then he eased them into taking precision aim at the targets and moved the targets further back once most of them had got the hang of it.

The few days of training were quite hectic—a crash course in guerrilla warfare. There was physical training, weapons handling and grenade training using rocks.

There were limited weapons during the month of April 1971 for the Mukti Bahini in Tripura, though there was a huge demand among both the freshly drafted guerrillas and the regular EPR and EBR troops. The defectors had carried their own weapons from East Pakistan when they had fled, but they had used up the ammunition while defending the city and district of Chittagong.

Meanwhile, at the bridge, Asstt Comdt Ghosh delegated the task of building bunkers to his subordinate officers. Both the BSF constables and the Mukti Bahini volunteers chipped in.

They carried sandbags, bricks and corrugated iron sheets to roof the bunkers. They dug trenches on the north bank of the Feni. The sandbags were used to cover the front, with peepholes for weapons. Corrugated galvanized iron sheets covered the top of the bunkers, camouflaged by leaves and branches.

On 21 April, a company of the Pakistan Army advanced to the bridge just before twilight. They were on the southern bank. One platoon of soldiers came close to the water, another stayed on the flood plain and another took position on the elevated embankment to give cover to the others.

As they got closer to the water, the Pakistan Army platoon that was heading to the riverfront began to move forward with guns blazing in the direction of the northern bank of the Feni. Asstt Comdt Ghosh had earlier told his mixed force to hold their positions and not retaliate till he gave the order so as not to give away that they were guarding the bridge. The Pakistan Army platoon at the waterfront fell for the subterfuge. They believed that the northern bank was empty and kept up their advance.

Just as they were about to cross the river, Asstt Comdt Ghosh, standing next to a machine gun section, told them to open fire. The others followed suit. The Pakistan Army soldiers were taken by surprise and some retreated to a safer location. Many of them died in the river; their corpses could not be recovered and floated downstream.

The Pakistan Army returned the next day to launch another attack. They wanted to eject the combined BSF and Mukti Bahini forces out in one go, but they failed. This time, they took up positions on the southern bank and built defences.

Regular exchanges of fire continued at random whenever one side spotted movement on the other. A few bursts from one side would launch both sides into a long round of exchanges. In the beginning, the Mukti Bahini civilian fighters were not comfortable with the volley of bullets and shelling. They would desert their posts, especially in the dark, and the next day, Nurul Afsar would have to coax them back to 'fight for our motherland'.

The Pakistan Army's attack from the south bank had led to a stalemate. They decided to initiate an attack from the north as well. The trunk road from Chittagong bifurcated at Feni town. A road turned west towards Dacca, another continued north to Comilla. The Pakistan Army base in Comilla sent a battalion south towards the bridge. The troop movement in Comilla alerted the BSF G branch (intelligence) operatives in Agartala and they passed the information on to Lt Col Ghosh, who went down to brief Major Zia and Asstt Comdt Ghosh in Srinagar. There, they planned how to stop the advance from the north. The Bangla Desh flag flew atop the Subhapur bridge, and holding it had become a point of prestige for the freedom fighters.

The Comilla troops of the Pakistan Army had to cross Feni town on the way to Subhapur. Major Zia tracked the movement of the Pakistan Army from Comilla to Subhapur. He delegated the task of securing the town to Capt. Enamul Haque, with a mixed group of regular soldiers and freedom fighters.

Capt. Haque put up a brave fight with the personnel and weapons he had. But it was a small force that couldn't stand for long against the thrust.

Major Zia was quite distraught when the Pakistan Army took Feni, because Subhapur was not far away. In the south, the Mukti Fauj had lost Chittagong, and the Pakistan Army was aggressively pushing north from there. The Subhapur bridge, which was in the middle of the battle, had become a symbol of the insurgency against the Pakistani junta's rule. Major Zia didn't want the freedom fighters to lose it.

Subhapur and Feni were connected by a 25-km-long, well-surfaced road. In between the two was a road bridge over the

Muhuri River at Rezumia. The Pakistan Army unit from Comilla was likely to cross the Rezumia road bridge the next morning on their way to Subhapur.

Lt Col Ghosh, Asstt Comdt Ghosh and Major Zia decided that the only immediate strategic move was to blow up the Rezumia road bridge. Asstt Comdt Ghosh didn't have explosives at his company HQ. They needed to retrieve explosives from the battalion headquarters in Bagafa.

Lt Col Ghosh left for Bagafa, from where he would send the explosives with BSF commandos from 92 Bn HQ. In the meanwhile, Major Zia sent a platoon of the Mukti Fauj, led by a naib subedar of his 8 EBR, to secure the Rezmuia bridge so that the demolition team could access it easily. Asstt Comdt Ghosh would lead the commandos, as soon as they arrived from Bagafa, to blow the bridge up.

Major Zia had commandeered an American-made CJ-5 jeep from his former commanding officer in Chittagong, Col Janjua, when he had arrested the latter on 25 March. It was a new and more powerful SUV than the Willys jeep that Asstt Comdt Ghosh used. Major Zia suggested that Asstt Comdt Ghosh use the CJ-5 jeep for the Rezumia bridge operation. The two exchanged cars along with their respective drivers, and Major Zia drove off in Asstt Comdt Ghosh's jeep.

Lt Col Ghosh reached his battalion headquarters in Bagafa and gave instructions to his commandos to immediately head to Srinagar with the explosives. Asstt Comdt Ghosh impatiently waited for the truck carrying the commandos and explosives at the Srinagar BOP, and it took much longer than he had estimated. At 10 p.m., a messenger arrived at the Srinagar BOP from across the border. He carried a message from the naib subedar of 8 EBR: the Mukti Fauj/8 EBR platoon had secured the bridge. However, there was still no sign of the truck from Bagafa.

A while later, a BSF constable came running up the road from Bagafa. The truck from the battalion headquarters had got bogged down in the soft mud of a canal not far from the Srinagar BOP. Asstt Comdt Ghosh sent men from his company with a vehicle to ferry the explosives from the truck to the border camp.

The commandos spent several hours packing the explosives into packets with detonators and fuse. They couldn't waste time in preparing the charges at the bridge. That took more time, with the risk of the Pakistani forces drawing closer. The Pakistanis were scheduled to begin their march to Subhapur early in the morning, and, as per the plan, Asstt Comdt Ghosh had to disable the bridge before that happened.

The estimate of explosives required was around 150 kg. Asstt Comdt Ghosh made them prepare 300 kg. They couldn't risk falling short.

The demolition team moved out after the explosives were ready. Asstt Comdt Ghosh rode shotgun in Major Zia's jeep with the latter's driver, Khurshid, while four commandos sat huddled in the back, clutching the ready-to-blow explosive charges. It was nearly dawn; the sky was still dark but a shade lighter on the eastern horizon.

They shot past the border and had just crossed Chhagalnaiya town when Khurshid jammed the brakes, bringing the jeep to a stop. A uniformed man had jumped on to the road and was waving frantically at the jeep. It was the platoon commander of the EBR, the naib subedar, 3.5 km from the Rezumia bridge.

'What happened?' Asstt Comdt Ghosh asked him.

'Sir, it's good that you didn't come last night, because the Pathans [Pakistani soldiers] are guarding the Rezumia bridge,' replied the naib subedar.

'But you sent me a message at 10 p.m. saying that the bridge is secure!'

'Err, that's because I was sure that I would secure it, sir. I had sent the messenger before I secured the bridge. When I arrived there, the Pathans were already guarding the bridge.'

'You would've sent us right into danger.'

'No, no, sir. That's why I was waiting here, to warn you.'

Asstt Comdt Ghosh was livid. 'Suppose I had missed you? I might have overshot your position, missed you and headed straight into the Pakistan Army soldiers guarding the bridge.'

The rest of the commandos were angry too.

'Sir, the Pakistani soldiers won't be there during the day. They were guarding it against a demolition attempt at night. If we go after sunrise, they will have left.'

'What if they don't? You head back to the bridge and secure it from both ends, and then come and get us. We will go there and blow it up.'

Khurshid pulled the jeep to the side of the road and parked it behind a bamboo grove. Asstt Comdt Ghosh told the commandos to load their Sten guns and remain still and alert.

Asstt Comdt Ghosh was already quite irritated with the operation not going to plan. The delays had made him angry, especially because of the naib subedar's message that the bridge was secured. This had been ticking in the back of his mind when he had supervised the commandos making the explosives through the night. He was also sleep deprived. The brief halt was refreshing, and he was using it to calm his nerves, which he would need to complete the operation.

That was when Khurshid broke his reverie: 'Sir, can you get off the seat?' Khurshid said, addressing Asstt Comdt Ghosh.

The company commander was already miffed, the irritation evident on his face, but he got off without a word.

Khurshid lifted the base of the seat to reveal about a dozen grenades right below where Asstt Comdt Ghosh had been seated.

The danger of sitting on top of grenades didn't even occur to him. Instead, he smiled.

'Khurshid! This is wonderful. Please hand out two each to all of us.'

Khurshid obliged with a benign smile, as if he were distributing Diwali sweets.

The naib subedar returned. 'Sir, we have secured the bridge. Let's go.'

Asstt Comdt Ghosh packed him into the front of the jeep, sandwiched in between Khurshid and him. He had already briefed the others that if the naib subedar tried to escape, the commandos could deal with him from the back.

When they got to the Rezumia bridge, the commandos got off first and checked for themselves if the area was clear. Once they were satisfied, Asstt Comdt Ghosh headed with them to the bridge to see where they could lay the charges to cause maximum damage to it. The bridge was supported by four pillars. The commandos tied the explosives to the base of each, securing them with ropes.

They laid out the fuse and checked the area from where they planned to trigger the fuse. They took cover and lit it, lying flat on the ground.

BOOM!

The charges exploded together, cutting through the pillars and propelling the bridge upwards. As the bridge jumped up, so did a giant ball of fire. It appeared as if a great fiery cloud was shooting towards the sky, pulling the bridge up with it.

Within seconds, the bridge cracked and fell into the Muhuri River with a giant thud. It set off a ripple that rocked a few boats that were tied to stakes on the riverbanks. The explosion triggered cries of fear from Rezumia.

The commando team remained concealed, flat on their bellies, for several minutes. Asstt Comdt Ghosh got up first and told the naib subedar that he was leaving with the commando team and that he should follow after fifteen minutes with the Mukti Fauj platoon.

On the way back, Asstt Comdt Ghosh drove the jeep with Khurshid riding shotgun. A cloud of smoke hung over Rezumia, which wouldn't have been visible at night. But now it was quite clear, even from a distance.

The six of them heard the drone of a plane and looked up. A PAF Sabre jet, probably out on patrol, was flying low overhead. Asstt Comdt Ghosh slowed down the jeep and pulled off the road, under the cover of some trees. The plane had probably been on patrol and had moved towards the column of smoke for a closer inspection. All six of them waited with bated breath, gripping their guns closely. The PAF jet made a few rounds of the area and sped off.

As soon as it did, Asstt Comdt Ghosh pressed the accelerator of the jeep and drove as fast as he could. It was the fastest he had driven during the entire liberation war.

Three kilometres later, they entered Chhagalnaiya and saw that a crowd of townsfolk had gathered. They had heard the explosion and were looking at the smoke on the horizon. They were standing outside a police station, and Asstt Comdt Ghosh got off to talk to them.

The local policemen told him that there were arms in the police station armoury. Asstt Comdt Ghosh felt both relief and worry on hearing of the weapons that could easily be accessed. Local criminals could have seized and misused them. But he was relieved because this meant that there was a supply of weapons for the Mukti Bahini recruits training to defend the Subhapur bridge. The policemen, eager to serve the liberation war effort, helped him load the arms into a jeep, and they moved off again.

They had just passed the town when they saw a BSF truck hurtling towards them. It stopped right in front of the jeep. Lt Col Ghosh stuck his head out and shot off the choicest expletives at Asstt Comdt Ghosh. Major Zia, who was seated next to him, cringed.

'Irresponsible fellow! I sent the explosives to you last evening, twelve hours ago. And there has been no response from you. At your BOP, I was told that you'd left at night and had still not returned while Pakistani troops are in close proximity of Rezumia bridge,' he shouted from the truck.

Major Zia was calmer and tried to pacify Lt Col Ghosh. 'Sir, let's head back to Srinagar, and we will sort him out over there,' he said.

The commandos loaded the weapons seized from the police station into the truck, and the vehicles headed back to the Srinagar BOP. Everybody was tired and sleep-deprived. Lt Col Ghosh had stayed up all night to hear about the operation. He had set off for Srinagar when he heard that Asstt Comdt Ghosh had not returned yet. After waiting a while, he had decided to go and find his company commander. He was worried that one of them had been captured.

They had no idea that the bridge hadn't been secured and that the truck had been delayed, bogged down into the muck of the canal. After listening to the entire episode of a night full of close shaves, over tea and breakfast, Lt Col Ghosh burst into peals of laughter and declared: 'You fellows are dangerous.'

* * *

The demolition of the Rezumia bridge deferred the operational plan of the Pakistan Army. The Subhapur road bridge could now be held a little while longer.

The battle had engaged most of 92 Bn personnel in East Pakistan. Lt Col Ghosh asked Rustamji for additional forces, and 104 Bn was moved from Assam to Tripura. Its companies were split over the Tripura border camps as additional companies that held the BOPs with 92 Bn personnel, who were in the bunkers in Subhapur.

Major Zia had been quite busy with multiple responsibilities. He coordinated with the political leaders and other military leaders of East Pakistan. But he was personally involved in the defence of the Subhapur bridge and worked closely with Asstt Comdt Ghosh. He left handwritten notes, like this one from 4 May 1971:

Captain Ali, kindly do the following:

1. When the mortars come with the supplies, they may please be sent to Hav Sikandar who has gone to reccee the area of the ghat.
2. Some troops from the rear positions at Subhapur are to be used for carrying more ammo. Some students of Barrister [Nurul Afsar] may be used also, for carrying ammo.

The notes had his signature, 'ZRahman', in a well-crafted autograph. The notes also show how busy he was with simultaneous operations.

The next day, his soldiers arrived with two men they had detained and a note from Zia, dated 5 May 1971, on the letterhead of the National Bank of Pakistan (Chhagalnaiya branch), that said: 'Captain Ali, Pl interrogate these two chaps for essential infos. I will give disposal orders tomorrow.'

Later that day, when Asstt Comdt Ghosh met Major Zia, he proposed a celebration.

'Celebrate what?' asked Major Zia with a smile.

'We have held the bridge for two weeks. That calls for a celebration.'

'How should we celebrate it? The men are in the trenches.'

'*Mishti, abar ki* [Sweets, what else]?'

The two of them called for boxes of sweets from Tripura and then went to each bunker, handing them out to the personnel of the four different forces, all holed up for two weeks. In between, they took a break under a mango tree, and a Pakistani machine gun section spotted them. They fired a burst at the two commanders. The bullets hit the tree and showered the two with mango leaves and flowers.

'*Ali, dekho, pushpo brishti hochhe* [Ali, it's raining flowers on us],' Major Zia said with a smile, and the two of them moved behind the cover of the tree, away from hostile eyes.

The supply between Chittagong to Dacca and Comilla had been completely stopped since early April. The demolished road bridge was under heavy fighting, with no chances of repair till the Pakistan Army reclaimed it. The alternative was the railway line, but the BSF had also blown up the Dhumghat railway bridge.

In the second week of May, the Pakistan Army sent reinforcements to dislodge the BSF and Mukti Bahini from the Subhapur bridge. Major Zia was in command and staved off the attack for as long as he could. He had the support of the other Mukti Fauj troops who had been fighting south of their position—a long, exhausting fight—since 25 March 1971.

11

The Fall of the Subhapur Bridge

The insurgency in Chittagong unfolded on multiple fronts because units of all the three armed forces of Pakistan were present in the city. The Pakistan Army also engaged with each of the rebel units and pushed them back along multiple axes. Asstt Comdt Ghosh was holding the trunk road to Chittagong with Major Zia at the Subhapur bridge. The BSF supported other Mukti Bahini units fighting along the other axes leading to Subhapur, such as the EPR forces led by Captain Rafiqul Islam.

Capt. Islam left his residence at the EPR officers' quarters in Chittagong for the last time on the night of 25 March. An emissary from the Awami League had just told him that the talks had failed, Gen. Yahya Khan had left for West Pakistan and the tanks were rolling out of the Dacca cantonment.

Islam rode shotgun, with two armed guards in the back, on the way to another EPR camp in the city. It was only the four of them who peacefully strode into the office of the West Pakistani officer and took over charge of the platoon. From there, he went to a larger EPR camp and captured that too.

By that time, the 20 Baluch Regiment of the Pakistan Army had moved into a garrison of Bengali soldiers and killed several of them. Some of the Bengali officers managed to escape and made contact with Islam. Others went to the cantonment of 8 EBR.

Major Zia had had a close escape here. Civilians had protested the unloading of arms at the docks, fearing these would be used against Bengalis in East Pakistan. Maj. Zia had been sent to get the weapons unloaded. He had been tipped off about Operation Searchlight on the way, and had returned to his cantonment and arrested his West Pakistani commandant, Colonel Janjua.

The mutiny had begun. The Bengali officers leading the EBR and EPR managed to communicate with each other and engaged the Pakistan Army.

In Comilla, the Pakistan Army surrounded 4 EBR with two battalions and trained its guns on their cantonment. By the time they made their move, the Bengali officers had been warned. The second-in-command in Comilla, Major Khaled, moved north, towards Brahmanbaria, with his troops.

Meanwhile, in Chittagong, the EBR officers and soldiers regrouped at Patiya, to the south-west of the port city. Capt. Rafiqul Islam held his position for another day. He moved out of the city when his ammunition supply started thinning, escaping an attack in which he was nearly killed.

The Pakistan Army took control of most of Chittagong by the morning of 29 March. The next day, PAF aircraft strafed and bombed the pro-liberation radio station, Swadhin Bangla Betaar Kendra, which had made the first announcement of Mujib's Declaration of Independence on the evening of 26 March. The final battle happened on 2 April, where a full battalion of Pakistan Army regulars, supported by artillery and naval guns, took out the remaining EPR platoon.

In the first week of April—around the time that Asstt Comdt Ghosh first met with Maj. Zia—Asstt Comdt J.N. Pradhan, also of 92 Bn BSF, met with Capt. Islam in Sabroom, South Tripura. Lt Col Ghosh arranged for the defected Bengali officers of the Pakistan Army to meet in Tripura, and also sent arms and ammunitions for Capt. Islam, who was headed back in the direction of Chittagong.

Brig. Pande and his Tekanpur commandos had begun their demolition operations by then. That stalled the military reinforcements from the north from marching towards Chittagong. The rest of the Pakistan Army cantonments, along the eastern border of East Pakistan, had their own problems. Most of the plans to wipe out the Bengali EBR and EPR troops had backfired, and the defectors were fighting back along the entire East Pakistan border with Tripura.

The Pakistan Army soldiers in Chittagong began to push northwards to claim the Chittagong–Dacca trunk road, which was being defended by the Mukti Fauj. The Pakistan Army used full battalions, the PAF, naval guns and artillery to attack the Mukti Fauj defences.

Kalurghat bridge, east of Chittagong city, fell on 11 April, despite reinforcements led by Major Showkat Ali, who'd come from Cox's Bazaar. The Pakistani forces used heavy artillery and naval guns from a great distance but with great accuracy, along with snipers and machine guns. The rebels lost the bridge by evening and, after a few losses, headed out of the vicinity of Chittagong. They moved towards Ramgarh, travelling through the Chittagong Hill Tracts (CHT).

A surprise awaited them on that route. The Pakistan Army had enlisted the support of the Mizo National Front (MNF) commandos, who were headquartered in the CHT, where the Pakistan spy outfit, Inter-Services Intelligence, had put them up.[30] Nearly 100 km from Kalurghat bridge, the Mukti Fauj troops fought against the Mizos and the Pakistani soldiers on their way out of the area.

The EBR had established two other bases on parallel routes from Chittagong to Dacca at Kumira and Udalia. Both of these were pulled out and moved to Sitakund, which now had a larger force to defend itself.

The defence at Sitakund would last another week, after which the Mukti Fauj fighters would be forced to move northwards to Mirsarai, which would fall to the advancing Pakistan Army two days later. The resources of the entire Mukti Fauj were stretched thin. They had lost a lot of men, and the troops were scattered, fighting the Pakistan Army along two axes.

The Mukti Fauj troops were running out of ammunition in places which were not well connected with Tripura. The rebel troops on the battlefield managed with a little dal and rice every day. With its limited resources, officers and troops, the Mukti Fauj was engaged in fighting a regular army. It was two full battalions of the Pakistan Army that recaptured Mirsarai from the Bengali rebels on 20 April 1971.

Capt. Rafiqul pulled back further north to Hinguli, where Asstt Comdt Pradhan of 92 Bn BSF joined him with a commando platoon. There was a bridge over a canal between Mirsarai and Hinguli, and Capt. Rafiqul decided to blow it up, with a view to slowing down the two Pakistan Army battalions that were now advancing with artillery and tanks.

The Mukti Fauj troops crossed the canal and reached Hinguli at midnight. Asstt Comdt Pradhan and Capt. Rafiqul prepared to blow up the bridge. It would take two hours to set up the charges. And Asstt Comdt Pradhan left for Sabroom when the charges were being fixed to the bridge. Later, Capt. Rafiqul lit the thirty-second fuse and ran for shelter.

But there was no explosion. His heart sank. They had only one more fuse, and that too turned out to be a dud. At dawn, the Pakistan Army would reach their position. He could hear the tanks clanking their way towards Hinguli. If the tanks crossed the bridge, it would lead to terrible losses for the Mukti Fauj.

Luckily, Maj. Pradhan contacted the Mukti Fauj fighters in Hinguli to ask if the bridge had been demolished. When he heard that the fuses were duds, he grabbed a handful of them and rushed alone in his jeep to the bridge, using only the vehicle's sidelights to guide his way.

He ditched the jeep about 300 metres from the canal and sprinted towards the bridge. Breathless, he held out the fuses. The first three of these also turned out to be duds. The fourth one hissed and sparkled merrily forward to the explosive charges and blew up the bridge.

It was just in time. The Pakistan Army tanks were a mere kilometre away from it. Capt. Rafiqul and Asstt Comdt Pradhan ran to the jeep and drove at breakneck speed back to Hinguli.

The Mukti Fauj was able to hold off these positions for a few days till around 24 April. It had a few companies which had been split up, and the troops were stretched thin across the three axes all of which led to Subhapur, where Asstt Comdt Ghosh and Major Zia held the Subhapur bridge.

Capt. Rafiqul held the main axis of the Chittagong–Dacca trunk road, with less than a hundred men, against two battalions of the Pakistan Army. On a parallel axis, a company held Narayanhat. And 100 km east, another Mukti Fauj unit was fighting with Pakistani troops and the Mizo rebels.[31] The Pakistan Army was advancing up all three axes at the same time, clearing any resistance it found.

Col Osmani, chief of staff of the Bangla Desh forces, emphasized that the Pakistan Army had to be stopped, but it seemed impossible. The Bengali rebel officers of the EBR and EPR had some manpower and a lot of spirit, but hardly any equipment to stop an entire brigade that was fanning across all of Chittagong district with the help of Mizo guerrillas to the east. Maj. Showkat Ali tried to hold them at Mahalchhari for as long as he could. The Chittagong insurgency was crumbling.

The ISI had trained the Mizos in guerrilla warfare and mountain warfare; the EBR soldiers had no experience in either of these tactics. The Pakistan Army pushed the Mizo guerrillas to the front in the east and captured the mountain route over the CHT to Ramgarh. Major Showkat's tactics kept their losses to the minimum, but ultimately, he managed to organize a retreat before they were encircled by the Mizo guerrillas and a Pakistani commando battalion.

The defence at Heyako also fell, and the two axes to Ramgarh had been cleared. If the Pakistan Army occupied Ramgarh in East Pakistan, it would stop the flow of refugees, who were using the Ramgarh–Sabroom route to enter India from Chittagong because of the fighting on the main highways.

The people fleeing the genocide and the civil war would often walk for more than 100 km to get to Ramgarh, where the East Pakistani police helped them cross over to India. There was only one bridge over the Feni at Ramgarh to cross the border into India, and the alternative was to use boats. Either of the two escape routes would make them sitting ducks for the Pakistan Army soldiers.

The Mukti Fauj was also pushed out of East Pakistan. On 30 April, Lt Col Ghosh created a base for them to operate from by putting them up in Harina in South Tripura, near a BSF camp. The EBR rebel soldiers created some defences at Ramgarh so that all their troops could withdraw to Harina.

That same day, the Mujibnagar government sent a direction to the EBR to hold Ramgarh, which was a difficult task. The Indian Army and the BSF moved its troops to Sabroom to ensure that the Pakistanis could not enter Indian territory, but the Indian Army could not engage the Pakistan Army column in a fight. Ramgarh fell to the Pakistan Army on 2 May.

The fighting continued for another ten days in that region before the Pakistan Army columns from Chittagong cleared the road right till the Subhapur bridge. The threat of a major assault on Subhapur became real. Till then, a battalion of the Pakistan Army had been engaging with a company of the BSF and about seventy-odd volunteers of the Mukti Bahini from the refugee camps. The Mukti Fauj had been engaged in fighting the Pakistan Army advance from the direction of Chittagong.

* * *

Early next morning, that is, on 12 May, two battalions of the Pakistan Army moved past Karerhat and Hinguli with its tanks and artillery. They used the heavy weaponry to shell the Subhapur bridge defences.

The Pakistan Army launched its first infantry attack from the west using two of its companies at 11 a.m. The BSF and the Mukti Fauj managed to repel this advance. After lunch, the Pakistan Army soldiers resorted to heavy artillery fire and pounded the bunkers. Many of the freedom fighters were injured with shell splinters and a few bunkers also collapsed on them.

The artillery fire stopped only at around 5 p.m., when the Pakistan Army assault parties were less than 300 yards from the bridge. The only threat to them were machine guns and the BSF mortars. And in another hour, the Pakistani troops were so close that hand-to-hand combat broke out, and the BSF and the freedom fighters began to withdraw.

The bridge fell that day after heavy shelling on the defences as well as on some of the Indian BOPs and villages. It killed many civilians, including asylum seekers, who were streaming past every day from East Pakistan. After the bridge fell, the BSF and the Mukti Bahini got busy evacuating the refugees from the camps.

A three-tonne truck had delivered ammunition the night before this final battle of the Chittagong insurgency. Since it was late by the time the cargo had been unloaded, Asstt Comdt Ghosh had asked the driver to stay back at the Srinagar BOP. The truck now came in handy to evacuate the injured people to a hospital in Minibazar, near Belonia in south Tripura. Even though they were themselves injured, the Mukti Fauj troops gave priority to the wounded refugees.

Asstt Comdt Ghosh, Inspector Lal Lachunga Lasai and two constables went around looking for injured soldiers and refugees. They administered first aid and then carried those with serious injuries to the three-tonne truck.

There was a girl of about fifteen who was whimpering, unable to cry properly because of her injury. The agony and shock of the injury made her unable to point out exactly where she had been hurt. Asstt Comdt Ghosh lifted her arms and saw that the bullet had pierced the side of her torso and she was bleeding profusely.

'She won't survive this wound,' he thought to himself.

Nevertheless, he wrapped her up with bandages and had two constables carry her to the truck. Some said that there was no point, that she would take up space that might help someone who would survive with timely treatment. But Asstt Comdt Ghosh decided that perhaps she still had a chance or the hospital could give her some relief till the end came.

After the fall of the Subhapur bridge, Lt Col Ghosh focused on a continuous assault on the East Pakistani roads that passed closed to the BOPs. All the company commanders had additional companies seconded from the BSF's 104 Bn, which would remain in South Tripura for several months. In November, when units of 4 Corps of the Indian Army moved in to execute their operational plans, 104 Bn was moved to bolster the BSF's troops in Khowai and Kamalpur in north Tripura.

The fight for Subhapur, between the Pakistani regular army and combined forces of the BSF, the Mukti Fauj regulars and the hurriedly trained Mukti Bahini guerrillas, lasted twenty-one days. The Mukti Fauj troops had held off the Pakistan Army column from advancing as long as they could. This entire battle and the fall of the Subhapur bridge to the Pakistan Army signified the end of the revolt of the EPR and EBR that had begun in Chittagong— the first call to arms of the Bengalis in East Pakistan against the genocide.

In his memoirs of the liberation war, Captain (later Major) Rafiqul Islam wrote about the changes to the strategy of the Bangladeshi liberation forces after the fall of the Subhapur bridge:

> Till then the future strategy of the war had not been decided and the operational responsibility of assisting us remained with the Indian Border Security Force (BSF) who had made their best and sincere effort to help us. In some cases they even went out of their way to assist us. But their resources were limited as compared to those normally available with an army facing such a war.

12

The Heroes of Killapara

The Bhogai River meandered south through Meghalaya along the Tura–Dalu road, just before Panihata (in Bangladesh), and then ran westwards along the international boundary for 3 km, till it hit Dalu, before curving southwards again. That 3-km stretch of the river formed a natural boundary between India and East Pakistan right up to Dalu and Killapara.

A company of the BSF's 83 Bn was posted at Dalu, commanded by Asstt Comdt Baljit Singh Tyagi. The camp was on elevated ground, which gave it a dominating position over the landscape. Down the grade and a kilometre south-west of Dalu was the Killapara BOP, right at the border itself.

The checkpost on the India–East Pakistan border at Dalu connected a large chunk of the northern part of East Pakistan to western Assam. The best and perhaps the quickest escape route into India from cities such as Mymensingh and Sherpur in northern East Pakistan, bound by the Brahmaputra on the west, was through Dalu.

This was why the Dalu BOP had been made a hotbed of political activity by the fleeing political leaders of the Awami League, especially those coming from or via Mymensingh, Jamalpur and Sherpur, among other places.

Deputy Commandant V.K. Gaur, the second-in-charge of 83 Bn, had been cautious of West Pakistanis or their spies infiltrating the refugee camps. There was a threat to the political leaders and other refugees. Besides, by April, the Mukti Bahini had begun some of their operations across the border.

A unit of the Pakistan Army's Baloch regiment was based in Haluaghat in East Pakistan, manning their side of the border adjacent to the jurisdiction of 83 Bn. On the afternoon of 25 May 1971, they sent soldiers dressed as refugees into the camp near Dalu to infiltrate it. The Pakistan Army also fired sporadic bursts from MMGs and mortars for two hours between 4 p.m. and 6 p.m. This was done to divert attention from the attempted infiltration along the border. The infiltrators were easily identified and ran, but so did the residents of Killapara village, because of the shelling by the Pakistan Army.

Back at the 83 Bn HQ, Dy Comdt Gaur was officiating as the commandant since the CO was busy at another part of the border. There were intelligence inputs, collected by the Mukti Bahini, that the Pakistan Army was likely to attack Dalu. Dy Comdt Gaur informed Asstt Comdt Tyagi and deployed additional weapons to Dalu for the Killapara BOP.

Asstt Comdt Tyagi's company headquarters was located at the Dalu BOP, which was linked to the Killapara BOP with a field telephone. There was no direct connection to the battalion headquarters in Tura. Asstt Comdt Tyagi asked the village postmaster in Berengapara village for assistance. The postmaster connected the field telephone terminal at Dalu to the civilian telephone line at his post office, which gave them a connection to the 83 Bn HQ in Tura. The telephone connection was required to send updates to Dy Comdt Gaur in case of a skirmish.

The firing on the evening of 25 May was a cause for concern. Dy Comdt Gaur and Asstt Comdt Tyagi decided to tighten their defences and keep a close watch. They suspected that this was a part of the Pakistan Army attack that the Mukti Bahini fighters had warned them of.

There was a hill next to Dalu, with a church on its peak. Asstt Comdt Tyagi placed MMGs and mortars on the hill so that they could cover a large span of the border from the elevated position. At Killapara, he placed a section of seven personnel with two LMGs. Head Constable Man Bahadur Rai of his company led the section comprising Constables Mandho Thapa, Man Bahadur Chhetri, Pramod Chandra Kalita, Kushal Singh Uprari, Kuladhar Saikia and Man Bahadur Singh.

It began to rain at around 3 a.m. on 26 May 1971—a heavy, torrential downpour. The BSF personnel used plastic sheets to cover themselves while they lay waiting in the trenches for the impending attack. They kept watch in shifts as the rain poured down and made sleep almost impossible.

A column of the Pakistan Army, two companies strong, arrived at Panihata on the East Pakistani side of the border at around 4 a.m. According to the sitrep filed later by Asstt Comdt Tyagi, the Pakistan Army opened fire at around 4:30 a.m. with mortars and MMGs.

The undulating landscape and the thick vegetation provided good cover for them to camouflage the weapons. The shelling alerted Asstt Comdt Tyagi who was sitting at his desk in Dalu. SI Man Bahadur Rai also called him using the field telephone to report the attack and ask for reinforcements.

Asstt Comdt Tyagi informed Dy Comdt Gaur in Tura and rushed to the Killapara BOP with SI Kirpal Singh, Naik Kalyan Singh, and constables Debendra Datta Bahaguna, Puran Bahadur Chand, Khem Bahadur Chand and M.J. Singh Damnik.

Meanwhile, the two companies of the Pakistan Army moved forward to within 250 yards of the border checkpost, spanning a width of around 500–600 yards. They were a mere 500 yards from the Dalu BOP, standing in the pouring rain. Their formation at the cusp of the India–East Pakistan border seemed like they were poised to attack.

The Killapara post, with two LMGs and fourteen men, and the church hill in Dalu lined with MMGs and mortars, had a tactical advantage over the two companies of the Pakistan Army. Asstt Comdt Tyagi directed MMG and mortar fire on the Pakistan Army from the church hill. The Dalu BOP also opened fire using their LMGs and rifles. The firing killed and maimed some of the Pakistani soldiers and scattered the remaining. The Pakistan Army responded by firing from four MMGs and four 3-inch mortars. The brunt of this firing was directed at Dalu to give cover to their withdrawing soldiers.

This exchange went on for close to an hour. Then, the Pakistan Army switched to the heavier 120-mm mortars to fire at the Killapara BOP. That gave some cover to the Pakistani infantry soldiers to completely withdraw from the checkpost near Dalu. By 6 a.m., they had regrouped closer to another side of the border.

The heavy rainfall did not let up, and completely soaked and damaged the field telephone batteries in Killapara. The rainwater had drained right into the trenches at Dalu and waterlogged them. This also damaged the telephone cables.

Asstt Cmdt Tyagi sent two teams from Dalu to restore the telephone connection. There was a junction box in a room between Dalu and Killapara; he sent SI Kirpal Singh and Constable Mandho Thapa to check and repair it. Simultaneously, constables Kushal Singh Bist and M.J. Singh Dumnik went to check the entire length of the telephone lines from Dalu to Killapara, and repair it where required.

With the two teams dispatched, Asstt Comdt Tyagi headed back to Dalu in his jeep to get an update regarding the rest of his area. The Pakistan Army spotted his jeep and suspected it was an officer. Machine-gun fire hit the side of the jeep and punctured its tyres. Asstt Comdt Tyagi veered to the side of the road and stopped. Just as he was about to jump off, he heard the whistling sound of an airborne shell followed by a loud explosion. The 120-mm shell missed the jeep by a few feet and hit the road next to it. The jeep was already in a precarious position on the edge of a waterlogged ditch, and then the impact of the explosion pushed the vehicle sideways into it.

The crash was mild, and the company commander survived it. Crouching next to the damaged jeep, Asstt Comdt Tyagi spotted a bicycle, possibly abandoned by a villager fleeing the Pakistani attack. He mounted it and began to pedal towards the post. The machine-gun fire followed the bicycle, which he had to abandon. The path to Dalu was uphill and the machine gun would have caught up with him.

Asstt Comdt Tyagi rode the bicycle into a ditch away from the fire, threw it aside and lay on the ground for a while. The firing didn't stop. Anticipating that the Pakistan Army might fire a mortar shell at him, he moved forward. He ran from one cover to the next amid the intermittent bursts until he made it to his company HQ at Dalu.

Here, he called Dy Comdt Gaur and gave him an update. The news was sent up the chain of command: the battle was still raging; the first attack had been pushed back.

Asstt Comdt Tyagi then headed east with his radio to observe the withdrawal of the Pakistan Army companies. He wanted to see where they would regroup and direct his mortar fire to push them back further.

Across the border, the two companies of the Pakistan Army had split up. One company advanced towards Dalu from Panihata. The other company moved westwards to Hathipagar (in East Pakistan), from where they could attack Killapara.

The second company attacked Killapara around 6.40 a.m. Asstt Comdt Tyagi sent another BSF section as reinforcements to Killapara. Besides them, a Mukti Bahini section also tried to reach

Killapara. Mohammad Ashfaq, the Mukti Bahini commander there, was a Bengali officer of the Pakistan Air Force. He was posted in West Pakistan when the genocide was launched. At the first opportunity, he defected, crossed the border into India and made his way to Meghalaya. He joined the Mukti Bahini camp in the jurisdiction of Asstt Comdt Tyagi's company and became the commander of the local unit.

When he heard of the Pakistan Army attack, Ashfaq gathered as many of his men as he could and headed for Killapara. Both his team and the BSF reinforcements found their way blocked by firing from machine-guns and mortars.

Meanwhile, the Pakistan Army company, attacking from Hathipagar, stormed the Killapara BOP. The ratio of soldiers was fifteen Pakistan Army soldiers to every BSF constable. The nine BSF men fought till their last bullet, and when their ammunition was exhausted, they didn't surrender but resorted to hand-to-hand combat till they were all killed.

Asstt Comdt Tyagi later found a rifle with its butt cracked in a trench at Dalu. This, to him, was evidence that the BSF men had fought till their last breath. 'One Rifle No 4169Y was broken at the butt was also recovered at the Morcha which shows that in hand to hand fight, BSF personnel fought gallantly till the rifle was broken,' he later wrote in his situation report.

Asstt Comdt Tyagi called Dy Comdt Gaur in Tura to tell him that there were nine casualties. The news was again passed up the chain of command. Within a few minutes, the BSF's head of Intelligence, IG P.R. Rajgopal, called to inquire about the number of casualties and their names. 'Who are the people who were killed? Where has the Pakistan Army reached, and how many of them are there?' he asked.

Dy Comdt Gaur had no details. He couldn't leave the phone and couldn't pester Asstt Comdt Tyagi for details in the midst of battle.

Asstt Comdt Tyagi had sent two teams, each comprising two BSF personnel, to repair the lines. In one of the teams were SI Kirpal Singh and Constable Mandho Thapa, who were at work when the Pakistan Army company moved further into Indian territory from Killapara BOP and spotted them. The Pakistan Army soldiers overpowered and took the two BSF men prisoner.

The other team of BSF personnel—Constables Kushal Singh Bist and M.J. Singh Dumnik—had concealed themselves in a deserted cabin and saw the capture of their colleagues. When the coast was clear, the two escaped and reported the capture to their company commander.

Asstt Comdt Tyagi gathered the BSF personnel from another position. He led a platoon to the Killapara BOP and reoccupied the post at around 9 a.m., four hours after the first advance that morning.

Meanwhile, at the Bn HQ in Tura, Dy Comdt Gaur continued fending off calls from senior officers. Asstt Comdt Tyagi was busy conducting the battle, and the telephone lines between Dalu and Killapara were down, the details would not be accurate.

After IG Rajgopal, the next call came from IG Ranjit Sinha, who had recently been appointed the IG BSF of Assam. IG Sinha said that he was on his way to Tura in a helicopter with his DIG and that from there they would head to Dalu by road.

Dy Comdt Gaur had to quickly figure out how to dissuade the senior officer from heading to a battlefront because of the risk involved. He made breakfast arrangements for IG Sinha, hoping to delay him from heading too close to the fighting in Killapara.

The border was 60 km away, and it would take a two-hour-long drive across hilly terrain to get there. As soon as he landed, IG Sinha impatiently said he should get there immediately to verify the details. IG Sinha and DIG Barua, who had also come from the headquarters in Assam, headed off to Dalu in the only two jeeps available with the 83 Bn HQ.

Dy Comdt Gaur gave a heads-up to Asstt Comdt Tyagi about the impending arrival of the two officers. The Pakistan Army had just retreated, but it still wasn't safe.

IG Sinha and Major Rangarajan, the commandant of 83 Bn, arrived almost simultaneously. The BSF personnel at Dalu were exchanging fire with the Army's assaulting team at the time. The Pakistan Army was firing with machine guns and mortars from the safety of a thick forest across the border.

IG Sinha insisted on going right to the Killapara BOP during a brief respite in the firing. He was at the trenches, being briefed, when the Pakistan Army opened fire. They had spotted the flag car and the arrival of the officers. In that chaos, the IG's entourage fled on foot to Dalu, leaving IG Sinha stranded with Asstt Comdt Tyagi in the trenches of the Killapara BOP. Thanks to his experience from that morning, Asstt Comdt Tyagi knew how to make it safely back to Dalu.

Dodging bullets, all of them ran, with Asstt Comdt Tyagi in the lead. They crawled past rocks, slid through crevices and crouched through a canal, and finally emerged at Dalu, safe and sound. They later surfaced at the Berengapara post office with soiled uniforms and pants torn at the knees.

The firing continued at the border. The tyres of the jeeps the IG and his team had travelled in had been punctured in the heavy firing and could not be recovered. The two senior officers waited for another two hours till Dy Comdt Gaur got hold of a spare jeep from the state police.

Asstt Comdt Tyagi and the nine slain BSF personnel were awarded medals of gallantry. The names of the BSF personnel killed at Killapara on 26 May 1971 are:

Head Constable Man Bahadur Rai
Naik Kalyan Singh Negi
Constable Man Bahadur Chhetri

Constable Pramod Chandra Kalita
Devendra Datta Bahuguna
Purna Bahadur Chand
Khem Bahadur Chand
Kuladhar Saikia
Man Bahadur Singha

Both SI Kirpal Singh and Constable Mandho Thapa were taken prisoners of war and shifted to a jail in Dacca, where they were tortured. Thapa managed to escape and fled to his native place in Nepal, where he died after 2–3 months. Singh was freed after the Pakistan Army surrendered in Dacca in December 1971. They found him blinded in one eye from the torture.

After the attack at Killapara was over, the Mukti Bahini commander Md Ashfaq was found dead between Dalu and Killapara. He was killed in action by machine-gun fire and splinters from mortar shells while on the way to Killapara.

Asstt Comdt Tyagi's story did not end there but he had a glorious role to play in the war on the eastern frontier in December 1971. With the Indian Army, he first commanded companies that captured cities in East Pakistan from the Pakistan Army, and then he was part of the final trump card that the Indian Army played that led to Lt Gen. Niazi's surrender of Dacca.

***

The Brahmputra River flows from east to west past Guwahati in Assam till it reaches Goalpara, from where it begins to curve gently, completing the turn at the western border of Assam. From there, it flows southwards into Bangladesh.

In 1971, 82 Bn of the BSF had charge of the riverine border formed at the curve, where the river entered East Pakistan.

They were neighbours of 83 Bn, which was headquartered in Tura. Four of 82 Bn's six companies were on the north bank of the Brahmputra, and two were on the river's south bank. These two companies were based in Mankachar, Assam, and in Hallydayganj, Meghalaya. The headquarters of 82 Bn was in Gauripur, West Bengal.

Inspector K.S. Yadav was posted at the Sonahat BOP in Assam. A large number of asylum seekers had used that border to seek refuge in India right from the beginning. The area was critical. From May 1971, the Indian Army had kept a close watch on it, since it was to the east of the Siliguri–Jalpaiguri 'chicken's neck', a critical security zone for India. The northern tip of East Pakistan's Kurigram district bulges into Assam and West Bengal, and the Indian Army wanted to keep it from the control of the Pakistan Army. By the time India and Pakistan went to war, a total of 2700 Mukti Bahini fighters had been recruited and trained in the jurisdiction of 82 Bn.

A railway line from Bhurungamari connected to Dhubri in Assam. But because of the hostilities between the two nations, the train that used to run on this line had been suspended. The Mukti Bahini conducted several operations here with the BSF to decommission the railway connection and blew up several road and rail bridges to keep the Pakistan Army from taking over the bulge.

From March to June, the Mukti Bahini and the BSF inflicted heavy casualties on the Pakistan Army here—with the estimated toll of around 150 soldiers.

The Indian Army gave the Sonahat BOP an objective to blow up a bridge connecting Bhurungamari to the India–East Pakistan border. They procured explosives from the public works department in Dhubri. A former Indian Army engineer at 82 Bn, Asstt Comdt J.S. Jaura, knew how to handle explosives. The operation was planned and led by Asstt Comdt James Parshuram and Inspector Yadav, the latter being an experienced commando who had served in the 1962 and 1965 wars.

The bridge extended around 16 km inside East Pakistani territory. The demolition team was hand-picked from among 82 Bn's commandos with the support of the Mukti Bahini.

The Mukti Bahini guerrillas first went to observe the area, and brought back a detailed description of the bridge and the local terrain. They also scanned the entire area to understand the patrolling pattern of the Pakistan Army.

The BSF commandos, too, had gone on two recce missions when the Pakistan Army platoon close by spotted them and fired mortar shells. The recce missions had possibly alerted the Pakistan Army that this bridge was a target, and they had increased their strength there to two companies.

The bridge stood on five pairs of pillars, with four spans along its length. Asstt Comdt Jaura said that they would have to blow up at least two of the spans. On the day of the operation, a platoon of commandos went with the prepared explosive charges to the bridge.

Only those who were to lay the charges got close to the bridge along the side of the road. As they got to the riverbank, Asstt Comdt Jaura descended the gradient of the bank to the water, causing a few ripples. The Pakistan Army was positioned on the opposite bank; so the BSF commandos waited till the ripples had become gentler.

Then, they stealthily walked to the base of the pillars and strapped on the charges to the base of three pairs of the pillars. These three pairs supported two spans of the bridge in the centre. The six Cordtex wires, from each of the charges, were joined together at the pillar closest to the eastern bank, creating a junction.

Asstt Comdt Jaura connected two fuse wires to this junction of six Cordtex wires. He held the two fuse wires above his head and walked back to the eastern bank of the river, careful not to make any noise. He looped the fuse wire around a pillar so that it was safely above water level. They climbed up the bank, releasing more of the fuse wire to increase its length.

Once they were a safe distance away, the fuse was triggered, and Inspector Yadav felt the blast cause a mini tremor where the commandos stood.

The Pakistan Army companies opened fire once they realized that the bridge had been blown up right under their nose. The BSF commandos spread out into small groups on the eastern bank and responded with their Sten guns. They were not carrying any heavy firearms and could move quickly, but they didn't want the Pakistani soldiers to follow. Each of the small groups fired in rotation, and then they began to withdraw one by one before the Pakistani soldiers could realize what was going on.

The Indian Army's brigade commander was quite happy that the BSF had pulled off the task, and that too without casualties. He turned up the next day and wanted to visit the bridge. Inspector Yadav dissuaded him and said that they should wait a week.

A week later, the brigadier returned. He wanted to see the demolished bridge. In the meantime, since the bridge had been blown up, the Pakistan Army had withdrawn the additional company it had posted to guard it.

Inspector Yadav organized two of his platoons and accompanied the brigadier, his staff officers and security detail to the India–East Pakistan border. They went as close as 50 yards from the eastern end of the bridge, and stood behind the embankment. The BSF platoon spread along the embankment, and then the brigadier and the other officers came close to the bridge, remaining behind the embankment.

The Pakistani soldiers had spotted them but waited till the officers were closer. They then opened fire from machine guns and mortars. The BSF platoons responded with their own machine guns and mortars. But there was time enough for the brigadier to see the damage on the Sonahat railway bridge before he made it back to the safety of Indian territory.

13

Radio Revolution

Belal Mohammad heard Mujib's 7 March speech as carefully as millions of other Bengalis who wanted freedom from West Pakistan. Their elected leader had directed the East Pakistanis to begin a civil disobedience movement. There was a specific direction for mediapersons: 'If the plight of Bengalis is not represented on radio and TV, Bengalis should boycott those mediums.'

Belal Mohammad took it as a guideline, as did several other radio professionals across East Pakistan. It was a call to boycott Radio Pakistan. But they didn't take the direction in a literal manner.

The radio stations in East Pakistan used to broadcast with their regional names suffixed to Radio Pakistan. So Chittagong radio presenters would announce the station name as 'Radio Pakistan Chattogram', the radio station in Dacca as 'Radio Pakistan Dacca'. After Mujib's speech, they dropped the word 'Pakistan' from their broadcasts. In Chittagong, they rolled off programmes with the opening words: '*Shuru hochhey Chattogram Betar kendrer anushthan* [The following is a programme of Radio Chittagong].'

Pakistan observes its Republic Day on 23 March. In 1971, East Pakistanis declared it as 'Resistance Day'. The radio station in Dacca played 'Amar Sonar Bangla', announcing itself as Radio Dacca. Two nights later, East Pakistan was thrown into civil war.

Radio Chittagong played the song 'Joi Bangla, Banglar Joi' (Victory to Bengal), which was the theme song from the banned film *Joi Bangla*.

Belal Mohammad woke up on the morning of 26 March to loudspeakers proclaiming that the Pakistan Army had attacked Bengalis in Dacca and elsewhere, and that Mujib had announced the independence of Bengalis from Pakistani rule.

He hurriedly turned on the radio to learn more and found a different narrative playing out on it. The Pakistan Army had taken control of the radio station in Dacca and was using the station to run its own propaganda.

The radio station in Dacca transmitted through a powerful 100 kW transmitter. Belal wondered if they could use their low-powered 10 kW transmitter to broadcast content that would counter the Pakistan Army's propaganda. It was worth trying, he decided.

Nobody was in charge of the radio station in Chittagong at the time. The Pakistan Army was fighting the Mukti Fauj troops. M.A. Hannan, a local Awami League leader, got hold of the text of Mujib's message. He went to the radio station and, with the help of a technician, announced that Mujib had declared independence from Pakistani rule. Hardly anybody heard it.

Belal Mohammad went to Mahbub Hassan, who was in the drama section of Radio Chittagong. They needed technical staff to run the radio station. The two of them located two radio technicians and took them along to the Kalurghat transmitting centre.

Though the studio was in Agrabad, they decided to run all their operations from Kalurghat, which was east of Chittagong city and under the control of the Mukti Fauj at the time. Kalurghat would suffice as both studio and transmitting centre; the studio in Agrabad was within the range of the Pakistan Navy's weapons at the port.

Before 1971, there had been at least two instances of rebel forces using clandestine radio stations successfully, both in South America. The CIA had used a radio station to topple the Guatemalan government, and the South American guerrilla leader Ernesto 'Che' Guevara created an underground radio station, Radio Rebelde, to share news and updates about the Cuban revolution.

Belal wrote down the name 'Swadhin Bangla Betaar Kendra' (Independent Bengal Radio Station). Abdul Kashem Sandwip, Belal's friend and vice principal of Fatikchhari College, added the word 'Biplobi' (Revolutionary) to it. It was anointed Swadhin Bangla Biplobi Betaar Kendra (literally, Independent Bengal Revolutionary Radio Station).

The radio station was completely independent at the time. It was not affiliated to any political party or the liberation forces. A handful of radio staff decided to make an unaffiliated radio station to contribute to the liberation effort.

They decided that the first broadcast of the clandestine radio station would be to make multiple announcements of Mujib's message, a cyclostyled copy of which Belal had procured. Hanan returned to the station. Since he was general secretary of the party's Chittagong unit, all of them decided that he should make the announcement. Belal later said in an interview[32] that the broadcasts by the clandestine radio station were the first institutional response to the genocide and Mujib's call for liberation.

The next day, they found out about a Bengali officer who was commanding defected Bengali soldiers, Major Ziaur Rahman. They went to the Patiya police station and asked his help to secure the radio station. Major Zia immediately agreed and went there along with his unit. It even became a temporary headquarters for Major Zia.

Belal suggested that an army officer announcing the Proclamation of Independence would carry a lot of weight. Major

Zia agreed but told them to drop 'Biplobi' (revolutionary) from the name of the radio station. The clandestine station's name switched back to what Belal had suggested: Swadhin Bangla Betaar Kendra.

Major Zia announced Mujib's Proclamation of Independence shortly after 7 p.m. on 27 March. The next day they made other announcements, which gave away the position of the Mukti Fauj troops to the Pakistan Army. Programmes continued through 29 March and on the morning of 30 March. That day, just after lunch, the PAF bombed the Kalurghat radio station.

The staff of the radio station were resting inside when the bombs hit the building. They hid below the tables and the consoles as long as the bombing and strafing continued. The bombs hit the aerial mast, killing any further transmission from the Kalurghat station.

Major Zia left the radio station building with his force, and the radio staff, too, decided to leave Chittagong. The local MPA, Nurul Islam Choudhary, suggested that they go to the India–East Pakistan border. There, the PAF wouldn't dare to bomb or strafe them, as such an attack would likely violate the Indian airspace.

The radio station had a Collins 1 kW medium-wave transmitter kept as a back-up for emergency use. It had a range of only 10 miles, but something was better than nothing. The radio station staff went back to Kalurghat to retrieve the 1 kW transmitter and, with help from the Mukti Fauj, headed to Ramgarh, walking part of the way with the dismantled transmitter. Besides that, there were microphones, cables, record players, tape recorders, tools, spare parts and a host of other bulky equipment required to operate a radio station.

The kit also consisted of EP records made in Dacca with the 'Joy Bangla' theme song, 'Sonar Bangla' and several patriotic Nazrulgeeti.

The ten of them reached Ramgarh on 3 April. They were:

Belal Mohammad, scriptwriter
Abdul Kashem Sandwip, vice principal, Fatikchari College

Mustafa Anwar, producer
Abdullah al-Farooq, producer
Sharfuzzaman, technical operator
Syed Abdus Shakeer, radio engineer
Rashidul Hussain, technical assistant
Aminur Rahman, technical assistant
Rezaul Karim Choudhury, technical operator
Kazi Habibuddin, staff artist

All of them were staff of Radio Pakistan Chittagong, except Sandwip, who was vice principal of a college. He had helped Belal from the beginning and had become an integral part of producing the radio shows.

Three of them, Belal, Sandwip and Farooq, crossed the border on a ferry and went to the Sabroom police station. The deputy commissioner of Rangamati division of East Pakistan was there. He recognized Belal and introduced him to the police station in-charge.

The BSF camp in Sabroom sent an encrypted wireless message to the headquarters of BSF's 92 Bn in Bagafa. There, Lt Col Ghosh already had his hands full. He was busy overseeing commando operations by assistant commandants P.K. Ghosh, D.K. Pradhan and C.P. Arora, and facilitating the central commando team led by Brig. B.C. Pande.

Rustamji's response was to immediately work out how to set up the radio station and run it from Tripura. He dispatched Sub-Inspector Amar Singh from the Tekanpur BSF Academy with a 200-watt shortwave transmitter to start the broadcasts.

The 92 Bn HQ was already bursting at the seams, with Brig. Pande and his Tekanpur commandos taking up almost all the spare space for their operations. More teams, such as the central communications team, visited Tripura and other battalions to make sure that the infrastructure was up to date and fully operational. Despite the space crunch, Lt Col Ghosh set up the radio equipment in a room in his barracks. Five of the East Pakistani radio staff travelled up from Sabroom, where the rest remained along with the 1 kW medium-wave radio transmitter stashed in the Sabroom police station. Lt Col Ghosh lent his battalion's dilapidated record player and Swadhin Bangla Betaar Kendra started rolling out its radio programmes.

SI Amar Singh was the only one who knew how to operate his old shortwave radio transmitter—a World War II relic—and it could only run for 1.5 hours in a day. The team of engineers and scriptwriters put together programmes for daily broadcasts. In the initial days, they read bulletins from newspapers, followed by appeals for help from the world and inspirational Nazrulgeeti songs.

They ran two-hour sessions, one in the morning and one in the evening. Every half an hour, they would break for ten minutes because the vintage transmitter would be at risk of overheating. The bigger problem was that the shortwave transmissions could only be picked up by radio sets that had shortwave radio bands. Those were expensive and not everyone could afford them.

In the meanwhile, Rustamji went through the rolls and looked for officers who could efficiently run a radio station. He settled on a Bengali deputy commandant, S.P. Bannerjee, who was posted at the BSF weapons and technical unit (CSWT) in Indore, and Asstt Comdt M.R. Deshmukh.

The two officers were to help the Bangladeshi radio team set up a studio to record their own programmes of speeches, news and patriotic songs, and install the transmitter to broadcast the productions. Rustamji told Dy Comdt Banerjee that he was to keep the BSF's participation secret. Apart from the radio crew, only a few in the BSF knew that the force was going to assist the radio station.

Dy Comdt Banerjee reached Agartala on 8 April and was faced with several hurdles. The secrecy made it very difficult for Banerjee and his team to operate.

Other officers from the BSF's Indore unit easily found accommodation and offices waiting for them, but Banerjee and Deshmukh had no place to sleep. Frustrated, they reached out to the Tripura chief secretary I.P. Gupta, who found them a place at the circuit house and a jeep for transport. The only problem was that journalists from outside Tripura were also staying at the circuit house. It wasn't going to be easy to operate a clandestine radio station while living among nosy reporters.

Banerjee assumed the cover of a publicity officer for the Madhya Pradesh government tasked with assessing the number of refugees, so that they could be set up in rehabilitation centres in the state. The cover initially backfired. The reporters quizzed him about the refugees and the government's plans for them.

The unmarked jeep loaned by the chief secretary also proved a problem, though it was a great asset. Banerjee had returned one afternoon for a quick halt to retrieve some items from the circuit house before heading towards another task. He collected what he needed and rushed back out to find that the jeep was missing.

An assistant commandant of the BSF had seen the jeep and asked the driver whom it belonged to.

'Publicity officer, sir.'

'*Theek hai. Kya farq padta hai* [Fine. Doesn't matter],' the assistant commandant said and sped off in it, unaware that he had temporarily requisitioned the vehicle of a senior officer. Banerjee was left fuming outside the circuit house.

The BSF HQ in New Delhi had promised Banerjee a high-powered 400-watt SSB radio transmitter, which was at the headquarters at Agartala. But BSF IG, Tripura, V.K. Kalia's aide refused to part with it since it was a standby machine for their own headquarters. So the 400-watt transmitter remained disassembled and packed in crates till Banerjee directly contacted IG Kalia, who took pity on Banerjee and handed it over. Kalia and Banerjee had been batchmates.

Unpacking and setting up the transmitter became a difficult mission. The lieutenant governor of Tripura was afraid that Pakistani bombs would level Agartala if they set up a radio station there to broadcast pro-Bangladesh programmes. Someone had told the governor that the Pakistanis had a 'direction finder' and could track the broadcasts to their source. But though the BSF IG's headquarters were 10 km away from the city, the governor did not have faith in the PAF's accuracy, and he did not want the clandestine radio station anywhere close to Agartala.

Till the time Banerjee arrived, Belal, Sandwip, Mustafa Anwar, Abdullah al-Farooq and Sarfuzzaman were operating Swadhin Bangla Betaar Kendra from the 92 Bn HQ in Bagafa, where Lt Col Ghosh had set them up. Upon Banerjee's arrival in Tripura, Lt Col Ghosh sent the five radio station staffers north to the headquarters of 91 Bn in Agartala. Amar Singh packed up the vintage shortwave transmitter from the BSF Academy and took it with them.

But there was no space in the 91 Bn HQ either. The only available room where the transmitter could be set up was an empty office at the 90 Bn HQ in Bishalgarh, 30 km south of Agartala.

Asstt Comdt H.C.S. Rawat was posted as the adjutant of 90 Bn in Gokulnagar at the time. Early in the morning of 27 March, an officer from the DIG (sector) HQ arrived with a large group of West Pakistani officers. 'I have some Pakistani officers with me who have surrendered. The order is that you must keep them confined within your battalion headquarters,' the officer told Asstt Comdt Rawat.

The West Pakistani officers had fled their respective commands when the Bengali officers of their army had rebelled. Asstt Comdt Rawat set up a POW camp within the Bn HQ, deploying additional sentries to confine them and keep them safe.

On 1 April, Asstt Comdt Rawat learnt that Brig. Pande was on his way to Tripura with commandos. Rawat had worked under the brigadier as an instructor at the BSF Academy and was eager to meet him.

A few days after the first briefing, Brig. Pande called him with instructions. 'Harish, get hold of a vehicle and head to Bagafa. Lt Col Ghosh will introduce you to a Major Ziaur Rahman. Tomorrow, please get him along with you to meet me here in Agartala.'

Asstt Comdt Rawat had no idea who Major Zia was. He took his jeep and reported to Lt Col Ghosh at the veranda of the mess. A smart young man in uniform was walking up to the mess, with an elderly gentleman and two young women in tow. Lt Col Ghosh introduced the young man as Major Zia and the elderly gentleman as Rahman, the superintendent of police of Rangamati district in East Pakistan. The two young women were Rahman's daughters.

After the introductions, Major Zia looked at the other three with him and said, 'Okay, let's proceed with the job.'

They headed to a hut behind the mess, where some equipment of the Swadhin Bangla Betaar Kendra had been set up. Asstt Comdt Rawat followed them and saw the two women were singing the liberation war anthem, 'Amar Sonar Bangla', into microphones. It was being aired live over shortwave radio, and the broadcast was overseen by two men in civvies.

Next, Major Zia took the microphone and spoke into it, first in Bengali and then in English, 'My dear countrymen . . .'

He detailed the upcoming plans for the liberation war. When Major Zia was done, Lt Col Ghosh pulled Asstt Comdt Rawat aside and said, 'Harish, you have to escort Major Zia to Agartala. We are helping them, but he is not yet fully convinced of our intentions. He will be wary that something may go wrong. To win his confidence, I would suggest that you share the same room tonight.'

Asstt Comdt Rawat agreed, and the two shared a room with twin beds, talking into the night. Though Major Zia was senior to the adjutant, the two got along well. The major spent the night telling Asstt Comdt Rawat about how the West Pakistanis had ill-treated the Bengalis out of racial prejudice.

After breakfast, Asstt Comdt Rawat asked Major Zia to accompany him.

'Where to?'

'Sir, to meet my boss. He is going to conduct operations, and he wants to consult you.'

The two headed to Agartala for the conference with Brig. Pande to plan the black ops in East Pakistan.

The Indian government was worried about the POWs who had been put up in the 90 Bn HQ. They lived in thatched huts under the watchful eyes of armed BSF personnel. The order was to confine them within that perimeter, and if any of them tried to escape, to shoot the person.

The orders were revised sometime later, and they were shifted to a bungalow right beside Asstt Comdt Rawat's residence. When the Swadhin Bangla Betaar Kendra was shifted to 90 Bn, the staff of the clandestine radio station also stayed there. They occupied another adjacent bungalow, on the left of Asstt Comdt Rawat's bungalow, which was now flanked by West Pakistani officers on one side and, on the other, a very important organ of the mass movement to liberate Bangladesh.

Subsequently, Brig. Pande moved to the 90 Bn HQ in Bishalgarh to supervise his commando force. So, no civilian was allowed in there and the clandestine radio team had to move again. While the transmitter remained in the vacant room at Bishalgarh, the radio team could no longer broadcast live. They would have to record the radio programmes elsewhere.

Every day, Dy Comdt Banerjee crowded all the artistes into his room, at the circuit house, Room No. 6, tightly shut all its windows and recorded the news, announcements and songs. Then, either

Dy Comdt Banerjee or Asstt Comdt Deshmukh would drive an hour each way to Bishalgarh to transmit the recording from there with the help of SI Amar Singh.

They followed this routine every day, but 10 April was special—the announcer ditched his deadpan voice to excitedly announce that a government-in-exile of Bangladesh had been formed. This was perhaps the first major scoop of the Swadhin Bangla Betaar Kendra. Tajuddin Ahmed had met with the leader and legislators of his party in Agartala. The radio station staff were told, and they broke the news on their clandestine radio station.

On 11 April, just after a special recording session had ended, there was a knock on the door of Dy Comdt Banerjee's room in the circuit house. Asstt Comdt Deshmukh was the only person in the room and opened the door to find a young man who introduced himself as the district magistrate (DM). The DM said that he had been told of secret radio broadcasts made from this room using a clandestine transmitter. Deshmukh was surprised but let the man in. Someone may have heard the loud chants of 'Joi Bangla' coming from the room during the recordings.

The DM searched the room and found no transmitter. He paid no attention to the tape recorder resting innocently on a table, with a tape full of songs of freedom, news of the liberation war and one of the most important announcements for the liberation movement. That tape contained the very first address of Tajuddin since he crossed over to India for assistance and the first mass address by any of the elected legislators of East Pakistan.

The speech began with:

JOI BANGLA
JOI INDEPENDENT BANGLA DESH

Tajuddin's speech was prescient and covered several topics that would become burning issues later. He called for all East Pakistani political parties to unite in their common cause of a Bangladesh liberated from Pakistan. His reference was to both party colleagues and political parties, such as the Communist Party of Bangladesh and the two factions of the National Awami Party, one of which was led by Maulana Bhashani.

Tajuddin called upon all Bengalis of East Pakistan to join the liberation movement, saying that it would be formed around the nucleus of the defected EBR and EPR personnel working under Colonel Osmani, retired from the Pakistan Army and an elected MPA of East Pakistan. He mentioned majors Ziaur Rahman, Khaled Musharraf, Kazi Mohammad Shafiullah, and others by name, and announced that the officers were already in charge of certain sectors.

Across the border, that transmission was taped and played several times, sending many a youth across the border to India, to take up arms for the liberation of Bangladesh.

The transmissions were still being made through the old World War II-era transmitter. Another BSF officer flew down from Bangalore to set up the 400-watt transmitter, but it did not work. The radio station was transmitting on shortwave band, and most of the target audience in East Pakistan had low-cost sets that only picked up medium-wave frequency. So, there was an immediate need to broadcast the radio programmes on medium-wave frequency.

As a temporary fix, Banerjee took the tapes to the All India Radio station in Agartala and asked the station director if they would rebroadcast the Swadhin Bangla Betaar Kendra programmes. The AIR director was sceptical about the authenticity of the request. He asked his producer to play the tapes. The producer had been listening to every broadcast of the clandestine radio station and immediately recognized the voices. That convinced the AIR station director, and he agreed to rebroadcast the programmes.

On 13 April, IG Kalia told Banerjee to move the working shortwave transmitter, operated by Amar Singh, from the 90 Bn HQ in Bishalgarh to a 'dak bungalow' (forest rest house) outside the town.

Banerjee immediately agreed. They would now have a studio and a station. He excitedly drove down to the rest house and found that it was a single-room hut of the forest department. It had no electricity and no security, and was located right on a main road. The forest department officials who showed him the room understood his plight. They offered a space in their Forest Training School, but there was no power connection in that particular area.

On 15 April, Dy Comdt Banerjee, Asstt Comdt Deshmukh and SI Chaman Lal went to Bishalgarh to transmit the broadcast. The battalion commandant had evicted SI Amar Singh and locked him out of the room with the transmitter. Faced with a series of hurdles, Dy Comdt Banerjee was livid with rage. He called Kalia and asked him to remove the locks, threatening to call up Rustamji if it was not done within the next half hour.

The Swadhin Bangla Betaar Kendra had become an important organ of the liberation movement. East Pakistanis would record the programmes and listen to them discreetly at night, for fear of being caught by the Pakistanis. Missing a broadcast would cut off the East Pakistanis from the liberation movement and lead to speculations about its fate.

The five staff of the clandestine radio station became better at producing content over time. Their objective was to create the content while the BSF team worked out the logistics. Meanwhile, the other five radio staffers from Chittagong, who had remained in Sabroom, with nothing to do, were eager to contribute to the clandestine radio station.

The Rangamati deputy commissioner, Imam, who had helped them cross the border, and the Ramgarh (East Pakistan) MNA, Mohammad Siddique, asked Banerjee to involve those five too.

At the time, Banerjee was busy fighting fires and trying to work out where to set up the studio and install the transmitter. There was both a long- and short-term need for space to house the studio and transmitter.

The AIR would not run all the programmes of the clandestine radio station. Banerjee asked SI Chaman Lal if they could boost the range of the 1 kW medium-wave transmitter. But before solving this technical problem, they still had the most basic logistical need for space to house the transmitter. If they could find space, they could get the medium-wave transmitter working with the help of the five staff members of the clandestine radio station who were in Sabroom. So, the radio could be broadcast over both short- and medium-wave frequencies.

Pushed to the wall, Dy Comdt Banerjee requested Lt Col Ghosh in Bagafa for help. The Bn HQ had adequate security from Pakistan Army commando raids, but Ghosh declined to install the transmitter there. As an alternative, Dy Comdt Banerjee asked for his help to locate and rent a private residence in Bagafa which they could use. Even the low-frequency 1 kW transmitter could transmit to the Belonia Bulge from Bagafa.

Meanwhile, the shortwave station continued running with programmes produced by Belal, Sandwip and the three others who had been creating content. Still under an eviction notice from their base in Bishalgarh, Dy Comdt Banerjee got busy hunting for space to relocate the shortwave station as well. The Tripura chief secretary pitched in by deputing his director of panchayat to find a place for the shortwave radio station.

Together, they looked at many places but found nothing adequate. The owner of a tea estate in north Tripura offered space, but all he had were leaky huts and no power supply.

Another potential space at an engineering college turned out to be too close to an army camp. Finally, they found a school at Champak Nagar, about 20 km from Agartala. The chief secretary arranged for a power connection there.

The BSF's centre in Indore sent another high-powered medium-wave radio transmitter in the custody of an assistant commandant. They set it up at the school on 20 April, but it too failed to work.

The same day, Lt Col Ghosh located a place in Bagafa for the medium-wave station. The second team of radio staffers, who had been waiting in Sabroom all these weeks, finally moved the Chittagong transmitter and shifted it to Bagafa. They reassembled it at the new station house—a room in an under-construction residential quarter of the Tripura forest department.

Dy Comdt Banerjee handed them another tape recorder with the songs that were played by the shortwave station. This way, nobody could tell the difference between the transmissions of the two stations. A few days later, the BSF HQ in New Delhi sent an expert who was able to restore the powerful BSF transmitter at the school in Champak Nagar by 25 April.

Just as the logistical nightmare of transmissions and space was sorted out, a new radio station started to operate in Agartala on both shortwave and medium-wave bands. The radio station, too, called itself Swadhin Bangla Betaar Kendra.

Its content was strange, too. The announcer used a non-Bengali accent and pronunciations to read banal news stories, such as, 'Yahya's wife fasting to influence the Pakistani dictator to stop the genocide in East Pakistan.' The station played Bengali songs that sounded like they were recorded in Calcutta. The Bengali spoken in Calcutta differs from the Bengali spoken in Dhaka, both in terms of dialect and pronunciation.

The new station's biggest gaffe was to play Shyamasangeet—Hindu devotional songs in Bengali—that would not resonate with the Bengali Muslim population in East Pakistan.

Dy Comdt Banerjee's team and the members of the Swadhin Bangla Betaar Kendra were aghast, and wondered if this was an ISI ploy to run its propaganda and confuse listeners.

A week or so later, the BSF's intelligence chief, P.R. Rajgopal, dropped into Tripura. Along with Brig. Pande and other senior officers, he visited both the shortwave and medium-wave radio stations, in Chamak Nagar and Bagafa, respectively, and was quite impressed. By that time, the infrastructure was in a better position.

The senior officers suggested that Banerjee should organize a powerful shortwave transmission, which could be picked up by AIR in Calcutta and retransmitted using their powerful medium-wave transmitters. That would solve the issue of not having a powerful medium-wave transmitter. The only embarrassment to their efforts was the other clandestine Swadhin Bangla Betaar Kendra.

The genuine Swadhin Bangla Betaar Kendra was a hit. Three influential people walked all the way from Dacca to meet with the team—two East Pakistani MNAs and Jamil Choudhury, the director general of Dacca TV. One of the MNAs, Tahiruddin, had brought with him an Islamic preacher.

Dy Comdt Banerjee was considering introducing some religious flavour into the radio broadcasts. But the Awami League politicians and the defected Bengali military leaders were against it. Banerjee met with the Awami League MNAs and Jamil Chaudhury once again at a dinner party at Chief Secretary I.P. Gupta's house. The other guests included a number of Bangladesh liberation movement leaders, such as Colonel (later Major General) M.A. Rab, and MNAs Mahboob Alam and Tahiruddin Thakur.

Gupta introduced Dy Comdt Banerjee to one Bhattacharjee, a bureaucrat of the cabinet secretariat (possibly the subordinate of senior R&AW officer P.N. Banerjee, who was in charge of the agency's Bangladesh desk). Dy Comdt Banerjee mentioned the fake radio station to Bhattacharjee and asked if the R&AW knew about it. Bhattacharjee said that not only did he know about it, but he had also set it up himself. Thankfully, Bhattacharjee promised Dy Comdt Banerjee that he would shut it down.

Ever since he had been in Tripura, Dy Comdt Banerjee had bounced between several accommodations. Just as the radio station was forced to hop multiple locations, so was he. He had to clear his room whenever any VIP visited.

On 10 May, Banerjee was again asked to move out. Gupta had been helping Dy Comdt Banerjee all this while and put the BSF officer up at his own residence. There was more good news. Dy Comdt Banerjee went to meet Sachindra Lal Singha, the chief minister of Tripura. Triguna Sen, union cabinet minister and Rajya Sabha MP from Tripura, promised a high-powered medium-wave transmitter for the Swadhin Bangla Betaar Kendra.

Meanwhile, Brig. Pande wrapped up his operations in Tripura on 13 May, when the Indian Army assumed operational control of the BSF. The fate of the clandestine radio station was in question. Nobody knew if the Indian Army would continue to run it.

While the answer was being worked out by BSF HQ in New Delhi, Dy Comdt Banerjee and his team continued to assist the Swadhin Betaar Kendra staff in running the station. Rustamji took the matter up with Indira Gandhi, and All India Radio was roped in for help. They had earmarked a 50-kW medium-wave transmitter of AIR for the clandestine radio station. It was located in Amtolla, 25 km south of Calcutta. The Swadhin Bangla Betaar Kendra, with staff and infrastructure, would be transferred there.

The mystery around the sudden developments cleared on 16 May, when Mrs Gandhi came down to visit the radio station and met with the BSF officers running it. The next day, BSF PRO Samar Basu went to Agartala with a contingent of foreign reporters. He met Dy Comdt Banerjee and told him that the 50-kW medium-wave transmitter in Amtolla had been handed over to the R&AW. Basu told Dy Comdt Banerjee that the R&AW didn't have the requisite staff to make content or run the transmitter.

Dy Comdt Banerjee headed to Calcutta to convince the R&AW to employ Belal Mohammad and his crew to run the clandestine radio station for the liberation movement. Tajuddin and his war cabinet were operating out of the BSF safe house on Theatre Road. Tajuddin and a few of the ministers stayed there, while others in the Mujibnagar government stayed at a BSF office on Ballygunge Circular Road in south Calcutta. A team from the R&AW also spent a lot of time there—it almost became their camp office.

Dy Comdt Banerjee met with the R&AW joint secretary, Phanindra Nath Banerjee, who also served as joint director, IB, and was known as Nath Babu. Nath Babu was with his subordinate officer, Saradendu Chatterjee. With them was another R&AW operative, whom Dy Comdt Banerjee had met a month earlier in Tripura and knew only by his last name—Sharma.

In Tripura, Sharma had been introduced to Dy Comdt Banerjee as a technical officer with the R&AW, experienced in radio engineering. Now, he learnt that Sharma was running the fake Swadhin Bangla Betaar Kendra from Agartala with medium-wave and shortwave transmitters. But Sharma didn't have anyone to run the programmes or create content. So, he got one of his technicians to act as announcer and play the records bought in Calcutta. Nath Babu had now assigned the task of operating the clandestine radio station in Calcutta to Sharma.

Dy Comdt Banerjee made a quick pitch to Nath Babu about the authentic Swadhin Bangla Betaar Kendra. He told the R&AW officer that the experienced radio staffers ran the content for the radio station and described how they had trekked with their equipment all the way from Chittagong after making the announcement of the liberation there. Nath Babu was impressed. He agreed to take them on as long as the BSF shifted them to Calcutta.

A BSF officer training Mukti Bahini guerrillas

Mukti Bahini guerrillas being trained on LMGs by the BSF at a BOP

A Mukti Bahini fighter guarding farmers in a liberated zone in East Pakistan

A Mukti Bahini guerrilla before an ambush in East Pakistan

Brig. B.C. Pande briefing Gen. Sam Manekshaw and other senior officials in Tripura

Ashwini Kumar (IG, BSF, Western Frontier), on the left, with senior army officials in 1971

(*L–R*) K.F. Rustamji (DG, BSF), Maj. Gen. B.N. 'Jimmy' Sarkar, Tajuddin Ahmed and Col M.A.G. Osmani

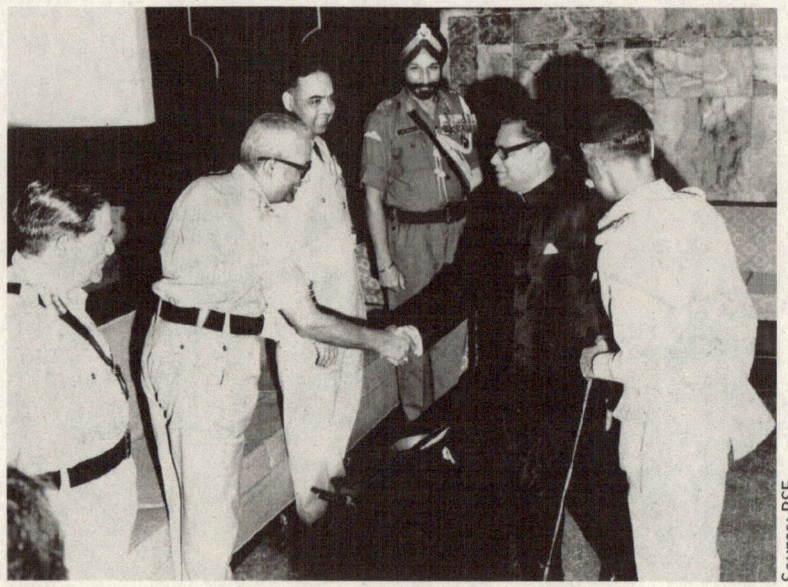

(*L–R*) Brig. B.C. Pande, Golak Majumdar (IG, BSF), a senior air force official, Lt Gen. J.S. Aurora, Tajuddin Ahmed and Col M.A.G. Osmani

An officer briefs K.F. Rustamji (DG, BSF) and Gen. Sam Manekshaw (COAS) in an Indian Army signals office

Rustamji at a test-firing of BSF-made rockets

(*L–R*) Lt Col A.K. Ghosh, Maj. Ziaur Rahman, Maj. Gen. B.F. Gonsalves and Brig. Shant Singh in the Chandgazi (East Pakistan) liberated zone

(*L–R*) Maj. Gen. B.F. Gonsalves, Lt Gen. J.S. Aurora and V.K. Kalia, IG, BSF (see Chapter 14) in Srinagar (Tripura), July 1971

The Subhapur bridge (Noakhali) after it was demolished by BSF commandos in a clandestine operation

BSF commando team rigging a rail bridge with explosives in East Pakistan, April 1971

Demolition experts: Assistant commandants L.R. Rana and P.K. Sharma in East Pakistan, April 1971

Asstt Comdt P.K. Ghosh
before a clandestine mission
in East Pakistan, May 1971

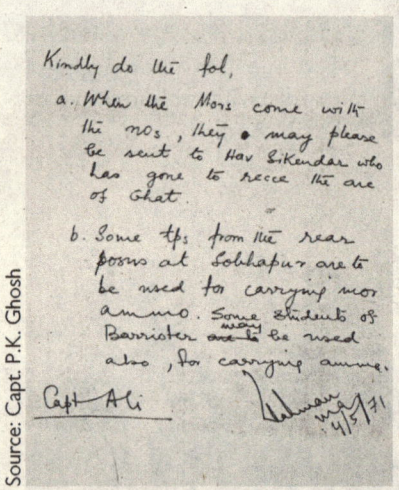

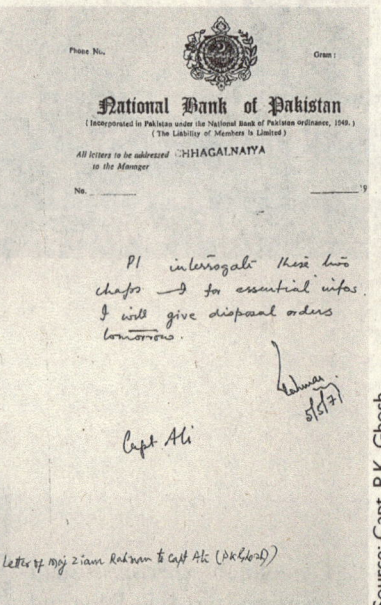

Handwritten notes from Maj. Ziaur Rahman to Asstt Comdt P.K. Ghosh
about coordinating India–Bangla Desh joint ops

(*L–R*) Brig. B.C. Pande, Maj. Ziaur Rahman, Asstt Comdt P.K. Ghosh and Lt Col A.K. Ghosh inspecting a demolished rail bridge

(*L–R*) Asstt Comdt Ashok Gupta, Capt. A.Y.M. Mahfuzur Rahman, Capt. Enamul Haq, Maj. Mir Shawkat Ali, Asstt Comdt P.K. Ghosh (Capt. Ali) and Maj. Rafiqul Islam in Chittagong after the war

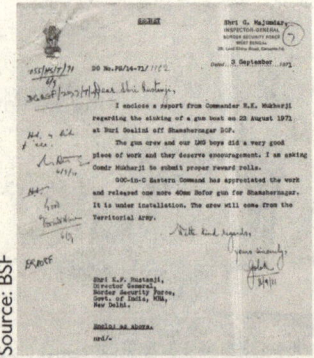

Classified report of Golak Majumdar, IG, BSF, to Rustamji on the sinking of a Pakistani gunboat by a BSF crew

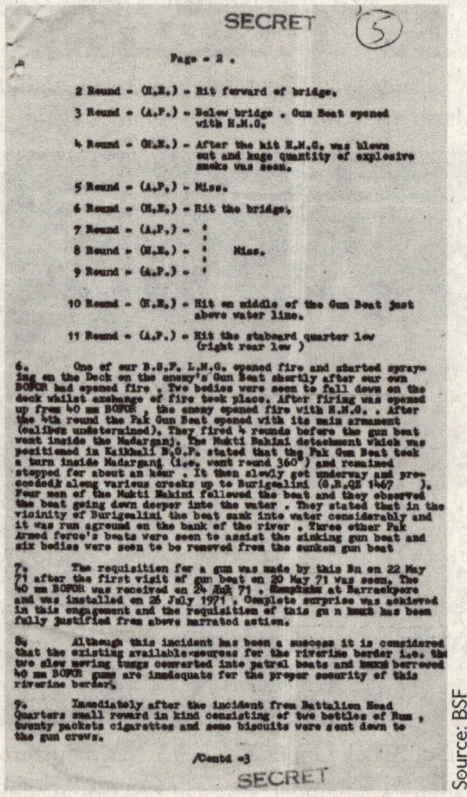

BSF commandant's report on the sinking of the Pakistani gunboat in August 1971

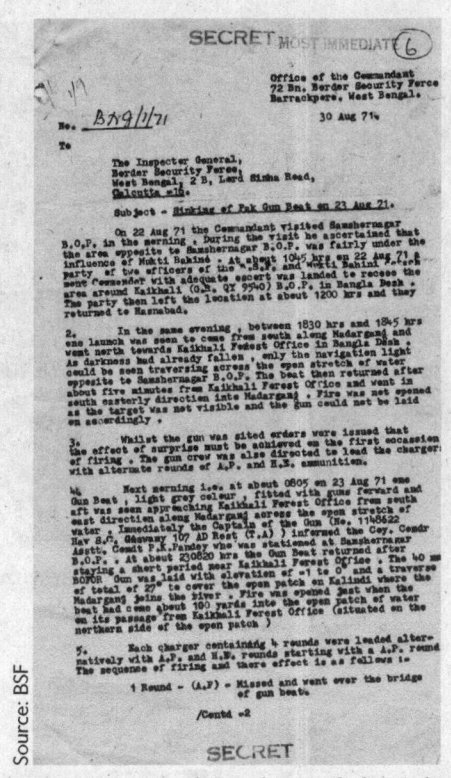

SECRET MOST IMMEDIATE (6)

Office of the Commandant
72 Bn. Border Security Force
Barrackpore, West Bengal.

No. BN9/1/71   30 Aug 71.

To

The Inspector General,
Border Security Force,
West Bengal, 2 B, Lord Sinha Road,
Calcutta -12.

Subject - Sinking of Pak Gun Boat on 23 Aug 71.

On 22 Aug 71 the Commandant visited Samshernagar
B.O.P. in the morning . During the visit he ascertained that
the area opposite to Samshernagar B.O.P. was fairly under the
influence of Mukti Bahini . At about 1230 hrs on 22 Aug 71 a
party of two officers of the Army and Mukti Bahini along with
some commander with adequate escort was landed to recee the
area around Kaikhali (G.R. QT 9540) B.O.P. in Bangla Desh .
The party then left the location at about 1200 hrs and they
returned to Hasnabad.

2.   In the same evening , between 1830 hrs and 1845 hrs
one launch was seen to come from south along Madargang and
went north towards Kaikhali Forest Office in Bengla Desh.
As darkness had already fallen , only the navigation light
could be seen traversing across the open stretch of water
opposite to Samshernagar B.O.P. The boat then returned after
about five minutes from Kaikhali Forest Office and went in
south easterly direction into Madargang . Fire was not opened
as the target was not visible and the gun could not be laid
an accordingly.

3.   Whilst the gun was sited orders were issued that
the effect of surprise must be achieved on the first occasion
of firing . The gun crew was also directed to load the charger
with alternate rounds of A.P. and H.E. ammunition.

4.   Next morning i.e. at about 0805 on 23 Aug 71 one
Gun Boat , light grey colour , fitted with guns forward and
aft was seen approaching Kaikhali Forest Office from south
-east direction along Madargang across the open stretch of
water . Immediately the Captain of the Gun (No. 1145622
Nak S/L Ganpay (?) AD Rest (T.A.)) informed the Coy. Comdr
Asstt. Comdt P.K.Pandey who was stationed at Samshernagar
B.O.P. . At about 230820 hrs the Gun Boat returned after
staying a short period near Kaikhali Forest Office . The 40 mm
BOFR Gun was laid with elevation of -1 to 0° and a traverse
of total 27° to cover the open patch on Kaikhali where the
Madargang joins the river . Fire was opened just when the
boat had come about 100 yards into the open patch of water
on its passage from Kaikhali Forest Office (situated on the
northern side of the open patch)

5.   Each charger containing 4 rounds were loaded alter-
natively with A.P. and H.E. rounds starting with a A.P. round
The sequence of firing and there effect is as follows :-

1 Round - (A.P) - Missed and went over the bridge
of gun boat.

/Contd -2

SECRET

BSF commandant's report on the sinking of the Pakistani gunboat in
August 1971

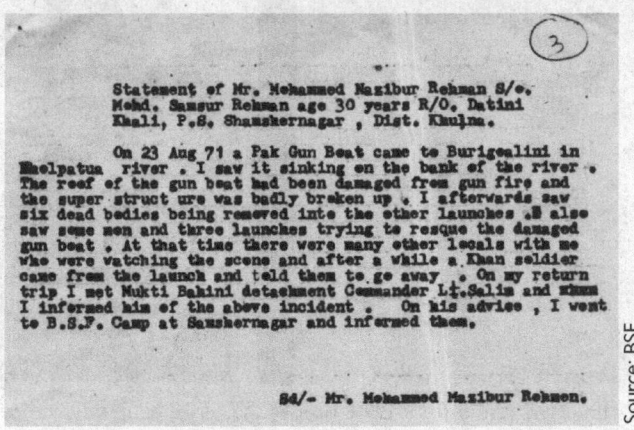

Statement of Mr. Mohammed Mazibur Rehman S/o.
Mohd. Samsur Rehman age 30 years R/O. Datini
Khali, P.S. Shamshernagar , Dist. Khulna.

On 23 Aug 71 a Pak Gun Boat came to Burigoalini in
Bhelpatua river . I saw it sinking on the bank of the river .
The reef of the gun boat had been damaged from gun fire and
the super struct ure was badly broken up . I afterwards saw
six dead bodies being removed into the other launches .I also
saw some men and three launches trying to resque the damaged
gun boat . At that time there were many other locals with me
who were watching the scene and after a while a Khan soldier
came from the launch and told them to go away . On my return
trip I met Mukti Bahini detachment Commander Lt.Salim and whom
I informed him of the above incident . On his advice , I went
to B.S.F. Camp at Samshernagar and informed them.

Sd/- Mr. Mohammed Mazibur Rehman.

Civilian eyewitness report of the damage and casualties on the gunboat

Dy Comdt P.K. Chatterjee with a Pakistan Army howitzer captured in the black op

Mujib's handwritten note to Dy Comdt Chatterjee from when they met in Dacca after the war

A BSF LMG operator in a bunker

BSF personnel checking comms and weapons in the field during the 1971 India–Pakistan war

A BSF mortar section with a 3-inch mortar

A BSF MMG detachment near Chittagong

BSF personnel with a rifle grenade launcher during deployment in the India–Pakistan war, 1971

Pakistani POWs with seized landmines under the BSF's watch

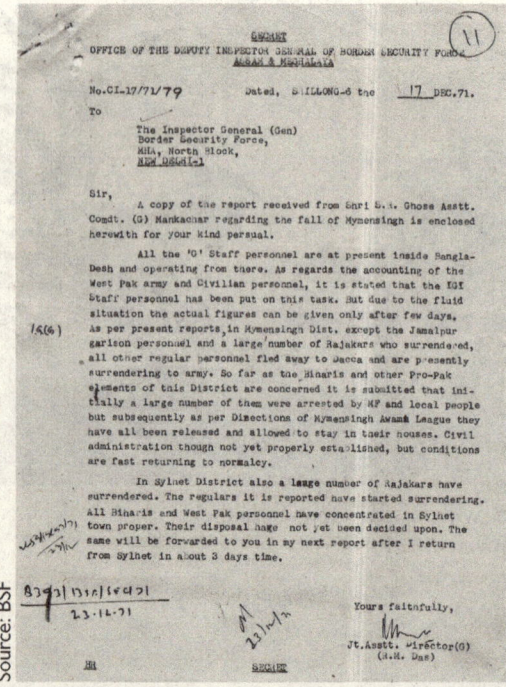

Classified BSF intel report on Mymensingh after the surrender in Dacca

K.F. Rustamji (DG, BSF) meets Sheikh Mujibur Rahman in Dacca after the war

Dy Comdt Banerjee went to the transmission centre at Amtolla and found it had a studio and a guest house. Samar Basu, the BSF's PRO, convinced the AIR director to allot the guest house to the Swadhin Bangla Betaar Kendra staff. They could stay on the premises, record their programmes and transmit from there.

But the R&AW nixed this idea. The R&AW agreed to transmit pre-recorded programmes, but the Swadhin Bangla Betaar Kendra staff had to stay and record their programmes elsewhere. Dy Comdt Banerjee was back to square one in Calcutta. Where would the Bangladeshi staff stay? How would they record their daily programmes?

He rushed over to M. Hossain Ali in the month-old Bangladeshi diplomatic mission and called for a meeting with some of the political leaders. The Dacca TV director general, Jamil Choudhury, offered to run the radio station. He asked for some equipment, a vehicle, office space and a budget. The indirect expenses to run the station came to Rs 15,000 per month, including staff salaries. The direct expenses to operate the station varied between Rs 9000 per month for one-hour-long programmes each day and Rs 43,200 per month for eight-hour-long programmes each day.

The R&AW operative, Sharma, backed out when he saw this budget. Dy Comdt Banerjee felt that he could work out a solution for the Swadhin Bangla Betaar Kendra team. The only issue was that Calcutta was too hot and humid for them to record programmes without an electric fan. And recording with an electric fan would introduce a background hum in the audio. The Swadhin Bangla Betaar Kendra needed an air conditioner.

Three radio staffers from Radio Pakistan, Dacca, were in Calcutta: Ashfaqur Rehman, Tahir Sultan and T. Sikder. They had earlier said that they wanted to be part of the Swadhin Bangla

Betaar Kendra. Dy Comdt Banerjee recruited them to start recording for the broadcasts from Amtolla.

Next, he went to meet with Nath Babu and convinced him to start off the radio transmission from Amtolla with pre-recorded content. Sharma got hold of two tape recorders for the Dacca radio staffers but couldn't make them work. One of the Bangladeshis, Tahir Sultan, learnt how to operate it within minutes, and they recorded songs from the other tapes and announcements that Dy Comdt Banerjee had carried with him from Agartala.

The first recording for the new station in Calcutta was done on the night between 24 and 25 April at the Bangladeshi diplomatic mission in Park Circus, Calcutta. Head of the mission, M. Hossain Ali, lent his car to Dy Comdt Banerjee to carry the recordings to Amtolla at 5.30 a.m., and the first broadcast hit the airwaves at 6.30 a.m.

Nath Babu tuned in. He was happy and thanked Dy Comdt Banerjee for finally launching the clandestine radio station from Calcutta. It was an important project for the R&AW, which stressed on 'psy-war' campaigns.

Later that afternoon, Belal Mohammad and Mustafa Anwar flew down to Calcutta. The three of them recruited Hasan Imam to read the news. He used the pseudonym 'Saleh', because he feared for the lives of his family and friends still living in East Pakistan, as would other future announcers of the clandestine radio station.

They also recruited M.R. Aktar Mukul, who devised the first satirical show for the Swadhin Bangla Betaar Kendra. Called *Chorom Potro*, it was a spoof on the Pakistan Army.

Dy Comdt Banerjee finally bid farewell to the staff on 29 May, after nearly two months of working with the Swadhin Bangla Betaar Kendra.

The rest of the radio team in Agartala were shifted to the BSF office on Ballygunge Circular Road, where they remained till the end of the liberation war. They stayed in a single room and recorded there, working through the morning for the evening show and all through the night for the morning broadcast. Two R&AW operatives would carry the tapes to Amtolla.

Their location was kept a secret for several years. After the surrender of the Pakistani forces, the staff of the Swadhin Bangla Betaar Kendra were rushed to Dacca to broadcast the first radio programme for a free Bangladesh.

14

Lt Gen. Aurora's Monsoon Message

After Subhapur fell, the Pakistan Army was quick to reorganize its defences and restart the supply route from Chittagong. They brought in their engineers and repaired the road bridge first and then the railway bridge. It re-established communication with Chittagong.

In the meantime, the Pakistanis shifted to using riverine routes to cart their supplies to Dacca. It took the Pakistan Army engineers around two weeks, working day and night, to repair the bridge and make it operational. The military convoys then started using the trunk road, which passed very close to both the Srinagar and Amlighat BOPs.

The BSF's firepower was limited to mortars and machine guns, which could not do much damage to the convoys from that distance. At first, Asstt Comdt Ghosh used these. He positioned each of his two MMGs on either side of the camp. They would point at two different ends of the stretch of the trunk road visible from the camp. If the Pakistan Army convoy was travelling from south to north, he would first open fire from the one at the north to make the head of the convoy halt. Then he would fire from the south side at the rear end of the convoy. This would create confusion. He would then start the mortar fire at the entire convoy. After a few vehicles had been damaged, the BSF would stop the fire. The Pakistani soldiers would also stop their firing soon after the BSF withdrew their fire. This light attack irritated the Pakistanis but did not do any great damage.

On 1 July 1971, Lt Gen. Jagjit Singh Aurora, chief of the Indian Army's Eastern Command, was in Tripura with divisional commander Maj. Gen. B.F. Gonsalves and one of the latter's commandants, Colonel Sharma. Lt Gen. Aurora visited the Srinagar BOP, and Asstt Comdt Ghosh showed him around.

'You are also Ghosh, like your commandant. Can I call you PK?' Lt Gen Aurora asked.

The guard commander interrupted the briefing and said that a Pakistan Army convoy was passing. As company commander, Asstt Comdt Ghosh would order the engagement using machine guns.

'PK, can I have a look?' Lt Gen. Aurora asked.

'Of course, sir.'

Lt Gen. Aurora asked the major general and the colonel to stay back, and accompanied Asstt Comdt Ghosh to a bunker up front. He was surprised to see the Pakistan Army passing so close by.

'PK, what are they carrying?'

'Sir, these are all supplies from the Chittagong port—arms, ammunitions and rations.'

'The arms and ammunitions are to be used against whom?'

'Sir, against the Indian forces,' replied Asstt Comdt Ghosh.

'So, why are you allowing them to pass while they carry bullets meant for our soldiers?'

'Sir, I have one company under my command and a company of Mukti Bahini guerrilla fighters. I do not have the firepower or manpower to stop them,' Asstt Comdt Ghosh said in a matter-of-fact tone. 'I do not have any artillery. If I unleash a heavy attack on them, they will return the next day with tanks. This is level terrain in front of the BOP. They will mow us down with a short fight, because all I have are some machine guns and three-inch mortar shells to stop tanks and artillery.' Asstt Comdt

Ghosh was completely aware of his limitations and operated within his means.

'Okay. What do you need?'

'First, a recoilless [RCL] gun.'

'Done. Next?'

'I have two companies right now with the Mukti Bahini. To be stronger, I need four more companies.'

Once they returned to the BOP visitor's area, the general briefed his officers. 'I want PK to stop the Pakistan Army convoy from passing through here. He says he needs a battalion's strength, artillery guns and anti-tank guns,' Lt Gen. Aurora told his officers.

'Yes, I agree,' said Maj. Gen. Gonsalves. The brigadier and colonel, too, agreed.

'The artillery and anti-tank gun should be here tomorrow. Next, Colonel Sharma, you have to strengthen PK's deployment. How much time would you require?'

'Sir, fifteen days,' said Sharma.

Lt Gen. Aurora gave him a grace period of seven days and set the deadline for 21 July. All guns and personnel should be in place by that date, as per Lt Gen. Aurora's orders, and Asstt Comdt Ghosh could launch an attack on the Pakistan Army cavalcade passing within firing distance of the Srinagar BOP.

'The road should be denied to the Pakistan Army at all costs,' said Lt Gen. Aurora, ending the conference at the Srinagar BOP.

In less than a week, Mrs Gandhi's foreign policy adviser, P.N. Haksar, would be arguing with his American counterpart, Henry Kissinger, over continuing supply of US arms to Pakistan. Kissinger, in turn, accused India of supplying weapons to the Bengali guerrillas. The two situations were not comparable, but Haksar denied that they had given any guns to the Mukti Bahini.

Four companies of the 19 Rajputana Rifles were deployed at the Srinagar BOP in support. There were four RCL guns, six artillery guns and a three-inch mortar. The BSF had an outdated mortar, 86 mm, which wasn't as effective.

The additional deployments were parked next to the BOP and took positions on either side of it. This was in the third week of July 1971.

Since all the guns and personnel were in place, the date of the operation was as fixed earlier—21 July. The bunkers were prepared a day before the attack. The entire Indian and Bangladeshi Forces were briefed—it was the first time that the Indian Army would also participate, in battalion-strength, in a battle that year. The constables, guerrilla fighters, jawans, all classes of soldiers and their junior, non-commissioned and commissioned officers were briefed about the mission. Asstt Comdt Ghosh led the tactical briefing since he knew the BOP, the road and the mission ahead.

The ammunition was sorted out for the next day. The meals were prepared the evening before. This was to ensure that nobody left their bunkers for any reason. The Pakistan Army convoy would be prepared to retaliate and could call for reinforcements from the nearby camp. There was a history of firing from the Srinagar BOP, besides the risk of the Mukti Bahini and BSF ambushes.

On the morning of the operation, everyone woke up to rain—the kind of torrential rain that is common during monsoon in tropical South Asia. The rain began pouring down noisily on the corrugated tin sheets, sounding like machine-gun fire. The packed lunches were handed out with breakfast on the day of the operation. The ground around the camp had become a large patch of mud. The path inside the camp was paved with loose stones and allowed everyone to get to the border. The trenches were wet and difficult to get into. The wide-brimmed steel helmets of the constables kept the rain out of their eyes. They held up sheets of plastic over their heads to get to the bunkers and trenches.

The BSF was at the front line of the attack, followed by the Indian Army. The order was to open fire as soon as the convoy was spotted. South Tripura is on the same latitude as North Vietnam. And here, the BSF, the Mukti Bahini and the Indian Army were facing the same conditions as the Viet Cong fighters and the US Army soldiers, five countries due east.

The visibility was down to about 50 metres due to heavy rain. Beyond that distance it was hazy, and the constables strained to mark the vehicles and the Pakistan Army soldiers. As the first few vehicles of the Pakistan Army convoy came into the line of sight, the machine guns opened fire. Within seconds of the first burst, cries rang out.

'*Darao darao, mero na, mero na* [Stop the fire, don't shoot]!'

A large group of refugees was making its way up the road— the same road that the BSF constables had dug up when Inspector Leela Ram Rana had blown up the Subhapur bridge.

A head constable ran back and informed Asstt Comdt Ghosh about the refugees. The BSF constables and Indian Army jawans had ceased fire, but the Pakistani soldiers didn't care about the *gaddars* (traitors) fleeing the country and had already begun to retaliate. The Indian forces also resumed fire. The asylum seekers were now stuck almost in the line of fire.

Asstt Comdt Ghosh told the head constable to stop the BSF fire. He also requested Colonel Sharma for the Indian Army to cease fire. Bengali-speaking constables stood as close to the edge of the camp as possible and shouted at the asylum seekers to move.

Many of the asylum seekers made a break for the camp. The bullets flying close by made them turn sideways and take cover behind trees. Some lay flat on the ground and crawled to the safety of the BOP. It took a while before all the asylum seekers cleared out of the line of fire. Then, a voice croaked loudly from within a bundle of cloth, quite close to the bunkers.

'What should I do?'

By that time, Asstt Comdt Ghosh had gone up close to the front. He saw an old man crouched into a foetal position on the ground. He seemed to be in a sort of DIY palanquin, made out of bed sheets tied around two large poles. Asstt Comdt Ghosh realized that the man was an invalid and had almost made it to the camp when the firing started. The old man was being carried across the border by able-bodied men, who had ditched him when they heard the bullets.

There was nothing to be done. The firing and the rain had made any chance of a rescue difficult. The man lay in his wretched state. A mis-calibrated mortar or stray bullet could kill him any minute.

'Should I try?' volunteered one of the constables.

'How?'

'Leave it to us.'

The constable, joined by another volunteer, got hold of a thick rope lying in the bunker. The two of them crawled on their bellies through the slush, pushing with their hands and moving forward as if they were hand-paddling a surfboard on the sea.

One of the two constables got close to the 'palanquin' and tied one end of the rope to it. He crawled back, and the two of them together pulled the palanquin towards them, with the old man tucked in the cloth pouch inside.

They got him to the bunker and freed him from the soaking wet cloth he had been carried in. The man was old, wrinkled and frail. He was covered in mud and completely soaked too. He was shivering, from both the wetness of his clothes and the firing. They stripped the wet clothes off him, helped him into an oversized combat uniform and covered him with another set and a plastic sheet. They gave him food from their packed lunch and told him to stick close to the wall of the bunker. He held the food to his chest and stayed frozen for a while, unable to speak. Carrying him inside to the barracks would be both difficult and dangerous during the continuous exchange of fire.

Meanwhile, the battle raged on. Soon after the warning, the asylum seekers had moved to safer positions and crawled into the camp. The Indian forces and the Mukti Bahini had resumed firing at full power.

The Pakistan Army faced the brunt of the Indian Army mortar and artillery attack. The recoilless gun delivered by Lt Gen. Aurora had blown up several trucks. Machine guns and mortars of the BSF and the Indian Army had killed several Pakistani soldiers. Much of the cargo headed for the cantonment in Dacca had been lost to that day's firing. The rain had made it difficult for them to turn around and get out of the range of fire from the Srinagar BOP.

The firing continued through the day and let up around dusk. Nobody had left their posts or the bunkers except to attend to nature's call. When the firing stopped, Asstt Comdt Ghosh stepped out of his observation post, from where he had been directing the BSF fire. He cautiously headed to the administrative area of the camp to take stock of the damage. The way was littered with the bodies of stray dogs that had been killed by bullets and shrapnel.

A woman stood waiting near the administrative area. Earlier, one of his head constables had told Asstt Comdt Ghosh that a woman was waiting there looking for the company commander. She was searching for her husband, who had not made it through during the firing and was probably stuck near the paddy fields outside the camp. Her daughter, too, was missing. The other refugees had been led to the safety of the refugee camps. Split from her family, she refused to go to the refugee camp till she could locate them.

She had been waiting since morning. She was served food and made to sit in hutments at the camp, away from the firing. Once she saw the company commander, she went up to him and, using all the Hindi she could muster up, gave Asstt Comdt Ghosh a description of her husband and asked for help to locate the missing man. The description was unmistakably that of the old man whom the two constables had pulled into their bunker.

The pronounced East Bengali accent in her Hindi was unmistakable. Asstt Comdt Ghosh responded in Bengali. '*Apnar chintar kono karon nei. Uni amare kachhei achhen, theek achhen* [Don't worry. He is with us, safe and sound],' he said.

The woman expressed some relief but wanted to go to her husband right away. But Asstt Comdt Ghosh was firm in his refusal. 'It could still be dangerous to get him out of the bunker right now. We will retrieve him later in the night, when it is safer.'

Later that evening, the old man was carried out of the bunker. Husband and wife were reunited and kept in the hutments at the far end of the BSF camp.

She came to speak with Asstt Comdt Ghosh again. That he was responding to her in Bengali finally registered with the woman. 'Oh! *Apni Bangla bojhen* [You can speak Bengali]?'

'*Hyan, kichhu kichhu* [Yes, a little],' Asstt Comdt Ghosh replied, a smile curving the corner of his lips.

'*Apnake dhonyobaad janata chai* [I want to thank you],' she said.

'*Dhonyobaad pore janaben, ekhon oidike chole jaan. Je kono shomoy abar guli cholte pare* [You can thank me later. You should head to the hut there. The firing may resume at any moment],' he said.

'There is a problem. My daughter is still missing,' she responded.

'We will send you to the refugee camp early tomorrow. Why don't you look there first? We had sent the entire group there but for the two of you,' he replied.

Before dawn the next morning, Asstt Comdt Ghosh was preparing to send the two of them to the nearby refugee camp. The woman was worried about her daughter and how to get word to Asstt Comdt Ghosh in case she wasn't at the refugee camp. A few young men from the group of asylum seekers who had also arrived the day before had returned to the BSF camp. They brought news that the daughter was safe and at the refugee camp.

The old couple were finally on their way to the refugee camp, and before leaving, they thanked Asstt Comdt Ghosh profusely.

'Where do you stay?' the woman asked him.

'Barahanagar, very close to the Dakshineswar Kali temple.'

'Oh, I know that place well. Where exactly?'

Asstt Comdt Ghosh's residence in Baranagar was easy to locate. Dulaler Taal Misri is a brand of date palm candy (made by crystallizing sap from the palmyra palm available in the winter months). Across Bengal, the brand is a household name that became synonymous with palm candy in the early twentieth century. It is claimed as a magic pill for ailments, from sore throat to fertility issues, among others.

Asstt Comdt Ghosh's house was across from Dulal's factory in Baranagar. Where the wall of the factory begins, there was a board which bears the brand name and logo—the smiling face and bald head of the founder, Dulal Chandra Bhar. Asstt Comdt Ghosh's residence was in the lane opposite this board. One couldn't miss it; Dulal Chandra Bhar's smiling face ensured it.

Realizing he had shared more than he should have, Asstt Comdt Ghosh asked the woman why she wanted his address.

'*Maaer kachhe monnot korechhilam jano amra benche berote pari. Ekhan theke Dakshineswar mondirey pujo ditey jabo. Tahole tokhon apnar bari giye dhonoyboad janabo* [I had made a vow to Goddess Kali in return for her help in safely fleeing [East Pakistan]. I will go there to offer Her prayers in Dakshineswar temple. So, I thought I would visit your house then and thank your family too],' she said.

'Please don't do any such thing.' Asstt Comdt Ghosh was quite aghast at the suggestion that the woman would land up at his house after having seen the action in south Tripura. He had not told his family that he was in the midst of raging battles. They had no idea that the fighting had begun there—the missions and the fighting at the borders were classified, and they would worry for his safety.

The old couple left after this exchange, having once again expressed the gratitude they felt. Asstt Comdt Ghosh forgot about this incident.

Meanwhile, the woman located her daughter at the refugee camp. They belonged to a wealthy family of East Pakistan with a home in Calcutta. From Srinagar, she made her way to Calcutta and visited the Dakshineswar temple to offer a prayer of thanks. After the puja, she went to Baranagar, despite having been told not to. She located Asstt Comdt Ghosh's house and knocked on the door. The BSF officer's mother answered the door.

'*Apni Parimal Kumar Ghosher ma* [Are you Parimal Kumar Ghosh's mother]?' she asked.

'Yes, who are you?'

Though older of the two, the woman bent over and touched the feet of Asstt Comdt Ghosh's mother, in a sign of veneration. Asstt Comdt Ghosh's mother was stunned. An unknown woman had arrived unannounced, mentioned her son's name and touched her feet. Mrs Ghosh asked what was going on.

The visitor narrated the entire incident of her escape from East Pakistan to Mrs Ghosh. 'We are alive only because of your son. He saved my entire family,' she said, in tears.

Mrs Ghosh had no idea what her son was up to. She shot off a letter to Asstt Comdt Ghosh that day itself, inquiring about her son's well-being and requested to see him.

Asstt Comdt Ghosh took special leave and headed to Calcutta for a brief time-off to pacify his mother.

* * *

Gen. Yahya Khan had been seething in Pakistan. He had made several comments bordering on brinkmanship. On 30 July, he said that 'a total war with India is very near'. On 9 August, India signed a treaty with the USSR that assured mutual assistance in case of external threats. PM Gandhi responded from the ramparts of the Red Fort in New Delhi to Yahya Khan's threat on the Indian Independence Day, 1971. She said that India wasn't afraid of threats and was prepared to respond to any act of aggression.

15

When Is Winter Coming?

The field visits by international delegates were of great importance to the Bangladesh liberation movement. There was widespread support for the movement, and the world was becoming aware of the massive humanitarian crisis that the genocide had started and the civil war carried forward.

The BSF had facilitated reporting on the crisis by foreign and Indian journalists at the refugee camps and at the camps of the Mukti Bahini guerrillas at the borders. Some reporters insisted on crossing the border into East Pakistan without papers, but the BSF could not allow that. Many journalists still managed to slip into East Pakistan. The reports brought a number of aid workers and researchers to India. The BSF and the administrative officials of various districts also facilitated their efforts to document the refugee crisis. The number of refugees had reached 7 million by August 1971.

Perhaps the most damning report on the genocide in East Pakistan came, ironically, from a junket organized by the Pakistan Army in the summer of 1971. The Pakistan Army took eight journalists from West Pakistan to report from East Pakistan. The junket, like most are, was a curated tour of certain areas in East Pakistan, carefully selected to churn propaganda using the reporters. But unfortunately for the Pakistan Army, one of the reporters, Anthony Mascarenhas, assistant editor of the *Morning News* in Karachi, saw and heard a little more than the Pakistan Army wanted him to.

When he went back to West Pakistan, Mascarenhas sent his family to the UK and then fled himself. His report was published by *The Sunday Times* in London. It documented his own experiences as well as the boastful accounts of Pakistan Army officers. Mascarenhas had seen first-hand how the Pakistan Army profiled Bengalis to weed out guerrillas and Awami League politicians and supporters. This reinforced earlier reports on targeted killings, mass killings, forced disappearances and sexual assault and mutilation of women.

The report ignited a chain of reactions across the world and generated more concern for the East Pakistanis, who refused any compromise on their self-determination. Prime Minister Indira Gandhi later said that the report had also triggered her to initiate diplomatic-level talks with the USSR and European countries to lay the pitch for war against Pakistan to liberate Bangladesh.

India had estimated that the cost of supplies to refugees was close to $400 million for the first six months.[33] The United Nations and other organizations had pledged around $177 million by August, but it was not close to half the estimation. And in August, no one really knew when the conflict and the consequent crisis would end.

The third visit by British MPs to South Asia was in July of 1971. The delegation included the previous UK overseas development minister, Reginald Prentice. After his visit, Prentice spoke in the UK parliament, on 5 August 1971, about the status of the refugees and praised India for its efforts:

> They are doing a job on behalf of the rest of the human race which
> is beyond praise but they are doing it at enormous costs. Over
> 5 million of these refugees are in West Bengal, one of the poorest

and most over-crowded parts of the world. The whole area is packed with people, not merely in the camps but in the villages. There are refugees living in the schools so that the children cannot go to school, there are refugees in the offices so that normal office activities cannot continue.[34]

The British MPs wanted the UK government to pressure the US into stopping its arms supply to the Pakistani regime, since those were being used to kill East Pakistanis. Prentice also made observations on the guerrilla action, which was being supported by the BSF:

> The guerrilla activity in East Bengal is being intensified, as one would expect from the basic political facts of the situation. There are many reports in the Press in the past few days—the report from Clare Hollingworth in today's *Daily Telegraph* is an example—showing the growing activity and the growing success of the guerrillas, who can train in border areas, who are drawing their recruits from among the refugees, and who have the bulk of the population on their side. I suggest to the House that they will win in the end. The only question is how many deaths and how much suffering will take place before that happens.

Clare Hollingworth was an eminent war journalist. She had famously reported the outbreak of World War II. In June 1971, she had met with Gen. Tikka Khan, and the Pakistan Army had taken her on a low-flying helicopter ride through East Pakistan.

'I tried to count the burnt-out villages,' she later said. 'But I just lost count.'

On the same trip, Hollingworth reported from camps in the Petrapole–Benapole border, facilitated by 72 Bn of BSF, and wrote[35] on 9 July for the *Daily Telegraph*:

> Six weeks ago, just a few hundred yards further down this three-lane main truck road inside India I witnessed six or seven mortar

bombs land from the Pakistan side and noted the Indian army had constructed well camouflaged bunkers in defensive positions. Bangladesh guerrillas cross the frontier every night to lay mines, leave time bombs in deserted villages which the [Pakistani] army patrols, and throw hand grenades into outposts. The guerrillas are becoming an increasing menace to communication in border areas, where almost all telephone wires and electric cables have now been cut.

In the same edition, the *Daily Telegraph* carried[36] a report from Tripura by journalist Peter Gill, who wrote:

Now the Pakistan Army is involved in a full-scale war against its guerrilla enemies. And massive reprisals against villages suspected of harbouring guerrillas are driving out both Hindus and Moslems.

Refugee accounts of the scale of the fighting in East Pakistan are amply corroborated by senior officers in the Indian Border Security Force. Long range artillery, using 'air burst' shells as anti-personnel weapons, mortar bombs and machine guns have all been deployed by the Pakistan Army against villages.

The flow of information built global pressure on Pakistan and the US. The latter country was one of the biggest diplomatic hurdles for India to launch a war against Pakistan. The Mujibnagar government also asked Indian officials several times when the war would begin. On the ground, this question had been posed by East Pakistanis to the BSF officers right from the beginning. The BSF officers also wondered when the Indian government planned to go to war. The answer came to Rustamji in August through Golak Majumdar.

On 31 August, Mrs Gandhi visited the Indian Army station in Siliguri and then headed to a refugee camp in Tapurhat, Cooch Behar (West Bengal). Majumdar went with her and accompanied her to the Mukti Bahini camp, where the guerrilla fighters asked her about India's plans to go to war with Pakistan.

On the way back, she asked[37] Majumdar if the progress of the
BSF and the Mukti Bahini would take them all the way to Dacca.
He replied that it would not be possible without the three Indian
defence services because they would be up against the Pakistan
Army, Navy and Air Force.

But the prime minister was concerned that there would be
repercussions on India's western frontier—Gujarat, Rajasthan,
Punjab and Jammu and Kashmir. Indian military action in East
Pakistan would mean a war with Pakistan, which would respond
with an attack on all frontiers. Majumdar agreed and noted that the
conditions should be conducive for Indian tanks to operate at its
western border. According to Majumdar, the conversation indicated
the possibility that the war would be some time in winter. Senior
planners of the Indian Army had been working on plans for a winter
war since July 1971, based on the Indian government's policy[38].

A day later, Majumdar went to New Delhi and reported this
conversation to Rustamji, R.N. Kao, IB chief M.M. Hooja, as
well as to the defence secretary of India, the home secretary and
the three service chiefs.

16

'The BSF Is Making History'

By around September 1971, General Niazi's command was frustrated by the lack of intelligence from the field. Except for a scant minority, who had allied with the Pakistanis, the Bengalis in East Pakistan were not cooperating. The psy-war launched by the R&AW helped. The Swadhin Bangla Betaar Kendra dominated the airwaves. The growing global cultural and diplomatic support was a big boost to the exiled Bangladesh government.

On the ground, the Mukti Bahini guerrillas had become more effective. The Indian Army had increased the intake of recruits and shortened the training period. The EBR and EPR had been grouped into battalions with specialized objectives. The newly trained fighters were mixed with them.

In Tangail, the Kader Bahini—the guerrillas led by Abdul Kader Siddique—was a very effective force deep inside East Pakistan. And in the border areas, the BSF commandos made joint attacks with the Mukti Bahini. This confined the Pakistani soldiers to their camps and cantonments, and they kept away, using Razakars and other irregulars to engage with the Mukti Bahini and to man the borders.

Saidpur, in the north-west of East Pakistan, was a town with a 1,00,000-strong population. Non-Bengalis dominated three-fourths of the population, and the city was a stronghold of the

Razakars. The Indian territory bordering this part was manned by 70 Bn of the BSF, commanded by Lt Col Noel Gregory O'Connor.

Both his father and grandfather had been military men. But the young Noel Gregory O'Connor wanted to be a priest and was considering joining a seminary when World War II erupted. He signed up with the army, and after Independence, the Anglo–Indian continued to serve in the Indian Army. He was at the end of his service period when DG Rustamji inducted him into the border force. Many soldiers found the name O'Connor difficult to pronounce, so from his days in the army the lieutenant colonel came to be known as 'Onkar Sir'. That name continued in the BSF too.

In 1971, Lt Col O'Connor and his wife, Sylvia, were living at the Bn HQ in Raiganj. As the first wave of refugees trickled into India, Sylvia started coordinating aid at the camps. Over the next few months, this ballooned into a massive effort as an outbreak of cholera swept across the refugee camps.

By the end of the liberation war, India had given asylum to around 10 million refugees from East Pakistan. NGOs, missionaries and other aid workers had started going to the border areas as soon as the refugee crisis began. Global aid, in the form of people, money and necessary items, also trickled in to deal with the humanitarian crisis.

There were several aid workers engaged with the refugee camps close to Calcutta, but the ones farther away were neglected. Sylvia O'Connor had reached out to Mother Teresa and heads of other major organizations to send aid workers to West Dinajpur. Several, including the Missionaries of Charity, the religious institute founded by Mother Teresa, responded and sent aid workers who were then settled with the help of the BSF at the refugee camps. This was of great help to the district administration, which was overburdened with the responsibility of taking care of asylum seekers—close to a million had come into India through West Dinajpur.

British MP Michael Barnes toured[39] India in May 1971 to see the conditions of the refugees and the camps on behalf of War on Want, a charitable organization based in London. Lt Col O'Connor took him around. The British MP collected stories and data about the genocide from the East Pakistanis in the camps.

Barnes first travelled to Calcutta, where he met with Indian government officials to request a visit to the refugee camps at the border and Majumdar had sent him to West Dinajpur. Around this time, Lt Col O'Connor's daughter was engaged to be married, but he didn't want to leave his command. So he and Sylvia organized the wedding at a makeshift church next to his HQ in Raiganj during the monsoon. The wedding was attended by BSF personnel, policemen, priests and aid workers, as well as by some refugees and many Mukti Bahini freedom fighters who were at the camp close by.

After the monsoon, the Pakistan Army and the Razakars intensified their operations. Many of the East Pakistanis living in villages just across the border had not left their homes. But because of the increase in the number of raids and instances of crimes like torture by the Pakistan Army and Razakars, they too fled and came for part-time shelter at the refugee camps. There was also a massive shortage of food, and rations did not reach the border villages of East Pakistan. Some of them would live in the safety of the camps at night, and, at daybreak, they would go back to their villages in East Pakistan to tend to their fields and livestock.

The Mukti Bahini guerrilla units, too, increased their operations during and after the monsoon. When the Mukti Bahini would return from such operations, Pakistani fire chased them all the way into the Indian territory. The BOPs gave them cover to return to the base.

Sometime in September, while Lt Col O'Connor was visiting a company HQ close to the border in Dinajpur, he heard bursts of machine-gun fire from the Pakistani side. He rushed to the BOP and found a BSF sniper trying in vain to shoot at a treetop on the East Pakistani side. An LMG section sitting on a tree was shooting at a Mukti Bahini guerrilla squad returning from patrol.

Lt Col O'Connor told his men to cross the border and rush to their aid, but many of the Mukti Bahini guerrillas died before the BSF personnel could force the machine-gun operator to withdraw. Under cover of the BSF's guns, Lt Col O'Connor himself crossed the stream that served as the border and helped his men extract the corpses of the Mukti Bahini guerrillas.

As a response to such attacks, Lt Col O'Connor started sending BSF personnel, dressed in civilian clothes, with the Mukti Bahini guerrillas. Some of those raiding parties went as deep as 30 and 50 kilometres into Pakistani territory, aiming to hit military installations and blow up bridges.

After the joint teams had gained some experience, Lt Col O'Connor started leading larger missions into East Pakistan personally. In one such mission, he took a company each of the BSF and Mukti Bahini before dawn. They moved from the Goalgachh BOP and crossed the Nagri River on boats arranged by the Mukti Bahini.

The district commissioner and the police chief, who were at Goalgachh, wished them luck and waited for them to return. The assault party rowed across the river and moved up northwards close to the Pakistan Army base in Panchagarh. They organized bullock carts to lug the mortars and shells.

The Pakistan Army had built a camp for its additional forces outside its base in Panchagarh. The BSF and Mukti Bahini forces opened their attack with mortar fire at that camp. The Pakistani forces were taken by surprise, and the rain of fire forced them to run into the cantonment.

On the way back to Goalgachh, they spread out and used a different route. After Lt Col O'Connor and his men reached the river, one of his platoons hung back to give cover to those who would cross first. The boats were ready. The news of the attack had been relayed to other Pakistani BOPs, with orders to engage the assault party. Every Pakistani BOP was on the lookout, and the one opposite Goalgachh spotted the two companies. They began to fire shells on the BSF personnel and the Mukti Bahini guerrillas.

The two district officials waiting at Goalgachh rushed out of the camp as soon as the Pakistani soldiers began their shelling. This was more than they had signed up for. Those who had reached the boats on the eastern bank of the Nagri dove into the water and began to swim across. The shells began to hit the western bank just as the last of the raiding party made it back. An assistant commandant in O'Connor's battalion scooped up an unexploded mortar shell and buried it into the mud so that nobody would detonate it by accident.

Later, he retrieved it thinking it was a dud. Lt Col O'Connor saw him carrying it and snatched it away. In the safety of his cabin, he removed the detonator and emptied the explosive material from the missile head. But he did not keep it there for long. The next day, one of the district officials was back and absent-mindedly used the missile's emptied hollow end as an ashtray.

* * *

Maj. Gen. Nazar Shah, the chief of 16 Infantry Division, was the commander of Pakistani troops in north-western East Pakistan. He decided to keep the regular soldiers in their cantonments after the heavy losses because of the guerrilla operations and began to use the Razakars to conduct raids across the border. Taking a leaf out of the BSF's playbook, Maj. Gen. Shah mixed a few regular soldiers and paramilitary personnel into the Razakar units.

The regulars mixed with the Razakars wore civilian clothing or the uniform worn by the Razakars. When caught or spotted, it was easy to distinguish the Pathans by their features from the others in this part of the world. Dinajpur, Saidpur and other towns close by became a base for such operations shortly before the liberation war entered its third phase. The third phase was during the monsoon of 1971, when the Pakistan Army found that its soldiers, born and bred in a dry climate, were unable to navigate the muddy and waterlogged terrain of East Pakistan.

Later, Lt Gen. Niazi wrote:

> My troops belonged to dry areas of West Pakistan; many of them had not seen a big river before and did not know how to wade through water above their navels. There was a small stream or river every five or six miles, and big rivers looked like oceans to us. Swimming, rowing, and even wading had to be taught during operations. All this hindered our cross-country mobility, particularly during monsoons.[40]

The Pakistan Army considered Dinajpur and its adjoining areas along the India–East Pakistan border strategically important. Lt Gen. Niazi believed the Indian Army's Eastern Command would use this route to attack East Pakistan with tanks. In October 1971, a team of Razakars began to make raids at night by launching from random points across a 60-km stretch of the border, between Kukradha village and Bindol town in north Bengal. Kukradha was a few kilometres away from Kishanganj in Bihar—an important transport junction. Bindol was not far from Raiganj, the headquarters of 70 Bn.

Lt Col O'Connor sat down with his intelligence officer, and the two decided to send scouts to talk to villagers to locate the base of the Razakars. A few Mukti Bahini fighters, disguised as farmers, crossed the border and found that they were in a town called Haripur. There, a Pakistan Army platoon had holed itself up in a police station. They planned the operations from Haripur and used it as a launchpad for the Razakars.

The Pakistanis had evacuated residents living close to the police station for their security. So the Mukti Bahini spies were unable to get close and conduct a recce of the police station-turned-camp. A few nights later, a Mukti Bahini team, led by EPR personnel, conducted a raid on Haripur, but returned without making a dent. This established that the Haripur camp had been identified, and Pakistani soldiers fortified their camp better.

Since it was a base for regulars, Lt Col O'Connor decided to raid Haripur with a combined force that would have more BSF personnel than usually deployed for joint missions. There were forty-two men in total, along with two sections each of mortar and MMGs. Lt Col O'Connor expected a tough fight from the Pakistani soldiers, and he could not risk any Indian personnel being captured in Pakistani territory.

The Mukti Bahini had provided a detailed, hand-drawn map. The joint force of the BSF and Mukti Bahini guerrillas crossed the border at a point north-east of Haripur, while Lt Col O'Connor took a small team with him and sneaked into the south of Haripur to observe the operation. The mortar operators remained closer to Lt Col O'Connor, while the MMG operators took positions a few hundred metres from the camp. The attacking team went as close as possible to the camp without being detected and signalled for mortar fire.

Those first rounds of mortar were enough to dislodge the Pakistani platoon from the police station. They were caught by surprise, and Lt Col O'Connor saw that the Pakistani soldiers deserted the police station as soon as the MMGs opened fire at the sentries perched atop its wall. The machine-gun fire scattered them quicker. The rest of the BSF–Mukti Bahini personnel did not have to fire their weapons—it was a walkover.

The joint force demolished the police station building and set it on fire, to prevent the Pakistani soldiers from returning to it. Haripur was right at the border. So to reclaim that BOP, the Pakistanis would have to send a larger unit. But it was not a priority.

Further north, the Pakistan Army-backed Razakars had been conducting similar raids. Their aim was to stall the frequent and unpredictable Mukti Bahini ambushes. The reason was that the Pakistan Army was moving one of its columns to the north for a troop build-up at Panchagarh. The monsoon had taken a huge toll on the Pakistan Army soldiers who were used to fighting in drier conditions. Now that it was over, Lt Gen. Niazi was buffing up his troops for the coming war.

The Mukti Bahini had found out the real reason for the raids in Indian territory. The night following the successful Haripur raid, Lt Col O'Connor crossed the border once again with another joint team of the BSF and the Mukti Bahini. They walked for a few kilometres till they got close to the highway connecting Thakurgaon and Panchagarh. The Mukti Bahini scouts had picked an area which was free from patrolling Pakistani soldiers or Razakars. The men took positions on both sides of the highway and lay waiting, hidden by the trees, for the column moving north.

The terrain was flat, so the BSF snipers and MMGs took positions on treetops, which gave them an advantage of height and some natural camouflage. This section of the highway was a short and sharp curve. At dawn, the Pakistani troops began to move through the highway, unaware of the ambush party.

First came a road-opening party (ROP). The BSF company commander signalled the men to hold their fire till the main convoy appeared. The Pakistan Army ROP went past the curve and took positions there. Then came the rest of the formation, with two jeeps carrying officers and supplies.

When the jeeps nearly reached the middle of the curve, the company commander signalled the snipers and rifles on one side of the highway to hit the ROP, so that they could not return to the rescue of the officers in the jeeps. Next, he signalled the MMGs on the other side of the highway to fire at the jeeps. The ambushed soldiers and officers had nowhere to run.

Those in the rear were blindsided by the sharp curve and, as anticipated, could not come to the rescue of their officers and the ROP. They didn't know the size of the ambush. A Mukti Bahini fighter lobbed a grenade at one of the jeeps; it hit the bonnet, rolled to the far side and exploded, injuring its occupants. The chaos was enough for those on the eastern side of the highway to cross back to the western side (closer to the border). The ambush party regrouped and pulled out while some with rifles covered the withdrawal for a few more minutes.

The Pakistanis wanted revenge for the ambush. They sent a large team of Razakars to raid the Indian BOPs closest to Panchagarh, but the company commander was ready. Additional platoons from another BOP were prepared to rush to the defence of the one under attack.

The Mukti Bahini fighters spotted the advancing team of Razakars and told Lt Col O'Connor which Indian BOPs they were likely headed to. The company commander reorganized the machine guns and mortars on his flanks. He pulled them out of their nests and spread them wider, beyond the BOP's perimeter.

As the Razakars got closer, the company commander saw that they far outnumbered his platoon. He used his radio to launch a rain of fire from multiple locations, to make it appear that the BOP had more than a platoon. The MMGs and a few shell bursts scattered the Razakars and drove them back to the safety of their bunkers.

Meanwhile, the disruption at Haripur turned out to be a short-lived victory. The Pakistan Army increased the size of the Razakars to two companies and moved their local operational base from Haripur to Jadurani. Haripur town is a stone's throw from the border and within range of the BSF's mortars. Jadurani is 12 kilometres away from the border, shielded by populated villages. It was connected by a motorable road to the Pakistan Army strongholds at Pirganj and Thakurgaon. Transferring their base deeper into Pakistani territory gave the Razakars a safer base to operate from.

The Razakars resumed their raids on villages along the 60-km stretch of border between Bindol and Kukradha. To disable the Razakar raids, Lt Col O'Connor planned an attack on Jadurani.

* * *

The Pakistan Army had organized a ring of defences around Jadurani. The road between Pirganj town and Jadurani was protected by a platoon of the Pakistan Army, which was headquartered in Kamarpukur village, 2 km east of the Jadurani base. The southern access to Jadurani was through a wooden bridge over a canal, which was guarded by a platoon of Razakars. They had dug trenches and made bunkers near the bridge to cover all approaches.

Further south and closer to the border near Haripur, two platoons of Razakars were based in two different villages, both at a distance of 5 km from Jadurani. These two platoons used to conduct raids towards the south, near the Bhaturia BOP. There was real danger posed by the two platoons, which could be out on raids or patrols at night.

It took O'Connor close to a week to learn the entire defence layout and troop positions for Jadurani and Kamarpukur. To hit a base so deep inside East Pakistani territory, Lt Col O'Connor needed both approval and artillery cover from the Indian Army.

By then, the strategists in the Eastern Command were war-gaming their strategy and tactics for the impending war. The missions that Lt Col O'Connor was pulling off were important. Regular raids and attacks not only asserted the Mukti Bahini's presence but were also measures to prevent the Pakistani forces from rigging the roads and terrain with landmines that may later impede the Indian Army's attack when the war began.

The Eastern Command had decided 'that the border should be kept alive' through gradual escalation of attacks in two phases before a concentrated move.[41] This concentrated move was the Indian Army's assault plan as part of the Battle of Hilli—an attack on the north-western part of East Pakistan right up to the Jamuna–Brahmaputra River.

In the first two phases planned by it, the Indian Army wanted the Mukti Bahini and the BSF to conduct operations, backed by regular troops of the Indian Army. In the second phase, there would be low-risk escalation using regular troops. The 20 Mountain Division of the Indian Army approved the plan to attack Jadurani because it coincided with its first phase. The Indian Army began to send a few of their own commandos dressed as BSF and Mukti Bahini personnel for the BSF raids.

* * *

Lt Col O'Connor decided to employ a full company for this task and assigned command of the main raiding force (the BSF and Mukti Bahini) to his battalion's quartermaster, Assistant Commandant Singh. They would be supported by twenty MMGs and some mortar sections.

Jadurani was in a part of East Pakistan that shared borders with India both to its south and west. Asstt Comdt Singh's party would cross the border from the south. The company would hike due north-east, avoiding motorable roads, set up a position to the west of Jadurani and begin the attack on the Pakistani base.

Meanwhile Lt Col O'Connor would hold the position to the south with a platoon, and a section of mortar and two

MMGs. Once Asstt Comdt Singh had carried out the attack, Lt Col O'Connor would use his radio to contact the Indian Army for artillery fire on the Jadurani base. This would give fire cover to the assaulting company to retreat towards the south using the main road.

All the separate raiding teams would converge at a junction south of Jadurani close to the border and cross back into India together.

The plan, drawn by an officer who had tactical experience of three wars on different terrains, sounded brilliant. This would be easy for BSF veterans. The Mukti Bahini guerrillas had enough experience to pull off their part.

Lt Col O'Connor shared the plans for the clandestine mission, with the Indian Army brigadier supervising his battalion, who approved the plans. After all instructions were imparted to the commanders of the different parties, the teams assembled at the Bindol BOP a few hours after a light dinner. They were to trek through the night to take up positions according to assignments and then launch the attacks at dawn.

* * *

A. Ghosh, the additional district magistrate (ADM) of West Dinajpur district, was the liaison officer for the refugee camps. In that capacity, Ghosh visited Lt Col O'Connor quite frequently and was in awe of the secret missions that the BSF had been pulling off. Realizing that Jadurani was going to be another such black op, Ghosh asked O'Connor if he could tag along.

The latter tried dissuading him. District officials had been at the BOP during the shelling a few times. When the shelling became too intense, the district magistrate and the superintendent of police would retreat. The younger Ghosh, however, observed without panicking.

'There are too many risks. We will definitely attract fire, and it may be difficult to keep your wits like at the BOP,' O'Connor warned Ghosh.

'I will manage. I am sure your boys will keep me safe,' Ghosh replied.

O'Connor finally relented with several disclaimers for Ghosh's safety and said that the IAS officer must, at all times, obey his directions.

That night, Ghosh had dinner with the BSF men. Asstt Comdt Singh crossed over first, heading north-west through the Indian BOP at Bahor. Some of the BSF personnel wore *lungis* and singlets, and covering their heads with gamchhas, but all wore jungle boots. Lt Col O'Connor followed with his platoon of soldiers and Ghosh.

Across the border, Asstt Comdt Singh's team found the Mukti Bahini fighters waiting, and they made a quick march north-east to their destination. Lt Col O'Connor's platoon was not fast enough to catch up or communicate with them.

This was a clandestine operation, so there were no radios—they did not want to risk being heard by the Pakistanis. The only radio set was with Lt Col O'Connor to alert the army to fire the artillery guns to cover the return.

But there was a bigger problem. Lt Col O'Connor's mortar section had the shells, but those carrying mortars were in the group with Asstt Comdt Singh. By the time Lt Col O'Connor realized this, it was too late, and there was a three-hour hike's difference between the two teams.

That was when firing broke out but, but instead of from the north, where Jadurani was, it was to their east!

* * *

The Razakars were exchanging fire with the Indian BOP at the border near Bhaturia. Both Asstt Comdt Singh's and

Lt Col O'Connor's teams thought that the other was in danger and contemplated moving to each other's rescue. Communication between the two remained cut off till 8 a.m. the next morning.

Lt Col O'Connor now had just the platoon with MMG and a mortar section with only shells and no mortars. But instead of retreating, he decided to move forward and attack the Jadurani base with what he had. It was a bold move to pit forty-odd men against 250 with reserves close at hand. They got closer to the wooden bridge just south of Jadurani and took cover near some stacks of bricks.

It had started raining quite heavily by the time the constables with rifles took positions and began to fire from behind the brick stacks. The MMGs also began firing intermittently at the bridge. The Razakars returned fire.

Lt Col O'Connor decided to change the plan. He climbed atop a stack of bricks and used his radio to signal the Indian Army to start the artillery fire on both the bridge and the Razakar base.

ADM Ghosh, wearing a helmet, stayed behind the stack of bricks, with his back against it, sweating on the ground. 'Colonel, I don't envy you,' ADM Ghosh shouted out. 'I don't mind the rain, but there's also a rain of live bullets.'

'There's more of it up here,' Lt Col O'Connor replied. 'But don't worry. The shelling will clean up the bridge soon and then we can be off.'

Lt Col O'Connor jumped off the stack of bricks and took cover, lighting a cigarette. The artillery fire flushed out the Razakars from their bunkers at the wooden bridge. They ran to the Jadurani base only to find that it was being shelled too. Lt Col O'Connor's team found out later that the shelling had killed forty Razakars and four Pakistani soldiers. Satisfied, Lt Col O'Connor headed back south to the border.

En route, they came across Asstt Comdt Singh's platoons. They had heard the unexpected exchange of fire the night before and rushed towards Bhaturia, thinking that Lt Col O'Connor and his platoon were in danger. Thankfully, they came back with no losses, except one injury.

The operation was successful, even if not as per the exact plan they had set out with. All of them took a circuitous route to get to the border, stopping to eat fruits for lunch at an orchard. ADM Ghosh returned unharmed and with a story to tell.

In New Delhi, Rustamji read the report of the attacks for the month of October and sent an encrypted message to Lt Col O'Connor: 'BSF is making history.'[42]

17

Capture of Bantara and Bee Stings in Khanpur

Soon after the successful operation at Jadurani, the 20 Mountain Division of the Indian Army started to move in to the 'Balurghat Bulge'. The first phase of its operations was 'low-risk escalation', which involved employing the BSF and the Mukti Bahini to 'keep the border alive'.

The Indian Army kept some of its troops in reserve, in case back-up was required during these operations. They would support with light and medium artillery so as not to give away the locations of heavy artillery, and to avoid risk of discovery and sabotage by the Pakistani forces before the Indian Army's strike, which would come a couple of weeks later.

The first operation under the Indian Army's plan was to be carried out by a company each of the BSF and the Mukti Bahini. They were to attack two East Pakistani BOPs—Bantara and Mohonpur—both held by a platoon each of regular Pakistan Army soldiers and supported by a large number of Razakars from nearby bases. These two BOPs were in Dinajpur district of East Pakistan and bound by the Atrai River to their south, which served as the international border.

Dinajpur district was the remainder of an old kingdom, split into two by Partition. Dinajpur city was in East Pakistan. From Malda town in the south to Raiganj in the north in West Bengal,

India, a tapering mass of land, bulged into the north-western side of East Pakistan; this was called the Balurghat Bulge. At the tip of this mass was the 'Hilli complex'. The town of Hilli was in East Pakistan, and across the border was an Indian village of the same name. (The territorial map and position of Balurghat Bulge and the towns mentioned here are still the same, except, at the time of this writing, what was East Pakistan then is Bangladesh now.)

The EPR had claimed Hilli in March 1971, but Maj. Gen. Nazar Hussain Shah of the 16 Division of the Pakistan Army retook it by early May in a campaign that emptied the nearby towns for months. Lt Gen. A.A.K. Niazi had built several fortresses around this entire structure. From Hilli, the Jamuna–Brahmaputra River is 60 km away. It cut off northern East Pakistan from Dacca, and, it also provided support for the movement of Indian troops to Jessore and Rajshahi towns (to the south of Dinajpur).

The BSF and Mukti Bahini operations in October had increased the death toll of Pakistani soldiers. Every day, Brigadier Tajammul Hussain Malik would sit at his office in the Pakistan Army HQ in Rawalpindi and read about 30–40 soldiers being killed in action in East Pakistan. He was posted as director, Staff Duties, a coveted post in the Pakistan Army. Tajammul approached Gen. Abdul Hamid, Pakistan's then chief of army staff, and volunteered his services, while those who were issued transfer orders feigned sickness and parked themselves at hospitals.

In a later interview, Tajammul said that the situation was so ridiculous that the Pakistan Army issued a letter saying that they would not cancel the transfers to East Pakistan on medical grounds.[43] Officers would be carted from West Pakistan in stretchers if required, and genuine cases could be treated at hospitals in Dacca.

Maj. Gen. Nazar Shah had positioned two of his three brigades to defend attacks from West Bengal's West Dinajpur and Malda districts. Lt Gen. Niazi sent Brig. Tajammul to guard Hilli as commander of the 205 Brigade.

Brig. Tajammul created a deep defence of Hilli, which, according to the Indian Army's analysis, would be difficult to breach. Before the Indian Army could march to cut off the retreat from the north, Maj. Gen. Lachhman Singh Lehl decided to create breaches towards Dinajpur that would bypass Hilli through its northern side. The proposed attack on Bantara and Mohonpur was the first step to create bridgeheads into East Pakistan for the Indian Army.

Bantara and Mohonpur BOPs in East Pakistan were opposite Indian territory that was guarded by the BSF's 77 Bn, commanded by Lt Col B.P. Mukherjee. But 77 Bn was occupied in defensive positions in Hilli on the eastern extreme of the Balurghat Bulge.

Maj. Gen. Lachhman Singh tasked Lt Col O'Connor with attacking the Pakistani BOPs. They would launch at night, with support from four batteries of artillery and MMGs and mortars. Once the posts were taken, the Indian Army would relieve them.

Lt Col O'Connor sent his deputy to attend the briefing conference. But the deputy did not think the plan was sound. He felt that the general was asking too much of the BSF, and they may not be ready for set-piece attacks that are part of conventional warfare, though they had been successful at commando attacks and defences. The Mukti Bahini was a mixed force of regulars and civilians who had been hastily trained in guerrilla warfare. They had pulled off missions using guerrilla tactics, but it would require a different skill set—that of trained regular soldiers—to attempt set-piece attacks.

This lack of confidence was exactly what Maj. Gen. Lachhman Singh wanted to counter. The Indian Army's internal mission plan said that they wanted to pick easy targets to boost the confidence of the BSF and Mukti Bahini troops. The Indian Army needed the BSF and the Mukti Bahini because they knew the lay of the land and could both guide and fight alongside the Indian Army during the final assault for the Battle of Hilli.

The Bantara and Mohonpur BOPs were less than a kilometre apart. The terrain was flat and sheltered by mango orchards. The Pakistani soldiers had built a good defence—the embankment along the Atrai River provided a natural cover, and from there, the Pakistani soldiers had dug a trench connecting a network of roofed trenches to protect against artillery shelling.

Bantara was at the border and Mohonpur a kilometre to its rear. Lt Col O'Connor thought that consecutive attacks on Bantara and then Mohonpur would be difficult because the assault on Bantara would warn the unit in Mohonpur.

Simultaneous attacks on the two posts would be tough as well. The terrain was open, with no camouflage or mounds to provide cover. The approach to Mohonpur was past Bantara, so the company approaching Mohonpur would be spotted by sentries at Bantara. Lt Col O'Connor negotiated with the general and brought the objective down to occupying only Bantara. He also took clearance to act as the forward observing officer (FOO), since Indian Army officers couldn't cross the border.

Maps show that Bantara is across the northern perimeter of the Balurghat Bulge, and the Atrai forms a riverine border just south of Bantara. The Bantara BOP was situated behind an embankment along the river. That would make a direct approach to the Bantara BOP from the river in the south difficult. A sentry would easily spot an attacking party on the water, and the BSF and Mukti Bahini men would be sitting ducks.

But only a part of this border is bound by the Atrai, which meanders deeper into Indian territory after Bantara. The BSF outpost at Kamdebpur (a few kilometres south-west of Bantara) was across the river, so Lt Col O'Connor decided that it would be the best place to gather the forces and launch the attack.

Accordingly, he sent two companies of the BSF and one of the Mukti Bahini to Kamdebpur on the night of 3 November. The next night, he headed there with his wireless operator.

Sub-inspector Sukdev Choudhuri, a platoon commander of 77 Bn, was there that night, leading his platoon. Before they set off, there was a Kali puja. Once the rituals were over, Lt Col O'Connor cried 'Joy Ma Kali' and, using his field knife, pierced the tip of his finger and gave himself a tilak. Using the same finger, he applied blood tilaks on the foreheads of some of the men closest to him. His subordinate officers also did the same. They all set off after that, their foreheads marked with the dull red of their colleagues' blood.

After crossing the border, they moved in smaller groups till they were 6 km away from the Bantara BOP. From there, the trek was through open fields. It was just two days after the full moon, which meant that the fields were lit up. The Pakistani soldiers would be able to spot them and welcome them with machine-gun fire.

Lt Col O'Connor took a pause when he could make out the silhouette of the camp in the distance and called in for artillery fire. The Indian Army obliged; this would distract the Pakistani soldiers from the assaulting company, which began to move towards the Bantara BOP. Far from the safety of their bunkers, it was difficult for the BSF personnel to walk under the whistle and blast of the heavy shells. Lt Col O'Connor and the other officers egged the two companies on. The mortar bombs and artillery fire kept them safe and also guided them to their direction.

When they were 300 metres away from the Bantara BOP, Lt Col O'Connor called in to stop the shelling and to switch to MMG fire from the Indian BOPs. The machine-gun cover also had to be called off when they were less than 100 metres from the Bantara BOP.

Lt Col O'Connor was personally leading the forward Mukti Bahini platoons on the right side of the assault formation along the river embankment. Without the artillery cover, several of his men had slowed their pace, to Lt Col O'Connor's irritation.

Seeing their reluctance, he urged them forward to where he could get a better view of the camp. Most of them were fresh recruits, recently trained in guerrilla warfare and with little battle experience. One of them shouted 'Joy Bangla', despite the necessity for stealth, and lunged forward. Another gripped his rifle too tightly in his excitement and squeezed the trigger by accident.

The Pakistani soldiers heard the commotion and directed LMG fire at the noise from the sentry post. A company of the BSF and two Mukti Bahini platoons managed to get within 20 metres of the Bantara BOP, evading the LMG fire. Four BSF men died at close range and three more were injured.

One of the inspectors, injured by a bullet through his legs, lay on the ground. Unable to use it any more, he offered his Sten gun to anyone who needed it more. A head constable, the company bugler, was the first to reach the Bantara BOP but was hit in the face by LMG fire and died at the gate.

Lt Col O'Connor was behind the embankment when he saw his men being shot at. No one had managed to breach the camp as yet. He urged on the men, who had slowed down because of their fallen comrades.

'*Peechhey mat dekho, aagey badhte raho* [Don't look at who has fallen behind you. Keep charging forward].'

He had primed a few grenades, and stuck them in his pockets and ammunitions belt. He turned to the Mukti Bahini platoons he was leading and told them to follow him. Without waiting for a reaction, he jumped over the embankment and sprinted to the camp.

Sub-inspector Choudhuri saw Lt Col O'Connor run up to the perimeter wall of the camp. Without stopping and in a single motion, the lieutenant colonel placed one hand over the wall, crouched and jumped across in a graceful motion. He landed without losing his balance. Choudhuri, who was himself running towards the wall, could see Lt Col O'Connor's head bobbing on the other side of the wall.

The commanding officer had outrun them all and executed a nimble leap into the camp. The Pakistan Army soldiers were firing from within their bunkers. Only the muzzles of their guns were visible, projecting through a peephole in the front. O'Connor sneaked up to one of the bunkers, held the muzzle of the gun sticking out of the peephole and threw in one of the grenades. He repeated this with the few grenades he had in quick succession, the concrete bunker walls protecting him from the blasts.

By that time, the BSF personnel and Mukti Bahini fighters had scaled the wall and caught up with their commandant. They also began stuffing grenades into the bunkers. Seeing them behind him, Lt Col O'Connor jumped into the trenches for hand-to-hand combat, and the BSF–Mukti Bahini men followed. The adrenaline had drowned out their fears.

The grenade attack on their bunkers had taken the Pakistan Army soldiers by surprise. The platoon quickly deserted the BOP and withdrew towards the Mohonpur BOP, while their supporting company of Razakars scattered across the countryside. One of the fleeing Pakistan Army soldiers was caught and overpowered inside the BOP.

The BSF and Mukti Bahini team took control of the Bantara BOP just as daylight streaked the eastern sky with a dull pink. The Pakistani soldiers fired a few mortars in their direction from the Mohonpur BOP, but it didn't last long.

Lt Col O'Connor informed the Indian Army brigade commander that they had captured the post and asked for the relieving party, as had been agreed. Instead, the commander told them to move forward and capture the Mohonpur BOP.

The personnel and officers of 77 Bn had been watching the Mohonpur BOP from their camps. It appeared that the Pakistanis had vacated Mohonpur too and moved further away from the border. A few platoons from 77 Bn were on their way to check.

Lt Col O'Connor mixed a few platoons of the BSF and the Mukti Bahini, picking the men who had been cowering during the last attack, and headed towards the Mohonpur BOP. They found that the Pakistani soldiers had indeed emptied the BOP and regrouped at the Mohonpur bridge, 5 km upstream.

The BSF company held the two East Pakistani BOPs till they were relieved by a company of the Indian Army. The wounded were shifted to a field hospital set up by the army.

Lt Col O'Connor was supremely proud of how his men had performed. They were not trained for war but to guard borders. Many had carried out clandestine operations, but, for most of the BSF personnel, this was the first time they had pulled off a set-piece attack. It was the same for the Mukti Bahini fighters who had picked up guns out of desperation and necessity. The mission had been a success, but at the same time, the number of casualties saddened Lt Col O'Connor.

* * *

The next target set by Lt Gen Lachhman Singh was Khanpur, a small town 20 km west of Bantara. The BOP here was on a road leading directly to Dinajpur city, a stronghold of the Pakistan Army. This East Pakistani BOP was manned by a platoon of regular soldiers of the 26 Frontier Force supported by Razakars.

Lt Col B.P. Mukherjee, CO of 77 Bn BSF, sent a company of his men who had been engaged in guarding the Hilli complex for months and were eager to get some action. Their neighbours, 70 Bn, had just pulled off a successful operation in Bantara and were in high spirits. Lt Col Mukherjee wanted that his men, too, should be prepared for the coming war.

The mission was commanded by a colonel of the Indian Army who went as an observing officer. The attacking force comprised a company each of the BSF and Mukti Bahini.

Some Indian Army soldiers also donned BSF uniforms and went with the attacking party.

They headed to Khanpur from the east and circled to the north to attack from the rear, but the camp was well protected. The area around it was also open terrain, with hardly any natural protection for the attacking companies of the BSF and Mukti Bahini.

The attacking party reached the Khanpur BOP at around 4 a.m. on 13 November 1971. Pakistani soldiers spotted the BSF and Mukti Bahini men as they advanced towards the BOP and opened fire with machine guns, killing close to twenty-seven of them.

The officers of 4 Madras saw the massacre and took a call to send in a supporting company of the Indian Army. The reinforcements from the rear confused the Pakistan Army soldiers, and they divided their fire between the two groups.

Sub-Inspector Choudhuri was leading his platoon and they rushed to the BOP gate. As they stormed it, he felt what he thought were bee stings on his back, but the adrenaline kept him moving. Once they had cleared the camp, he called the wireless operator, Bibhash Dey, to report the success of the mission and to ask for help with evacuating the injured. His back was turned to Const. Dey, who noticed blood on his lower back.

'Sir, *rokto berochhe* [you are bleeding].'

'*Ki bolchho! Kichhu hoyeni* [What nonsense! Nothing has happened].'

Choudhuri touched his back, and, sure enough, he felt something warm on his uniform. He retrieved his hand and saw it covered in blood. He didn't want to make a fuss, but the wireless operator was adamant that he receive medical attention immediately. The ambulance couldn't come immediately to evacuate them. The Pakistani soldiers who had escaped had regrouped ahead.

Dey began to lead him back to the border. After walking a few metres, Choudhuri realized that he was unable to go any further.

He later learnt that there were two bullets lodged in his lower back. Dey picked up his platoon commander and carried him piggyback to the border.

Crossing the Atrai alone was fine for trained personnel, but carrying another person while doing so was tough. The BSF training includes a commando course, much of which is spent in hikes and other activities carrying a 30-kg load on the back. But carrying a six-foot-tall person is a different matter, and Dey managed it. He did not give up at the silty riverbank where his feet sank into the ground. He went down on all fours and crawled through the mud.

Sub-Inspector Choudhuri spent about two weeks in the hospital and was then posted to the G-branch at the Frontier HQ in Calcutta. His job was to assist the Mujibnagar government and the senior Awami League leaders working out of the BSF safe house in 8 Theatre Road.

These two missions by 70 Bn and 77 Bn of the BSF were the openers of the Battle of Hilli, which would go on for nearly three weeks. The Indian Army appreciated the efforts of the BSF and the Mukti Bahini in carrying out these missions.

Excerpts from the declassified 'After Action Report' of the 20 Mountain Division reads:

Capture of Bantara and Mohonpur Border Outpost

On night 4/5 November 1971, one company Border Security Force under Lt Col O'Connor and one company Mukti Bahini backed by 1 Guard and 64 Mtn Regiment attacked Bantara position which was captured in spite of heavy enemy fire and stiff opposition. The position was held by a platoon of 26 Frontier Force [of the Pakistan Army] supported by Razakars. We suffered five killed and three wounded. After the capture of Bantara position, the fire was shifted to Mohonpur Border Outpost. Border Security Force managed to capture the outpost without opposition. Later, 1 Guards moved

into the occupied positions to provide backing to Border Security
Force and Mukti Bahini.

Capture of Khanpurhat Border Outpost

It was reported that Khanpur was occupied by one platoon 26
Frontier Force and two platoons of Razakars, Mujahids and East
Pakistan Civil Armed Forces. This Border Outpost was attacked
twice earlier by Mukti Bahini but without success. The post was
planned to be occupied by using one company Border Security
Force and one company Mukti Bahini. Office Commanding 4
Madras was made responsible for controlling the operation and
providing the necessary backing.

The attack was put in as planned at 0400 hrs on 13 November
1971. Mukti Bahini scattered in the face of heavy enemy fire,
but Border Security Force pressed on the attack on to a part of
the objective. To save the situation and capture the major part
of the objective, Office Commanding 4 Madras launched one of
his companies and captured Khanpurhat. Our casualties were one
junior commissioned officer killed and three other ranks wounded
while the enemy losses were 12 killed and 12 wounded including
an officer. Mukti Bahini and Border Security Force suffered
27 casualties.[44]

The following honours were given for the Battle of Khanpur:

Lance Naik Amal Kumar Mandal: Vir Chakra (posthumous)
Lance Naik Kalipada Murmu: President's Police Medal for
Gallantry (PPMG) (posthumous)
Asstt Comdt K.S. Bisht: PPMG
Asstt Comdt H.N. Ghosh: PPMG
Asstt Comdt J.S. Sandhu: Sena Medal
HC Devi Singh: Sena Medal
Asstt Comdt I.M. Kumar: Mention in dispatch
SI Shamsher Singh: Mention in dispatch

The two missions helped the BSF men prepare for the weeks of battle ahead. In Lt Col O'Connor's own words:[45]

BATTLE OF BANTARA

Many battle experts might have shrugged their shoulders and many others might have posed the question: Is the BSF Jawan any better than a mere policeman? How will he react if he is thrown on the battle?

Well, all doubts about the BSF's ability were set at rest. The BSF can do it and they proved it in the Battle of Bantara. This was a watershed in the history of the BSF. It gave the BSF confidence and conviction.

Bantara, in Dinajpur like many other strongholds, was Pakistan's bridgehead. It was time to call the enemy's bluff. The enemy's sanctuary in Bantara needed to be crushed and the 70 Bn BSF was given the task.

Bantara was manned by Pakistan regulars. Hence, it was not going to be a walkover. The strategy of operation was carefully planned. A Coy 70 Bn BSF with Arty support of the Army, under overall command of Lt Col NG O'Connor, the then Comdt 70 Bn BSF, attacked and captured Pakistani regular defences after furious battle at Bantara and Mohanpur BOPs on 05 November 1971.

The Pakistan Army suffered ten casualties with one taken prisoner of war. Inspector B.L. Shah of the BSF was awarded a Sena Medal. Head Constable Rai Pada Das and Constable Amarendra Nath Mullick were both awarded the Sena Medal posthumously.

Lt Col N.G. O'Connor was awarded the Vir Chakra for his conspicuous gallantry.

18

The Big Gun of Akhaura

Akhaura, in Bangladesh, is just across the border from Agartala, the capital of Tripura state. A stroll down Jay Nagar in Agartala will bring one to the giant gates of the integrated checkpost. The international boundary has stalled the expansion of the city to its west. The waiting yard is packed with cargo trucks, and clearing customs can sometimes take a few days. Perishable cargo, mostly fish, gets priority. In the monsoon, the hilsa netted in the Padma is the most popular fish that crosses from Bangladesh to India.

A train track installed before Partition used to ply passengers and goods between East Pakistan and Tripura. In 1971, a few metres' length of the track was snapped, stalling the train indefinitely. Back then, residents of Agartala would often walk down to Akhaura to buy fish. The hilsa drew the biggest crowds at the border market during the monsoon, and its largest variety cost Rs 10 per kilo back then.

It was a great place for BSF intelligence operatives to pick up chatter about the Pakistan Army's movements and installations. The Mukti Bahini fighters also blended easily into the crowds of Bengali-speaking fishmongers and shoppers.

P.K. Chatterjee, joint assistant director, G-branch of the DIG (sector) HQ in Agartala, had built a good network of informers in the entire sector, including the Akhaura market.

By July–August, the Mukti Bahini ranks had swelled. The Indian Army had shortened the duration of the training course for the recruits and sharpened their content. This added a larger, robust band of guerrillas to the squads of the EBR and EPR personnel.

Dy Comdt Chatterjee spent a lot of time with the Mukti Bahini units operating from Tripura. They had good access to the locals, and could slip in and out of the border towns and villages to gather intelligence, which they would share with Dy Comdt Chatterjee. He would report back to his immediate superiors, including IG V.K. Kalia, and also brief the army intelligence officers in the Lichubagan cantonment, next to the DIG HQ in Salbagan, Agartala.

A veteran of the 1965 war, Dy Comdt Chatterjee had seen bloodshed and carnage at close quarters, especially at Kargil in May 1965, when he was Major P.K. Chatterjee of the 4 Rajput regiment. He led a mission to successfully capture three Pakistan Army posts in response to their shows of aggression and denigration of India and top government officials. But the horrors he saw in 1971—much before the war in December—scarred him deeply.

The Pakistan Army had installed a European howitzer gun somewhere near Brahmanbaria, but nobody was able to locate it. This big gun took a heavy toll on the BSF's positions and personnel at the border between September and November 1971. The Pakistan Army used the howitzer to fire at Agartala city too, maiming and killing Indian civilians and East Pakistani refugees, and destroying property.

Initially, the Indian forces had assumed that this was mortar fire. But mortars had a shorter range of a few hundred metres, and they could not spot a mortar section firing the large shells. They speculated that this was a smaller artillery gun. But the impact of the shells and their range of destruction dispelled that theory.

The shells would explode with a great impact, and the explosion would also cause a giant fireball. The fire would spread quickly to extend the area of damage by setting ablaze the nearby houses, causing a great deal of damage in civilian areas. The range and disruption caused by the attacks made Dy Comdt Chatterjee suspect that it was a howitzer. But there was no information of a howitzer at any of the known Pakistan Army camps close to the border. They suspected it was firing from deeper inside East Pakistan.

Attempts to locate the gun had failed, and Dy Comdt Chatterjee was assigned the task. Nobody that Dy Comdt Chatterjee initially asked knew how and when the gun had been brought there. The Mukti Bahini teams which patrolled the areas were also clueless. They did not venture into unknown territory without local villagers to guide them, since the Pakistan Army soldiers had riddled the terrain with both anti-tank and anti-personnel landmines.

Local villagers in East Pakistan were also scared of veering away from known roads, since some had died by stepping on landmines and triggering them. But there were Mukti Bahini informers everywhere, and someone would have noticed a huge gun being carted across the district.

Mukti Bahini spooks asked around in the Akhaura border market and managed to figure out where and how the gun was installed. The Pakistani forces had transported and installed it with stealth and cunning. Sometime in September 1971, the Pakistani soldiers had carted the howitzer on a large truck to the area, avoiding the main roads and highways where they might have been spotted. They took small, unpaved forest roads to reach their destination.

The only impediment was the Brahmanbaria–Comilla railway line, which they had to get across. The Pakistan Army soldiers undid a section of the tracks, drove the truck with the howitzer across and rejoined the tracks. They reached a school building which was already occupied by a Pakistan Army platoon. The school was around 2 km from the border.

By the time the Pakistan Army unit reached the school building, the villagers had retired for the night. The soldiers broke the wall to the school, pushed the howitzer into the compound and then repaired the wall. By the time the villagers woke up the next morning, all they saw was a fresh coat of paint on the wall and assumed it to be routine maintenance work.

The howitzer was hidden from view by the school building from the back and by the flanks of the compound. The Pakistani soldiers made a hole in the wall facing the border, large enough for the barrel of the howitzer to stick out. The outer part of that wall was camouflaged with wild bushes and shrubs, and they added a few more, ripped from elsewhere.

The only safe approach to the school building was to stick to the road that led right up to the gate, which was covered by sentries and two machine guns. Villagers didn't veer from that road because the area around the school compound was rigged with landmines, especially anti-tank mines.

The day Dy Comdt Chatterjee found out about the howitzer's location he had gone to the Akhaura market to meet with the Mukti Bahini spooks. This was sometime towards the end of November 1971. They gave him the lowdown about the gun, and then he used a different route to slip back into India. As he reached the boundary, he saw a BSF border patrol moving less than 50 metres from where he was.

Dy Comdt Chatterjee, with a G branch operative, was headed towards them when he heard a loud bang. A column of smoke shot up into the air and hung about for a while. A Sikh JCO, Bhagwan Singh, had been leading the patrol. He had stepped on an anti-personnel mine, below which an anti-tank mine was also concealed. The blast from the anti-personnel mine triggered the anti-tank mine, increasing the range of damage.

The blast blew off Bhagwan Singh's skull through the top of his head. His turban had come undone and was on the ground, the scalded skin of his face hung from his neck, and his long hair dangled at the back. Next to him, a constable lay motionless with his face to the sky, and an arm and a leg severed from his torso. His midriff had been blown away, his intestines dangled out of his belly. Dy Comdt Chatterjee and some jawans lifted the body, which made the intestines quiver like jelly. Lance Naik Chhetri had also died and was lying on his side, half his chest blown away. Other constables of the patrol team lay on the ground with other minor and major injuries.

The tiniest details of this gory scene stuck in Dy Comdt Chatterjee's memory. Any mention of the Bangladesh liberation war would trigger memories of that scene.

That day in 1971, the scene had made him very angry. The howitzer had given the Pakistanis cover to plant landmines close to the international boundary, and the artillery gun, which had maimed and killed civilians and damaged property, had to be decommissioned. He went straight to the inspector general of the BSF, told him that he had located the gun and volunteered to lead a stealth mission to disable it. Dy Comdt Chatterjee then spoke with the Mukti Bahini guerrillas and recruited twenty-five volunteers.

'Respected sir, I have worked out the plan. I will go there at night but with only a team of Mukti Bahini fighters. They are ready to take it on. They know every inch of the area and can avoid the landmines,' he told IG Kalia, who agreed.

In case the mission went awry or they were discovered, the Pakistanis were likely to respond with heavy shelling at the BSF and Indian Army positions. He told IG Kalia that they should be prepared for it and that the army should respond with its firepower.

On the night of the operation, Dy Comdt Chatterjee and the twenty-five Mukti Bahini guerrillas crossed the border at 2 a.m. They were armed with rifles, Sten guns and 8–10 grenades each. They trekked for around forty minutes to reach a spot a few hundred metres away from the school. From there, they could view the road. So they lay in the dirt, observing the location for several minutes.

They waited till they confirmed the positions of the Pakistan Army's machine guns and sentries watching the approach to the camp. They could make out almost nothing in the dark, though they had a rough map of the area marked with the positions of the guns and sentries. The area was rigged with landmines. If they crawled forward on their bellies, a larger surface area of their bodies would come in contact with the road surface and trigger undetected landmines.

The only way to ensure minimum contact with the ground was to tiptoe. That required balance, but, at the same time, they could not stand up straight to achieve that balance. The result of these conditions was a very awkward movement—they hunched their backs and walked forward on tiptoe for a few hundred yards in the dark.

They walked in that manner till they were nearly 50 yards from the building. That was when the Pakistan Army sentry spotted the moving shadows. The Mukti Bahini commander had refused to let Dy Comdt Chatterjee be at the front of the formation or right at the back. But even from the middle of the advancing formation, Dy Comdt Chatterjee could hear the metallic click on a gun. The others heard it too and froze where they were.

Too late.

The sentry fired a burst from an assault rifle. It woke up the other Pakistani soldiers. The firing gave away the position of the sentry. One of the guerrillas lobbed a grenade. The five right in front opened fire, which gave cover to the five behind them to move to the other side of the road.

The grenade had done the trick. There was a lull in the firing from the sentry, and around ten Mukti Bahini guerrillas rushed right up to the gate and took positions along it. Those at the rear, including Dy Comdt Chatterjee, kept up the firing, and those in front lobbed a few more grenades inside the compound.

There was no more firing from within the camp. The surprise of the attack had prevented the Pakistani soldiers from using their machine guns. The Mukti Bahini, with Dy Comdt Chatterjee, captured the camp by 3.30 a.m. in a twenty-minute casualty-free raid.

Dy Comdt Chatterjee went into the school compound with the first team when the firing ceased. The Pakistani soldiers had escaped from the rear of the building. He saw a few trails of blood from the sentry post to within the compound—they had wounded at least one sentry and some others inside. The Pakistani soldiers had ditched their machine guns, which were heavy and would have deterred a swift escape. The howitzer stood unattended.

The Mukti Bahini guerrillas stationed a few men to guard the compound while others salvaged the armoury for weapons and ammunition.

At first light, one of the guerrillas noticed a patch of grass in the compound that was lighter than the rest. He began to dig there, and a few others joined in. After digging a little, Dy Comdt Chatterjee saw a mud-stained sari and decomposing hair. Digging deeper, they found the remains of a woman. Dy Comdt Chatterjee surmised that the Pakistanis were kidnapping and raping women even in the gun positions.

They deflated the tires of the howitzer to prevent it from being carted away and left some Mukti Bahini fighters to guard the gun till the Indian Army took command over it. Dy Comdt Chatterjee headed back to Agartala with the rest of the Mukti Bahini unit. He went straight to the DIG HQ in Salbagan and told the deputy inspector general that the weapon had been captured. It meant less work for the Indian Army when it would march across the border a few weeks later. Rustamji awarded Dy Comdt P.K. Chatterjee the Police Medal for Gallantry for this successful mission.

19

Sabotaging Chengiz Khan

The official period of war between India and Pakistan is 3 December 1971 to 16 December 1971, the day Lt Gen. Niazi surrendered in Dacca. Elsewhere, some of the Pakistan Army units would only surrender the next day, that is 17 December. India would hold on to the captured territories in West Pakistan for longer.

Fighting between Indian and Pakistani forces in the eastern sector broke out earlier. There were battles in Hilli and near the East Pakistani borders with Meghalaya and Tripura from the night between 21 and 22 November 1971, when the Mukti Bahini decided to move in, with support from the BSF and the Indian Army.

As Indira Gandhi and her advisers had anticipated, the liberation of Bangladesh was marked with a pitched war between India and Pakistan in the western sector. This began with an air attack, named Operation Chengiz Khan, launched by the Pakistan Air Force that was aimed at demolishing Indian Air Force (IAF) bases, runways and aircraft. This would have dealt a severe blow to the Indian defences.

The Indian government may not have known the name of the operation, but it learnt of its aims and objectives in advance, and removed its aircraft from the airbases, replacing them with dummies. The counter-espionage operation that helped avert this disaster has two versions available in public domain, and now another has emerged.

Two books have detailed the R&AW's initial years. In his *The Kaoboys of RAW: Down Memory Lane*,[46] former R&AW officer B. Raman wrote that K. Sankaran Nair—later a director of the R&AW—was responsible for several assets within the Pakistani establishments. One such asset was a mole in the office of Yahya Khan himself. This mole, Raman wrote, warned Nair about the impending attack. He sent an encrypted message that the PAF was going to launch an air attack on Indian airbases on 1 December 1971. The date would later turn out to be an error in decrypting the message, which originally had the date of attack as 3 December 1971. The security writer Nitin Gokhale relies on the same account in his book *R.N. Kao: Gentleman Spymaster*.[47]

In his memoir, *The British, the Bandits and the Bordermen*,[48] P.V. Rajgopal wrote that the BSF intelligence team had learnt of a Pakistani national spying on Indian airbases by posing as a mendicant near the India–Pakistan border in Ganganagar district of Rajasthan. IG Ashwini Kumar had his men interrogate the fake godman. They were able to coax some information about him, including details on a plan to bomb the Indian airbases in the western sector on 3 December 1971. Rajgopal wrote that the BSF verified this information through a contact of Ashwini Kumar's in Pakistan.

IG (retd) V.K. Gaur had interviewed then IG Ashwini Kumar for his own book[49] on the liberation of Bangladesh sometime in the 2000s. IG Gaur narrated the substance of that interview, pertaining to the counter-espionage operation, to this author.

Inducted into the Imperial Police in 1942, Kumar had trained at a police academy in Phagwara, Punjab. There, one of his instructors had been a Muslim man who had settled in Pakistan after Partition. The instructor's son worked as a tea estate manager in Sylhet, East Pakistan. When the civil war made life difficult in East Pakistan, the instructor's son wanted to head back to West Pakistan.

He went over land from East Pakistan through India. He made it all the way to Punjab but was stopped and detained at the India–Pakistan border near Fazilka since he lacked the right papers. He got in touch with his father in Pakistan, who, in turn, reached out to Ashwini Kumar for help. The son was a civilian fleeing the civil war and not a spy or a criminal. Kumar was both IG-BSF (western frontier) and IG of Punjab Police at the time. He spoke with government officials but could get no help. So he reached out to R.N. Kao through Rustamji, saying that helping the Pakistani national might prove useful later. Kao obliged Rustamji.

Kumar told Gaur that this same man, the tea estate manager who had fled the civil war in East Pakistan, would be the one to verify the intelligence input on the impending attack on Indian airbases. Rustamji passed on the information to Kao, and Kumar spoke to Air Marshal M.M. Engineer and later spoke with Mrs Gandhi too.[50]

The IAF withdrew its planes from the forward bases, replacing them with dummies, which the PAF blew up thinking they were real fighter jets of the IAF. Later, the IAF planes retaliated in kind to Operation Chengiz Khan while the IAF personnel repaired the airbases almost overnight.

After the war, the Indian government awarded IG Ashwini Kumar with a Padma Bhushan and, in the official gazetted notification, credited him with stopping Operation Chengiz Khan:

> Besides constantly visiting the borders and infusing confidence and fighting spite into his men, Shri Ashwini Kumar provided a fund of information on the intelligence side and a considerable share of the credit for the failure of the pre-emptive strike of the Pak Air Force on Indian bases on 3rd December 1971 should go to the intelligence conveyed by him.

20

Small Ops

'*Khan astesey, Khan astesey* [the Pakistani soldiers are coming]!'

Sub-Inspector P.K. Halder, a platoon commander of 72 Bn in West Bengal, was at the Amudia BOP (close to the Petrapole–Benapole border) when he heard the refrain above a bedlam of shrieks and cries. The East Pakistani Bengalis referred to the West Pakistani soldiers as 'Khan' and the Pakistan Army as 'Khan Sena'. This was sometime in September, well after the monsoon had passed. Halder rushed to the observation post, pushed past the gathered constables and peered at the border. Villagers from East Pakistan were rushing towards the Indian side. There was no Pakistani uniform in sight.

A Mukti Bahini patrol had seen five or six jeeps and had rushed back to the border camp. On the way back, they warned the villagers, who panicked and started running to India with whatever belongings they could carry, including livestock. As they crossed the border, they warned of the approaching 'Khan Sena'.

The border camp in East Pakistan had been vacated in March, since the EPR had defected. The 12 Baloch Regiment of the Pakistan Army had built a stronghold in Satkhira—a town 12 kilometres away—and they had some camps close by. After the monsoon, they could sense that war was looming and the soldiers were now on their way to occupy their own border BOPs.

Halder sensed an opportunity. Both he and the local Mukti Bahini commander agreed that they should attack the Pakistanis and keep them away. They put together a team of twenty men and took positions around the border with two LMG sections. Halder placed two snipers on trees and put the two LMG sections on either side of the road. Once the Pakistani convoy was near, he would signal for fire.

Within a few minutes, a cloud of dust showed up, followed by the sound of the jeeps. One of the LMG sections was of the Mukti Bahini. As soon as that LMG operator saw the jeeps, he let loose a burst of fire, but the jeeps hadn't yet got close enough. Before the others could react, the LMG volley stopped midway. Its firing pin had jammed—a common complaint against some of the light machine guns. The ambushing party was as surprised as the Pakistani soldiers—a platoon travelling in six jeeps.

The Pakistani soldiers fired back from inside the vehicles. A few jumped off their jeeps, took cover behind their vehicles and fired back with automatic weapons. The snipers managed to hit the jeeps, making them drive away in reverse gear. The BSF's LMG section opened fire and, within a few minutes, all of the jeeps reversed and left. Cheers broke out. They had managed to send back the Khan Sena.

A week later, the sentry awoke Sub-Inspector Halder past midnight to the rumbling of several vehicles not too far in the distance. The Pakistani soldiers had returned with more troops in a large convoy of 25–30 vehicles, escorted by machine-gun-mounted jeeps. The BSF platoon in Amudia BOP stayed put.

The next afternoon, the Pakistani soldiers announced their arrival by opening MMG fire at the Hakimpur BOP, a few kilometres to the north. The BSF personnel took cover in their bunkers. But the Indian villagers were not that lucky. The firing continued for an hour, damaging huts, killing livestock and injuring several villagers.

Later, Halder saw the extent of the damage and had the injured transported so they could get medical attention. There had been no provocation for the attack. Villagers across the border seemed to be afraid too—the wailing could be heard at the BOP. But this time the East Pakistani villagers did not dare to cross the border into Indian territory to seek shelter.

From the first day itself, the Pakistanis began to build more bunkers in their BOPs. It was done within two days, and then they began shelling the Indian BOPs. When he heard the first whistle of a mortar, Halder was near the embankment on the edge of his BOP facing the border. He vaulted the mound of the embankment and dived into the trench below. On that first day, Halder had counted twenty-nine shells in thirty minutes. Some BSF personnel had been injured as well.

On 9 July, similar shelling at the Ghojadanga BOP (of 72 Bn) had killed BSF Constable Narendranath Burman of Sub-Inspector Halder's platoon. This had then forced Halder's platoon to vacate the Ghojadanga post in July 1971. They had moved back to a BSF camp away from the border, where they built more bunkers, and the Indian Army moved closer to the border.

Halder didn't want a repeat of losses at the Amudia BOP and issued precautionary instructions. Over the next few weeks, the Pakistan Army began taking back more of its previously deserted BOPs, building more bunkers in them and then shelling indiscriminately, without provocation. Or so Halder had thought at first. Actually, the Pakistanis had many reasons for the shelling.

For one, the war seemed imminent, and after the monsoon, Lt Gen Niazi had begun moving his troops to forward positions at the border to build and secure defences. The monsoon had been difficult for his soldiers, who were unused to navigating the terrain in that weather condition.

In Halder's area, the Pakistan Army camps were tired of the Mukti Bahini raids, some of which had been ingenious and had hit the Pakistanis' morale.

Early on, in the liberation war, the Mukti Bahini sneaked deep inside hostile territory and arranged for microphones, tape players and aluminium-coned speakers—the kind that delivers a raspy sound without any bass. At first, they would draw close to the camps and use the microphones to launch a volley of abuses and slurs in Bengali at the Pakistani soldiers, who would retaliate with fire. The retaliation was useless; the Mukti Bahini fighters were well hidden, which angered the Pakistani soldiers even more. The abuse was spaced with recordings of hundreds of boots crunching on gravel and announcements like, 'Freedom is coming, we are coming!'

Then, they devised more elaborate plans. The Mukti Bahini would sneak close to the Pakistani camps at night and plant the red-gold-and-green Bangladeshi flag. In the morning, the Pakistan Army camp commanders would task the soldiers with taking down the flag. As the soldiers moved close to the flags, the Mukti Bahini would shoot at them, injuring and killing quite a few.

These pranks also added to the list of reasons that the Pakistanis moved to occupy the border camps they had previously deserted. From there, they could dissuade the Mukti Bahini from crossing over from India. But the BSF and Mukti Bahini made it difficult for them to step out of the camp. The Pakistan Army patrols left their own camps surreptitiously. A few times, BSF and Mukti Bahini teams would circle around the camps and wait atop trees with Sten guns and rifles, and take down the soldiers leaving the camp.

The Pakistanis also had their dirty tricks department. In October, well before the India–Pakistan war, Radio Pakistan broadcast the following news from Dacca:

> Earlier today, the Pakistani Army crossed the border into West Bengal in India. They killed hundreds of Indian troops at the border and have reached the outskirts of Basirhat town. They will take it any day now.

Less than 50 km away from Basirhat, Sub-inspector Halder's family heard the news and were shell-shocked, because to get to Basirhat, the Pakistanis would have had to cross the India–East Pakistan border at Ghojadanga, where Halder was posted at the time. And, his parents had no way of immediately getting news of him.

Halder's parents kept the radio on every day during the nine months of the Bangladesh liberation war. Their son was at the border, and they scoured the airwaves for every news bulletin they could access. They regularly tuned into the Swadhin Bangla Betaar Kendra for details—Abdul Mannan's and Akhtar Mukul's voices boomed through their house, as though these were the voices of family members. They tuned in for the AIR broadcasts in Bengali, Hindi and English.

When they heard the newsflash on Pakistan Radio in October, they were heartbroken at the alleged fall of Basirhat. But there were no reports in the Indian newspapers over the next two days. On the second day, Halder's father was contemplating whether he should go to the 72 Bn HQ in Barrackpore for news of his son, when the latter appeared at his doorstep in uniform. Halder had some work at the battalion headquarters and made a quick stop home. He convinced his family members that he was safe and sound, mentioning nothing of the shelling or the commando operations he had led with the Mukti Bahini.

The Pakistanis also used the Mukti Bahini's tactic and prepared ambushes from tree branches. They built machans with wooden platforms, with space enough for a light-machine-gun operator and a spotter.

The Indian Army unit in operational control of Basirhat had tasked Halder with a mission to find routes to Satkhira—the closest stronghold of the Pakistan Army. Halder chose five men each from the BSF and Mukti Bahini. Like always, the men donned their lungis and vests, slung carbine pistols across their shoulders and concealed them with gamchhas draped around their necks.

The terrain there was flat and not hilly. A kilometre ahead, cries of 'Khan astese' sent them racing to the closest village. A knock on a door revealed a bewildered villager who quickly hid them in his house. Halder pried open a window that looked on to a garden, beyond which was open pastureland. And walking on its edge was a section of Pakistan Army soldiers, rifles on their backs, out on an 'area-domination patrol'.

Once the patrol had passed, Halder and his ten men moved out in single file and used the footpaths parallel to the Basirhat–Satkhira road to travel further into hostile territory. A little ahead, they turned a corner towards a clump of trees, when a staccato burst of LMG fire broke the silence.

Halder and the others hit the ground to take cover. They lay still for a few minutes, rolled to positions behind trees and returned fire. That stopped the LMG fire within a few minutes. They waited for some more minutes and then got up to check for injuries.

Dudu Miyan, EPR constable-turned-Mukti Bahini fighter, lay sprawled on the ground, groaning in agony. The lower half of his body was covered in blood. Though the earth was dry, the blood had turned the soil stuck on his lungi muddy. Dudu Miyan was a big man—six feet tall and weighing about 130 kg—and he had been right in front of the single file of eleven people. The Pakistani soldiers had spotted him first and fired the machine gun in his direction; the bullets had shattered his body from the waist down. The rest of the team picked Dudu Miyan up to take him back, but the excessive bleeding had already taken its toll; he was dead by the time they got him to the BOP.

The death dampened the spirits at the entire camp. Kali Puja was around the corner, and Halder thought that would help bring back a sense of normality. On the night of the celebrations, the Pakistani soldiers spotted the lights at the BOP. They began pummeling it with mortar fire. The Indian Army silenced them with 25-pound shells.

Unlike assistant commandants P.K. Ghosh, Leela Ram Rana and others who had served with the Indian Army, many of the BSF personnel hadn't seen action. There were several policemen who had been absorbed from the state border police and fresh recruits who had the heart but were experiencing heavy action for the first time. Many had joined the BSF at its inception, but this was their first tryst with war-like hostilities at the border.

Before the war, Halder's platoon had never engaged with the East Pakistan Rifles. He had met the EPR personnel for the first time sometime in 1969, a year after he had been posted as a platoon commander and given charge of a platoon at the India–East Pakistan border. They were armed, in uniform and had different names, but they spoke Bengali, just as he did, and were cordial.

There was no fence dividing the two countries; the international boundary was demarcated by white cones. On the roads connecting the two countries, there were hand-operated boom barriers marking the border (but there were some mud trails which didn't have any boom barriers). Along this border, the nationality of the villages could be distinguished by establishing if they had mosques or the houses had markings of Hindu households. That, too, did not stop one from celebrating the festivals of the other. The fairs during Durga Puja and Kali Puja drew crowds from everywhere. The BSF and EPR sent boxes of sweets to each other's BOPs.

Once, a young recruit to the EPR, on his way to join the East Pakistan BOP, walked down the connecting road and overshot the camp. It was late in the evening, and he had missed the turn to his camp. He crossed over, saw the lights at the Indian BOP and assumed it was the EPR camp in East Pakistan. He landed in front of the BSF sentry with his trunk, bedding and a rifle slung across his shoulder.

'Assalamwaleikum, sir. I am here to report for duty.'

The arrival had drawn the head constable to the sentry position. They understood that this was an EPR constable and had crossed the border by mistake. The head constable told him that he was at the Indian BOP and offered him a cup of tea. Meanwhile, Sub-Inspector Halder was informed and he came to meet the waiting EPR recruit, who had started feeling quite uncomfortable by then.

Halder reassured him that he had nothing to worry about and offered him tea again, which the EPR recruit declined. He wanted to be on his way. So Halder took him to the border, called for the commander of the camp and told him what had happened, saying that it was a human error. Anyone on his way to a border camp for the first time and that too in the dark could easily make such a mistake. They had a good laugh about it, and the EPR constable assumed his post without incident.

But the bonhomie at the border would soon end. The relations with the new occupants of the East Pakistani border camps grew colder still with the advent of winter in 1971 as the war loomed. The troops were building up, and the shelling became more frequent after Kali Puja, with several close shaves. A week or two after Kali Puja, Sub-Inspector Halder was standing next to a bunker, briefing a constable, when they heard a whistle and jumped into the bunker. Their backs were against the wall in the direction of the Pakistani BOP. The second shell hit the wall opposite them and exploded, and a burning piece of shrapnel hit Halder's midriff. The explosion had temporarily deafened them, but he felt the heat and brushed off the shrapnel.

Sometimes, the constables seemed on edge, and Halder did his best to keep them motivated. For many, the presence of a temple on the premises helped. One evening in November, the shelling and a thunderstorm till late into the evening had forced them to abstain from offering evening prayers at the temple, which was usually just past dusk. That night, several of the constables went to bed feeling uneasy. Then, late at night, a loud hum woke up the constables in their barracks and Halder in his room, where the LMGs were stored. He listened carefully, trying to make out what it was. It had sounded like a grunt. Suddenly something large moved in the dark near the door to his room. Halder, in a single motion, reached for his carbine pistol in the dark with one hand and used the other to spring out of bed. By the time he got to the door there was nobody there. He waited for a few minutes and then stepped out.

Outside, he saw Head Constable Prem Kumar Rai sitting in his cot, Sten gun in hand. He, too, had seen something or someone creeping in the dark. The two of them made their way to the barracks, causing a murmur among the constables who were awake. One of them held an SLR weapon, the first truckload of which had just been received by their platoon.

'Dost ho, dushman ho, chup ho jao warna goli marunga [Whether you are friend or foe, keep quiet or I will shoot at you],' said Halder loudly.

Halder called out loudly for Head Constable Moti Singh, who was the barracks in-charge, and asked who had crept into his room at night. HC Singh began to stammer nervously.

'Sir, someone jumped on me. I thought we were being attacked and went to get the LMG,' said HC Singh, who was one of the LMG operators.

It took a while, but PC Halder made sense of what had happened after he investigated the cause of the disturbance. A cat from the neighbouring village had come hunting for food. It had jumped from between the beams that supported the roof, lost its footing and fallen with a yowl on HC Moti Singh, who woke up and rolled from his bed on to a constable sleeping on the floor. In the dark, both grabbed each other's throats and began to struggle. The chokehold prevented them from speaking, and their grunts could be heard from across the barracks as well as in Halder's room. The constable who had been sleeping on the floor extricated himself from the melee and rushed to retrieve his assault rifle, which had replaced the 303 rifle he used earlier. And that saved them from a deadly accident.

The 303 rifles are bolt-action, with the bolt on the right side of the gun, which requires the shooter to pull and release the bolt with the right hand to load the barrel before firing. The SLR weapon had a loading lever to its left. Since he was new to the weapon, the constable's right hand had instinctively gone for the bolt and not found it. Otherwise, he might have opened fire.

In the meantime, HC Moti Singh, convinced of a commando raid by the Pakistanis, headed straight for his LMG and loomed in the dark at Sub-Inspector Halder's door. Hearing the tussle and the grunts, five constables sleeping close to the door ran out into the rain and out of the camp. A roll call and a few whistles later, they emerged sheepishly and said they were trying to see if they had been attacked and would have rushed to the company headquarters to sound the alarm. They had seen the cat slinking away when the commotion began.

Note: In times of hostile engagement, the situation is different. The BSF posts follow a strict safety protocol. Weapons and ammunitions are stored in separate, guarded buildings at every camp and HQ, when not assigned to personnel on active duty.

21

A Bullet for Lunch

The BSF Academy at Tekanpur is an hour's drive from Gwalior city. It is a beautiful, green campus sprawled over acres of land. At its heart is a lake with gharials, crocodiles and birds, whose number increases in winter with the arrival of their migratory cousins. There are several buildings that house training facilities, lecture halls, accommodations for officers, rescuers, staff and guests, stadia, a pool, and research and technical facilities for the BSF.

It was once part of the estate of the erstwhile royals of Gwalior and the BSF acquired it at the time of its founding in 1965. Back then, the academy grounds comprised the lake, set against a few hillocks, a well-forested estate and a building called the 'kothi' (bungalow). The kothi is on the lakeshore and now serves as a mess for the seniormost officers of the BSF. The BSF Academy launched with this building, and doubles as its administrative HQ and quarters for its senior staff members.

Brig. B.C. Pande took charge of it in 1965 as its first director and told Home Minister Y.B. Chavan that he would have the BSF Academy up and running in a few days. Sure enough, the grounds were cleared of shrubs, tents came up and training began. This was how things remained, until the buildings were constructed some time later.

The first batch of the ACDE (assistant commandant-direct entry) recruits arrived in December 1966, and among them was Samir Kumar Mitra, a science graduate from Calcutta University. He had grown up in Barasat, a town on the outskirts of Calcutta. He had been a senior cadet of the NCC during his college days. A witty young man, Mitra had impressed the recruiters with his ability to perfectly accomplish the task assigned to him.

The first batch had a motley crew of public service aspirants. Apart from fresh graduates, there was a public prosecutor, a professor and a police officer from Calcutta, plus several from the Central Reserve Police Force, Railway Police, etc. Mitra was the youngest among them.

They got off the same train at the Gwalior station and headed to the academy, expecting a grand welcome at the officers' quarters. The road to the academy was majestic—bright, green fields darkening in the twilight, with the hills looming in the distance and acting as a compass to their drive into their future.

Arriving at the academy, they were greeted by a senior officer who guided them to their respective tents with the help of a halogen lantern. It was cold and misty in the field, and the dull, low-watt bulbs inside the tents were not particularly cheering. The furniture for each of the occupants included a steel cot, a wooden chair and a smaller metal chair and table near the tentpole. The floor of the tents was made of bricks, and that insulated them from the damp but not the biting cold of central Indian winter. The recruits kept the living areas clean and were taught how to assemble and disassemble the tents. The toilets were 'thunder boxes' housed in separate, smaller tents.

It was an adventure for Mitra, who had never been exposed to living in harsh conditions, but he knew he was signing up for the paramilitary and that it would be tough. The courses were designed by military officers, and they used the same standards to train bordermen.

Brigadier Pande had served with the Indian Army since 1940 and served as commandant and colonel of the Assam Regiment before he was deputized to the BSF. There were also other expert trainers in the BSF Academy such as Colonel Megh Singh, who had raised India's first special forces unit.

The call would come at any time for the recruits to present themselves. There were almost no weekends off. Brig. Pande was soft-spoken and fatherly in his demeanour, and the recruits looked up to this polyglot intellectual. But he was an exception. The other trainers were hard taskmasters. One of them made it clear in his inaugural speech: 'We will teach you tactics, but unless there are bullets flying over your head, you will never learn how to fight.' In four years, the training would prove to be invaluable.

Mitra, who had lived all his life in the warm tropical climate of Calcutta, was not used to the cold weather of Tekanpur. The physical training at 6 a.m., kept his body warm against the bone-chilling cold. This was followed by more physical activities and weapons training. Unlike police officers, BSF officers are trained and issued the same weapons that constables handle—rifles, assault rifles, machine guns, grenade launchers and so forth. Back then, the new recruits were first trained on obsolete rifles, and only then were they given 303 bolt-action rifles or Sten guns.

The trainees included sports stars from across the country. Mitra was a boxing champion (Rustamji used to call him Boxer), and he was in august company—a basketball player from Andhra Pradesh and ranked hockey players from Punjab.

Just before the mid-term break in summer, Mitra mustered up enough courage and told the barber to go easy on his hair.

'*Aankh band karke baith jao* [Close your eyes and sit down],' the barber responded.

Mitra could not recognize himself in the mirror afterwards—he looked like everyone else, and all of them had become fit, their features made gaunt by the intense physical training.

The training ended in October with an investiture ceremony and a short end-of-term break. The break would coincide with the Durga Puja, so Mitra planned a trip back home to Calcutta. President Zakir Husain came for the investiture ceremony, the event that formalized the civilian Mitra into Asstt Comdt Mitra. But Mitra couldn't hang around to savour the moment with his batchmates at the special dinner organized for them. He had to board a train to Calcutta, and requested Brig. Pande for permission to depart early and head to the train station.

Brig. Pande came to see him off. 'Have fun. How much money do you have?'

'Sir, I have already spent all my pay for this month. But I won't say no to a loan.'

'Does a father give loans to his son?'

Brig. Pande took out his wallet and emptied all the cash into Asstt Comdt Mitra's hands. This deeply touched the young officer, and tears welled up in his eyes. Brig. Pande placed his hand on Asstt Comdt Mitra's head and blessed him.

* * *

During the liberation war, Asstt Comdt Mitra was posted at Sitalkuchi and Gitaldah in West Bengal's Cooch Behar region. He was in charge of a company of the BSF's 78 Bn that guarded the India–East Pakistan border there. The border was unfenced, and it was easier to track developments in East Pakistan.

Bengal has three frontiers now; in 1971, there were a few battalions in charge of the entire border that runs through West Bengal. And most of its strength comprised police personnel absorbed from the border guards of state police forces.

At Sitalkuchi, Asstt Comdt Mitra's office-cum-residence was a mud hut that had a cemented floor covered by bamboo mats and a roof made of thin corrugated iron sheets. It was common to all company commanders. The hut was about 100 yards from the company HQ, located on the premises of an abandoned jute godown in the middle of the Sitalkuchi market.

In Cooch Behar, clandestine operations conducted jointly by the BSF and the Mukti Bahini picked up pace in the summer of 1971. Just before one such mission, Asstt Comdt Mitra was briefing the Mukti Bahini guerrillas about the plans when suddenly the Pakistan Army began to fire from their mortars. A section of BSF men was patrolling close to the border, a few yards from where Asstt Comdt Mitra was. The shells hit the patrol and injured two constables. Asstt Comdt Mitra and others rushed to evacuate the patrol. The mortars at the Phulbari BOP started replying, which made the Pakistanis stop their shelling.

Splinters from the shells hit constables Wangchu and Pandey, killing the former almost immediately. Constable Pandey had fallen; he was bleeding profusely but was still alive. Asstt Comdt Mitra immediately rushed to where the patrol was and picked up Constable Pandey. The constable's body was limp, and his eyes had glazed over. He gasped a few words to his company commander, 'Sir, *unko chhodna nahin* [don't spare them].'

He was shifted to a hospital where he was declared 'brought dead'.

This infused a spirit of determination in the joint BSF–Mukti Bahini forces, and their operations forced the Pakistanis to withdraw from the Phulbari axis.

The clandestine operations began in April, when Col Rampal Singh was posted there as the DIG of the sector. The Mukti Bahini frequently used Sitalkuchi and other Indian BOPs there as launch pads. BSF constables and subordinate officers would accompany them for some of the operations.

The Mukti Bahini would conduct low-risk operations. After the guerrillas got used to working in hostile territory, Asstt Comdt Mitra decided to conduct joint missions with them. One of those was to decommission the railway line across the border to choke supplies of arms and rations to the Pakistan Army. He picked the railway line that ran right from the border to Lalmonirhat in East Pakistan.

There was no major railway bridge, so Asstt Comdt Mitra devised a plan with the Mukti Bahini to blow up key sections of the railway tracks and some of the culverts. That created gaps in the railway line. It would be difficult for the Pakistani forces to build them back, for fear of guerrilla attacks by the Mukti Bahini.

This restricted Pakistani forces to their camps and impeded supplies to them, and created pockets of 'liberated zones' in that part of East Pakistan. The Mukti Bahini could use that area to move freely, and it also cleared the passage for civilians fleeing East Pakistan.

* * *

While the Indian Army took operational command of the BSF in May 1971, they did not interfere much with 103 Bn at Sitalkuchi. Asstt Comdt Mitra had a free hand with his company and was also taking larger decisions for the entire battalion.

Today, each of the BSF sector HQs has an operations commander, a commandant with experience in BSF operations. Back then, Asstt Comdt Mitra had charge of the operations, though not an official designation. In their sector, they did not supply a lot of weapons to the Mukti Bahini in the early months of the liberation war, but there was no dearth of explosives.

Most of the operations focused on weeding out the Razakars. This was especially important, as the regular Pakistan Army soldiers had been restricted to their camps. The Razakars were troublemakers and also informers. The Mukti Bahini identified them and would ambush them. But the freedom fighters were not yet skilled enough to take on the Pakistani forces.

In July, the Indian Army began to speed up training of the guerrilla fighters. One day, the Indian Army commander Brig. Joshi turned up with a few officers. All were in civvies, mostly in shorts and a few in lungis. The bordermen made frequent forays into East Pakistan with the Mukti Bahini platoons, and the Indian Army soldiers were keen to get their share of the thrill. Asstt Comdt Mitra personally escorted them, having made the trip several times before. They set out from the camp and hiked towards the border.

The international boundary between India and East Pakistan at that place was a riverine border, which, according to the Thalweg Doctrine, is where the waterway separating two countries is at its greatest depth. A narrow bridge crafted from bamboo stems was the only way to get across. They climbed on to it in single file. The moment Brigadier Joshi got to the middle of the bridge, there was a familiar whistle, followed by a boom and splash of water. The Pakistanis had been watching the Indian personnel from their observation post. They had figured out that Indian officers were present and fired from one of their artillery guns. The 25-pounder shell landed several feet away from the senior officer.

The Pakistanis had set up their spotter at the observation post closest to the bridge. The observation officer, or spotter, had apparently issued corrections to the artillery gun's firing angle. Another loud explosion and splash—this time a few feet closer in the direction of the brigadier.

'Look at that, guys. What a beautiful correction!' said Brig. Joshi.

'Sir, you can admire it later. All of us will be killed. Let's head back and punish them from there,' Asstt Comdt Mitra shot back.

Brig. Joshi made a U-turn to head back to the BOP, but Asstt Comdt Mitra stopped him midway and said they should take a different route. The Pakistanis, Asstt Comdt Mitra said, would find it easier to correct the trajectory if they used the same route. They would all be sitting ducks.

Asstt Comdt Mitra issued an order to the BOP to start firing their mortars at the Pakistani camp, and that made the latter cease their shelling.

After Monsoon

Decommissioning the railway line choked supplies to the Pakistani forces across from Asstt Comdt Mitra's command area. Major Rao, an army officer of 100 Mountain Brigade, arrived with a battery of artillery guns to give things a final push. It was close to Diwali, and the major had come with his own fireworks. A few rounds were enough to send the Pakistani forces packing to Lalmonirhat, which was also the divisional HQ of Pakistan Railways.

With the area cleared, the 78 Bn HQ instructed Asstt Comdt Mitra to head to Gitaldaha from the Phulwari BOP. Things were heating up in Gitaldaha, and, since Asstt Comdt Mitra's leadership in Sitalkuchi had delivered effective results, the battalion commander wanted the company commander to now assume charge at Gitaldaha.

In November, the intensity of shelling between the BSF and the Pakistan Army increased at Gitaldaha. The defence in the BOP was limited. Asstt Comdt Mitra moved the defences to the embankment along the Dharla River, on either side of which were the border posts of India and Pakistan. The railway service between Gitaldaha, Mogolhat and Lalmonirhat had remained suspended for many years, but the railway tracks were still there.

The elevated mound for the railway tracks would give a defensive advantage. Asstt Comdt Mitra was mindful of Rustamji's advice to improvise and decided to make twenty foxholes on either side of the railway-track mound that could be used as bunkers. The BSF personnel dug foxholes into the earth so that there was a natural screen in front, reinforced with sandbags. The 'defence store' at the BSF camp had limited provisions. So, they stripped bamboo stems from the groves and used them, along with wooden planks borrowed from the villagers, to create overhead shelters for the bunkers. The bamboo-and-wood frames were covered with corrugated tin sheets. The army sent a few spare sheets, but these were few in number, so the bordermen added a layer of earth over the bamboo-wood framework.

Asstt Comdt Mitra kept the Pakistan Army soldiers busy, too. He devised innovative ways to make every mortar shell count. He kept the mortar section ready at twilight, when the Pakistan Army soldiers at the Mogolhat BOP would head to the riverbank for their morning ablutions. The BSF men would wait till they saw that the man was about to squat, and, at that very crucial moment, the sickening whistle and explosion would send the Pakistan Army soldier sprinting away with his pants around his ankles, much to the amusement of the BSF troops. The Pakistanis had to keep shifting the place where they could go to answer nature's call.

Comical as the scene may sound, this tactic also had a point. It brought down the morale, and these pesky attacks 'broke logical thinking', as Asstt Comdt Mitra explained to his commandant later.

The BOPs in Mogolhat (East Pakistan) and Gitaldaha (India) were diagonally opposite to each other, separated by the Dharla River. The railway tracks from Gitaldaha to Mogolhat in East Pakistan, along which they had constructed the foxhole bunkers, ran over a railway bridge over the Dharla. This rail bridge was in Indian territory. Asstt Comdt Mitra placed two MMG nests at the base of the pillars of the bridge to prevent any clandestine attacks by the Pakistani soldiers. But it was no easy task to maintain those machine gun nests over there. The MMG sections had to be alert at all times, and each day it was a challenge to send the meals and rations for the machine gun operators on a boat. The time for sending supplies or shift changes had to be shuffled at random, so that the Pakistan Army soldiers wouldn't identify a pattern and shoot during supply runs and shift changes.

By November, everyone in the border camp was used to living amid the sounds of shelling. The only time the shelling ceased was when it was substituted by bursts from machine guns, which meant the Pakistanis had spotted some of the bordermen.

One day, Asstt Comdt Mitra was at the mud hut that served as his living quarters for lunch. He was just about to dig into the afternoon ration when a machine gun broke the silence with its staccato beat. Asstt Comdt Mitra, without flinching, reached for his plate for the next fistful of rice and dal. A machine-gun bullet plonked on to his plate. He was quite hungry. He put the bullet aside, finished his lunch, and then picked up the bullet and kept it with him. It was going to be his personal souvenir from the war.

22

G-Men

Ashwini Kumar's contribution in stopping Operation Chengiz Khan was one of several successful intelligence operations carried out by the BSF. Clandestine ops require a great deal of planning, which is not possible without precise intelligence. The BSF's advantage was that most of the intelligence officers operating in the headquarters and with the field units were also experienced in field operations.

B.N. Chaturvedi, of 74 Bn in Malda, West Bengal, whom we briefly met in the prologue to this book, was promoted from assistant commandant to deputy commandant during the course of 1971. He was shifted to the Bengal Frontier headquarters. He was a great asset to the headquarters because he had studied in Calcutta and spoke Bengali fluently. He had combat experience from his stint with the Indian Army in the 1965 war and had also commanded a few clandestine operations at the start of the liberation movement.

At that time, he was Asstt Comdt B.N. Chaturvedi and in charge of a company of 74 Bn. A thousand East Pakistani asylum seekers had come to the India–East Pakistan border on the intervening night of 25 and 26 March 1971, fleeing Operation Searchlight. He remembered what they had said at the checkpost: 'Either give us refuge in India or else shoot us.'

The next day, they came to Asstt Comdt Chaturvedi again, but this time with their valuables: Pakistani currency, US dollars, gold bars and gold ornaments in kilos, 303 rifles, pistols, foreign-made firearms and so forth. They wanted him to use those to fight for their country. The company commander sent the valuables to the district administration for safekeeping, but it was proof how desperate they were for liberation.

On 27 March, Rustamji and General Sam Manekshaw went down to Malda. It was one of the first visits to the border that Rustamji made after the launch of the genocide. It had a World War II-era airstrip, which Asstt Comdt Chaturvedi hastily got prepared to receive the two security chiefs with some of their staff officers.

Asstt Comdt Chaturvedi returned with his VIP guests to the BSF camp at Mahadipur, which was right at the Indo–East Pakistan border. The East Pakistani BOP across the border was in Sonamasjid. This is a place steeped in history. The rulers of Gour Banga (literally, Golden Bengal) had built a fort here, south of Dinajpur, centuries ago. The Radcliffe Line had divided the remains of their ancient fort. A road called the Gour Road connects the two countries. At that time, a part of the dilapidated fort wall was in between the two BOPs.

Gour Road runs to Rajshahi city via Nawabgunj. And Rajshahi had seen its share of violent reactions to the civil disobedience movement since 7 March.

Gen. Manekshaw came straight to the point after a cup of tea. 'Can you undertake operations across the border against East Pakistan?' he asked.[51]

Rustamji answered for Chaturvedi: 'General Sa'ab, *sawal mat puchiye. Aap bataiye kya karna hai* [Please don't ask if they can do it. Just tell them what they have to do]. My boys will do it.'

Asstt Comdt Chaturvedi took it as a sign of how much his director general trusted his personnel. He had been posted to Malda after a stint in neighbouring Murshidabad district in West Bengal and was familiar with both places. He outlined two immediate objectives in the Pakistani territory across the border from Murshidabad. The first was to target the cantonment in Rajshahi. The second was to blow up a bridge to sever connection between the cantonment in Rajshahi with a larger one in Jessore, thus limiting reinforcements and replenishment of supplies to the former.

Rustamji and Gen. Manekshaw approved the idea, and Golak Majumdar sanctioned the extra personnel that Asstt Comdt Chaturvedi required.

Asstt Comdt Chaturvedi wanted to attack the Rajshahi cantonment on the first two nights to ensure that the Pakistan Army soldiers didn't step out on the third night, when he planned to demolish the bridge. He drew a company from 71 Bn and took them to the Kaharpara BOP in Murshidabad district on 29 March. For the same operation, 74 Bn also sent a company of BSF personnel there, including a medium-machine-gun section and a mortar section. Across the river, there were around two companies of regular Pakistan Army soldiers at the Rajshahi cantonment.

The first target was the Ayub (now Rajshahi) Cadet College, where there was a large number of Pakistan Army officers. To get close to it, they would have to first cross the mighty Padma River. The BSF personnel arranged cargo boats, which could carry close to a platoon each with their arms and ammunitions. They were dressed in lungis and vests, and had their necks and faces partially covered with gamchhas. All identity documents were to be left behind at the camp in Kaharpara.

Around 8 p.m. on 30 March 1971, the Mukti Fauj fighters signalled from across the Padma. The BSF personnel of 74 Bn helped the boatmen to carry the boats upstream so that they could use the river's current to row across the Padma. They carried their rifles, Sten guns and hand grenades. Asstt Comdt Chaturvedi sat in one of the boats, with two primed grenades stuck into the rolled-up waistband of his lungi.

They crossed the river and met at the rendezvous point, where the Mukti Fauj personnel were waiting. They went to the Rajshahi University area and, at around 10 p.m., began firing with mortars and machine guns. The firing continued till just before dawn.

At around 4 a.m., the BSF and Mukti Fauj wrapped up and were back in Indian territory before sunrise.

The next night, that is, on the night between 31 March and 1 April, Asstt Comdt Chaturvedi returned with the company from 71 Bn and repeated the attack of the previous night—a whole night of firing from mortar and machine guns—and returned to Indian territory before sunrise.

For the third night, 1 April 1971, Asstt Comdt Chaturvedi was prepared to take the company and demolish the bridge with the Mukti Fauj personnel. He had got hold of explosives. They would prepare the charges during the day, take them to the road bridge on the Jessore–Rajshahi highway, rig the bridge and blow it up. That was the plan.

On the morning of 1 April, the Bengal Frontier HQ sent a message calling Asstt Comdt Chaturvedi to its office in Calcutta. He rushed as soon as he got the message and reached just around lunchtime to find that the message was to summon Brig. Chatterjee to the frontier headquarters. Chatterjee had become Chaturvedi in the dictation.

The confusion proved to be a stroke of luck. Back at Kaharpara, Asstt Comdt Chaturvedi learnt that the Jessore cantonment had already sent a column as reinforcement to Rajshahi. They would not be able to target the bridge that night. In hindsight, he thought that they should have targeted the bridge and the cantonment at the same time, the night before. The intelligence input proved to be a lifesaver, otherwise there may have been high casualties.

Yet there was some success to the operation. The Pakistan Army personnel in Rajshahi did not venture out of the cantonment for a long time, allowing free movement to the Mukti Fauj at night.

* * *

In August, Asstt Comdt Chaturvedi was promoted and sent to supervise intelligence operations for the frontier headquarters in Calcutta, working closely with Golak Majumdar.

Majumdar was very protective of his officers and defended their efficiency and integrity. Once, a senior officer of the BSF had doubted the credibility of intelligence inputs from Dy Comdt Chaturvedi's office. Majumdar wouldn't hear of it. He was quick to defend Dy Comdt Chaturvedi's work.

When the generals of the Indian Army were preparing for the war, some of them greatly relied on inputs from the BSF, which knew the lay of the land because of the clandestine operations it had conducted throughout the year.

The Eastern Command was working out the routes to Dacca. Lt Gen. Niazi anticipated that the main thrust would be through Jessore Road past the Petrapole–Benapole border gate to Jessore city. The Pakistan Army had rigged many of the border areas and the land around their camps in all of East Pakistan with anti-personnel and anti-tank mines.

Dy Comdt Chaturvedi found out that they had prepared a deadlier defence along Jessore Road. The British had lined this historic road with trees, some of which were 100 years old at the time of the liberation war. The Pakistan Army had rigged the trees lining Jessore Road with explosives. The charges were secured to the trees with long fuse wires. The plan was that when Indian forces' personnel and armoured vehicles went down Jessore Road, these would be blown up. Dy Comdt Chaturvedi was able to get hold of this information and passed it up the chain.

Calcutta itself was a hotbed for the intelligence community. Dy Comdt Chaturvedi sometimes worked out of the 8 Theatre Road safe house. Foreign agents mounted surveillance on 8 Theatre Road to keep track of the Mujibnagar government. There were a few diplomatic consular and cultural offices close by and a private hotel bang opposite.

The BSF had been the first point of contact for the Bengali political leaders from East Pakistan, and the latter soon grew comfortable dealing with them, as both the government-in-exile and the Mukti Bahini worked with the BSF. Besides, most of the leaders were put up at BSF safe houses. Some BSF intelligence officers were deputed to address their needs.

Injured in the 'Battle of Bantara', Sub-Inspector Sukdev Choudhuri of 77 Bn spent about two weeks in the hospital. Following his discharge from hospital, Choudhuri was posted to the G-branch of the BSF and assigned to work at the 8 Theatre Road office of the Mujibnagar government.

DIG, communications, B.N. Bhattacharjee was assigned to coordinate with the PM-in-exile and his cabinet, and Sub-Inspector Choudhuri assisted him. It meant coordinating every task possible, from when he got out of the hospital in Balurghat to accompanying them to Dacca in a convoy of SUVs up Jessore Road for the official ceremony, in which Lt Gen. Niazi signed the instrument surrendering East Pakistan and his nearly 1,00,000 troops to Lt Gen. J.S. Aurora.

Maulana Bhashani was in his nineties during the liberation war and did not always keep well. He often required the use of a wheelchair and had to be physically aided. He had frequent coughing fits and would be quite impatient with Sub-Inspector Choudhuri and other BSF personnel.

Bhashani once asked Sub-Inspector Choudhuri to get him a radio set and three prayer caps. The BSF officer went to an HMV store for the radio set. That was the easy part. But he didn't know much about prayer caps and asked a friend for help. The friend sent him to Chitpur in central Calcutta, from where Sub-Inspector Choudhuri got three of the best caps from three different shops, to play it safe.

Bhashani accepted the radio but threw the caps aside. He called them rubbish and threatened to report Sub-Inspector Choudhuri to the highest office in the country.

'I'm going to tell madam that you guys are treating me poorly,' he said, employing a threat that he liberally used.

Sub-Inspector Choudhuri took the threat in his stride—the East Pakistani political leaders were under considerable stress themselves.

Golak Majumdar himself was a great asset as the BSF's IG, Bengal. As an IPS officer of the Bengal cadre, he had served at a number of positions in the state's police establishments. He had sources across the state and had his own steady stream of information through those sources, which greatly benefitted the BSF and the liberation war.

23

Home-Made Rockets

Any story of the BSF in its formative years is incomplete without mentioning its emphasis on innovation. The previous chapters give an idea of how BSF officers could improvise on the field with whatever resources were at their disposal. And K.F. Rustamji encouraged them to do so. He himself was a great believer in making the best use of what was available around him.

In 1965, the union finance ministry approved the first budget of the BSF, except one important item. Rustamji had asked for foreign exchange to procure radios and weapons from abroad. This was denied.

But this did not stop Rustamji, who decided to build both at home. He recruited IPS officer C.P. Joshi into his core team as the inspector general of communications. IG Joshi started a technical wing of the BSF at the academy in Tekanpur. The first project was to build radios, and it was a success, greatly aided by Vikram Sarabhai, the pioneer of Indian space technology.

The bigger challenge was making bombs and rockets. The only artillery that the BSF had were Indian Army hand-me-downs of World War II vintage. There was a two-inch (51 mm calibre) and a three-inch (81 mm calibre) mortar bomb.

A brief explanation of a mortar and its operation is in order here to understand why Rustamji wanted better firepower.

A mortar is a bomb launcher or a modern cannon. Except cannons, like artillery guns, can fire straight at targets. The mortar fires at an angle between 45 and 85 degrees, which gives the shell a parabolic trajectory and a sharp fall to the target. The mortar is a cylindrical metal pipe, with its base end blocked and a trigger pin sticking out of the base into the inside of the pipe. The pipe is fixed on to a base plate, which is placed on the ground. Soldiers dig a shallow hole in the ground so that the base plate is firmly in place. The lower end of the mortar is balanced using a bipod that can be adjusted to correct the aim.

One soldier operates the mortar and corrects the aim, while another drops the bombs into the mortar. The shell or bomb falls to the base, and a firing pin triggers the detonator at the base of the mortar. This sets off explosive charges on the waist of the bomb that propel it out of the mortar and towards the target. It lands nose first and sets off an impact fuse that is connected to a detonator, which runs through the bomb like its spine. The detonator triggers the high explosives packed into the torso of the shell.

The biggest advantage of the mortar is that it can shoot past an elevated fortification, such as a mound of land, a clump of trees or a high wall around a camp.

The two-inch mortar was obsolete in 1971 because of a number of issues. The barrel was short, and instead of a base pin, they were fired using a trigger. There was no bipod, so the mortar had to be held by a trained soldier. The shell itself was small and had low impact.

The three-inch mortar bomb was more effective, but the one the BSF used in 1971 was obsolete. It dated to World War II. Although it was heavier and had greater impact than the two-inch mortar bombs, there had been several upgrades to these shells by 1971. The BSF was fighting against a regular army, armed with the upgraded three-inch mortars, which were also available with the Indian Army but not with the BSF.

Rustamji wanted to upgrade to the new one and also have access to his own stocks. So the technical wing of the BSF began to develop and produce the three-inch mortars and bombs that it required. But the BSF had no access to heavy-artillery guns or rockets. Rockets have greater range and explosive power, and can be used to destroy tanks. IG Joshi was asked to build a rocketry division, and Dy Comdt G.P. Bhatnagar was recruited from 16 Bn to lead the division. Before joining the BSF, Dy Comdt Bhatnagar had served as an emergency commissioned officer of the Indian Army, where he had been an artillery officer.

In 1969, Rustamji sent Dy Comdt Bhatnagar to Trivandrum to meet with Vikram Sarabhai and begin the project. Sarabhai, who was leading India's space tech development, agreed to help.

The BSF men in the technical team were not scientists. They went to different institutes to study rocket science. They trained at the Pilani and Mesra (Ranchi) campuses of Birla Institute of Technology and Science. By 1970, they had gained some knowhow but had to regularly travel to the space research centre (now called the Vikram Sarabhai Space Research Centre) at Trivandrum, where the rocket was to be built, and also set up a liaison office there.

Rustamji has written[52] that both A.P.J. Abdul Kalam and Vikram Sarabhai greatly contributed to the development of the BSF's first rocket, which had a long aluminium body, filled with solid propellant.

They first began by developing small-range rockets that could fire up to 200, 300 and 400 yards to test whether they could design the rockets. The practice fire was on the parade ground at the BSF Academy Tekanpur, so that if the rockets overshot the range they would fall in the lake.

On the day of the first test fire, Rustamji turned up with R.N. Kao as a surprise guest for the event. With great ceremony, the guests were led to the firing area. There, the technical wing had set up two stationary launchers next to each other, loaded with rockets. The tests were meant to demonstrate the flight, and not explosive, capability of the rockets.

One of the officers began to count down from ten for the first launcher. The technical wing waited with bated breath as the countdown progressed, eager to see their experiment succeed. However, to their dismay, the rocket did not fly but exploded in the launcher. Since it was stationed next to the second launcher, the explosion of the first blew up the other rocket in the second launcher.

It was a very embarrassing moment. The DG was present and had brought his friend, who was the director of an important institution. Dy Comdt Bhatnagar was nonplussed and, after packing up, skipped the after-party and headed home.

Rustamji realized that Dy Comdt Bhatnagar was missing from the party. Sensing that Bhatnagar was embarrassed about the fiasco, Rustamji sent another officer to fetch him to the party. As soon as he arrived, Dy Comdt Bhatnagar headed straight for the bar to down a few pegs of rum. He was downing his third when he sensed two tall figures looming behind him. As he turned to see who it was, Kao and Rustamji took their seats on the bar stools on either side of him.

'What're you up to?' Rustamji asked.

'Sorry, sir. I could not demonstrate the firing of the rockets to you,' Dy Comdt Bhatnagar replied.

'How much money did Khusro give you?' Kao asked. He was on first-name terms with Rustamji.

Dy Comdt Bhatnagar shrunk in his seat with embarrassment. 'Sir, quite a few lakhs.'

'Do you know how much was spent on the Apollo mission?' Kao asked, referring to the US space programme.

'Must be in millions.'

'You have spent a fraction of that on the rockets. If the Apollo mission can fail, your rockets can too. At least you made the test fire in the presence of a VIP. That is a big achievement in itself. Keep at it and you will succeed.'

Dy Comdt Bhatnagar went back to the drawing board, and soon enough, the rockets were firing absolutely fine. From 200 and 400 yards, the range of the rockets was increased to hit targets 20 kilometres away. The formal test fire was done in Pokhran, Rajasthan, and travelled a distance of 90 kilometres.

These rockets were used in the 1971 war at the western front, and Dy Comdt Bhatnagar himself led a group at the Battle of Dera Baba Nanak.

24

Nothing's Quiet on the Western Frontier

The Indian Army began to ramp up its war plans in September and war-gamed its strategy the following month. There were build-ups by the armies of both India and Pakistan in the month of October. In some places at India's eastern frontier, the BSF and the Mukti Bahini increased the depth and potency of their raids. In November, the Indian Army also engaged in a few skirmishes.

By the third week of November, a few battles had been fought, such as in Belonia, Tripura, and in Hilli, West Bengal. Gen. Yahya Khan declared a state of emergency in Pakistan on 23 November 1971, giving a signal that war was around the corner.

The Pakistani forces launched the war on 3 December 1971 with Operation Chengiz Khan, the aerial attack by the Pakistan Air Force that was stymied thanks to the intelligence gathered by Ashwini Kumar and the quick action of the Indian armed forces.

Next, the Pakistan Army launched attacks on some of the border posts of the BSF in India's western frontier. On the western border of India, the Indian Army had operational control of the BSF, and the force had not conducted any operations of the kind that it had carried out in East Pakistan. Both countries had moved their respective armies close to the border at India's west in anticipation of the coming war.

The BSF's 31 Bn was posted at Mamdot in Ferozepur, Punjab. Asstt Comdt Ram Krishna Wadhwa led a company that was guarding two BOPs, including the Raja Mohtam BOP. When the 9 Baloch regiment of the Pakistan Army attacked the Raja Mohtam BOP on the evening of 3 December, the Indian Army directed Asstt Comdt Wadhwa to make a tactical withdrawal of the BSF personnel from the Raja Mohtam BOP.

The Pakistan Army occupied the Indian border post by 5 December and began to prepare defences to the east of the BOP. On 6 December, the Indian Army rethought its strategy, and the brigade commander directed Asstt Comdt Wadhwa to recapture the Raja Mohtam BOP before sunrise the next day.

Asstt Comdt Wadhwa took two platoons of BSF personnel from his company along with his second-in-charge, Inspector Bhagwat Singh, for the attack. He had had very little time to prepare for the attack. They left Mamdot in jeeps and trucks, with lights dimmed to avoid detection. They got off the trucks 5 km away from the BOP and hiked the rest of the way.

Asstt Comdt Wadhwa picked an ingenious way to storm the BOP. He picked the war cry of an Indian Army regiment to make it appear that a large unit of regular Indian Army soldiers were attacking the BOP. They got to the camp around 1 a.m. to see that the soldiers of the 9 Baloch regiment were digging a trench on the eastern side of the BOP. The Pakistan Army soldiers had laid barbed wire on the eastern approach to the camp and rigged the area with landmines.

Asstt Comdt Wadhwa was himself in the front, and all of them charged with the thunderous war cry of the Sikh regiment of the Indian Army: *'Jo bole so nihal, Sat Sri Akal!'*

This caused some confusion among the Pakistan Army soldiers. In the bedlam, the BSF platoons moved forward. The Pakistani soldiers began to fire at them from all directions; they had placed machine-gun nests on all sides.

Asstt Comdt Wadhwa, who was right in front, braved the rain of bullets, jumped into the trench, fired a few rounds and started fighting with his bare hands. The bravado of their officer galvanized the BSF platoons to rush after him. They fought with the Pakistan Army soldiers of 9 Baloch for close to three hours and recaptured their post by 4 a.m. on 7 December.

Three days later, 9 Baloch came back in full-battalion strength and hammered the Raja Mohtam BOP with machines guns, artillery and mortars. Asstt Comdt Wadhwa and Inspector Bhagwat Singh kept up the morale of their troops amid heavy fire by moving between the bunkers and trenches. On the morning of 11 December, as he was moving between bunkers, splinters from a shell pierced Asstt Comdt Wadhwa's throat and killed him. Inspector Bhagwat Singh also fell in a similar manner sometime later, as did seven others of their company.

Asstt Comdt Wadhwa was posthumously awarded the Maha Vir Chakra for his bravery in recapturing the Raja Mohtam border post. The eight others who were killed in action were also posthumously awarded for their gallantry. To this day, the BSF commemorates and pays homage to the brave soldiers every year on 11 December at the BOP (which remains in Indian territory) as Raja Mohtam Day.

* * *

The Sutlej River meanders along the India–Pakistan border for several kilometres in Punjab, between Gajjal and the border near Ferozepur. The river winds around the international boundary for around 40–45 km. During the 1971 war, the Pakistani forces captured Indian border posts that were west of the Sutlej. Similarly, the Indian forces captured the Pakistani border posts east of the Sutlej. The BSF held on to some of its BOPs despite the fact that these were across the river. They were cut off from their battalion headquarters and supplies, and survived by foraging for food close to the BOPs.

In *India's Wars Since Independence*,[53] Maj. Gen. Sukhwant Singh wrote that during the 1965 war, the Pakistan Army concentrated their forces north of the Sutlej. The Indian Army focused on fortifying Fazilka. They felt that the Pakistanis may attack Fazilka to defend the Sulaimanke Headworks on their side of the border. The Pakistani 1 Armoured Division was in Okara, opposite Fazilka, supported by two infantry divisions. The Indian Army positioned 67 Infantry Brigade, commanded by Brig. Surjit Singh, to defend Fazilka.

According to Maj. Gen. Sukhwant Singh, Brig. Surjit Singh Chowdhary had three infantry battalions, a field regiment, a medium battery of artillery, 'an armoured squadron of obsolete Sherman-75' tanks requisitioned from the infantry school and a squadron of T-54 tanks.

The BSF had three battalions in this sector: 22 Bn was positioned close to Fazilka; 25 Bn at the border near Ferozepur; and 31 Bn was positioned in an area between these two. The Pakistan Army was also fortified by the border-guarding Pakistani Rangers in sufficient numbers.

The Sherman tanks were deployed at Muazzam, where 22 Bn manned a BOP. The T-54 tanks were behind the position, closer to Fazilka town. The entire structure of the Indian formations was defensive, meant to hold positions. But in the eastern frontier, India was moving on an offensive.

On 3 December, the Pakistan Army began to shell the BSF posts after sunset and moved some infantry units towards India. By night, some of the defensive positions close to Fazilka had fallen. Many of the BSF posts also fell, and to strengthen the defence of Fazilka, the army commanders pulled the companies away from the border.

By the morning of 4 December, the BSF had lost most of its BOPs except four, including the one in Muazzam that was under the command area of Brig. Chowdhary. The Pakistanis had taken Indian territory, and three counterattacks had not been able to dislodge them as Brig. Chowdhary pulled back defences toward Fazilka.

Sub-Inspector (SI) Laxmi Narain Saini was the platoon commander in charge of the Muazzam BOP. In April, he had been seconded to Brig. Pande's commando unit in Tripura. From the 91 Bn HQ in Agartala, he had been sent to decommission a railway bridge in East Pakistan. But a family emergency pulled him away from commando operations. When he returned to duty, SI Saini was back with 22 Bn and posted at the Muazzam BOP, which was also the headquarters for the company that guarded the Muazzam and Maharsana BOPs.

SI Saini had a free hand in running both these border posts. His company commander was from a state police force and his family was in Fazilka, and due to some pressing family matters the company commander spent little time at the border posts. Brig. Surjit Singh Chowdhary did not consider that part of the border to be a great threat and gave the BSF company greater responsibility in managing its defences.

In October, SI Saini organized the defences of Muazzam. He renovated and reinforced the bunkers. The men in his platoon there dug a seven-foot-deep and three-foot-wide trench to connect each bunker to the constables' barracks and the kitchen, running up to Muazzam village. This was to protect against snipers and machine-gun fire while walking between bunkers, or between bunkers and barracks. Since the terrain was flat, the company also built an underground dumping store for the weapons and ammo.

During the last week of November, the Indian Army mixed army soldiers, in BSF uniforms, with the BSF constables at all BOPs there, except Muazzam. A platoon of BSF constables was added to the Muazzam BOP, and an artillery unit was stationed there. The Pakistan Army did the same at their BOP across the border. It mixed regular soldiers of its Frontier Force Regiment, with the Pakistani Rangers guarding the Gazi BOP.

SI Saini began to randomly change the timings of meals, removing any patterns that would give the Pakistani troops an opportunity to attack BSF personnel. In the north-west of Muazzam, Saini also had charge of the BOP at Bhaini Dilawar that could only be accessed by boats since it was across a distributary of the Sutlej. The platoon at Bhaini Dilawar was stationed only during the day and stayed at Muazzam at night. Before leaving at the end of their watch, the BSF personnel left helmets on sticks to fool the enemy into thinking that they were still around. SI Saini also used the helmet-on-a-stick decoy at other BOPs where BSF personnel remained through the day and night. This helped the BSF constables to remain concealed from surprise enemy fire.

The first assault in SI Saini's jurisdiction began at 6.30 p.m. on 3 December with a rocket fired from a launcher from the Gazi BOP of Pakistan, followed by several rounds of artillery fire. The Muazzam BOP returned fire, and the exchange continued till late at night.

SI Saini used the trench to get to each bunker through the night to ensure that the constables were fine. At night, he shifted the platoons at the Maharsana BOP to Muazzam, since the latter was better equipped to handle the onslaught. Apart from the reinforced defences, a canal facing the border, called Landa Bund, provided a natural advantage. The Pakistanis sent a platoon or two to attack Muazzam, but they retreated quickly. A small commando team of the Pakistan Army also tried to get close to lob grenades into the BOP and storm it, but the constables fended off the assaults. The exchange of fire between Muazzam and Gazi stopped at 5 a.m. the next day.

The other BOPs had not been as lucky. As many as nineteen BOPs in the sector fell to Pakistani forces on the first night of the war, with the BSF pulling back from all of them. There were two major attacks—one on the Pakka and Jhangar BOPs, and the other further south, between Asafwala and Shatirwala. The Pakistan Army used tanks and infantry units to overrun the BOPs and pushed back the Indian Army regular units to occupy their positions well into Indian territories.

Brig. Chowdhary attempted counterattacks, but these failed. He also issued orders to withdraw his troops from several key positions and destroy bridges and roads during their retreat to defend Fazilka. Much later, the Indian Army would learn that the Pakistanis did not want to claim Fazilka but wanted to increase their territory around Suleimanke Headworks, to expand its defensive perimeter. In this debacle, many Indian soldiers were killed and several taken prisoners of war along with civilians.

As the Pakistanis strengthened their breach and fortified their strongholds, it became difficult for SI Saini to continue to hold the Muazzam BOP with the manpower and firepower that he had. The Pakistanis began to focus their firepower on this one BOP that continued to hold out against the assault. He managed for two days and then sent a request for augmenting the BOP with regular army infantry, tanks and artillery units.

Instead, Brig. Chowdhary directed them to withdraw from the border, and they headed to their battalion headquarters on 6 December. Early next morning, the Pakistanis claimed the deserted BOP and set fire to it. Reacting late, the Indian Army asked 22 Bn to send a platoon to guard the village. Saini led a platoon of BSF constables accompanied by two Sherman tanks.

Brig. Chowdhary's failed strategy made the Indian Army divisional commander, Maj. Gen. Ram Singh, take over command of the Fazilka sector himself. He worked close to the war zone and was wounded by Pakistani shelling while supervising the battle from the trenches.

At Muazzam, half of Saini's BSF platoon was occupied in protecting the crew of the Sherman tanks. The tanks were old and of questionable reliability, and the Pakistan Army had destroyed some Sherman tanks in the same sector.

Gen. Manekshaw was disappointed by the performance at Fazilka. He replaced Brig. Chowdhary with Brig. Piara Singh, a veteran who had been parked as a director of the NCC. On 9 December, Maj. Gen. Ram Singh and Brig. Piara Singh called for a conference of the operational commanders. Saini was sent to represent 22 Bn.

Maj. Gen. Ram Singh wanted to retaliate by recapturing the Muazzam BOP and capturing the Pak Rangers' Gazi BOP with the 3/11 Gorkha Rifles (an infantry battalion). SI Saini offered to lead this attack, and Maj. Gen. Ram Singh agreed, since SI Saini had commanded the BOP and knew the area well.

Late on the night of 10 December, SI Saini, leading the BSF, and Maj. Mall, leading a company of the 3/11 Gorkha Rifles, headed for Muazzam. Saini was wearing a khaki overcoat over his khaki uniform to protect himself from the harsh north Indian winter. This was risky, because the Gorkhas may have mistaken him for a Pakistani soldier. He tied his belt to Maj. Mall's with a rope, so that they were close together. The front of the attack was led by a section helmed by a lieutenant of the Indian Army.

SI Saini came up from the northern side of the bund, crossed the Sutlej distributary into Pakistan and took the company 500 yards behind Gazi post. To cover any escape attempts, SI Saini posted a platoon there. SI Saini and Maj. Mall began to stealthily head towards the Gazi post with the rest of the company when they spotted a lone, unarmed Pakistani soldier and overpowered him.

They made out from his uniform that the Pakistani soldier was a lance naik (a non-commissioned officer rank) with the Pakistani Rangers. He said that he had been carrying bed tea to wake up the relieving officers at the post. It meant that they had picked the right time to attack—during the change in shifts. The soldiers gagged the Pakistani lance naik and made him lead them to the bunker where the officers were sleeping. Four Gorkha Regiment soldiers held down the officers while others pummeled them with bare fists. These three—two officers and the lance naik—were marched back and handed to the platoon posted at the possible escape route of the Pakistanis.

Maj. Mall signalled to the artillery unit to shell the Gazi post till they were 50 yards away from the post. The Indian soldiers then lobbed grenades into the bunkers to disable the soldiers in them. Shortly after, they rushed in.

SI Saini saw the famed fighting abilities of the Gorkha soldiers first-hand. They fired weapons with one hand and slashed away at the Pakistani soldiers with *khukris* in the other. The operation was over in less than ten minutes, with several Pakistani soldiers killed and wounded. Many fled into the night taking cover of the elephant grass growing outside the border post.

Some of the Indians gathered the fourteen alive and remaining Pakistani soldiers as prisoners of war. A few of them headed to the flagstaff, pulling down the Pakistani flag and hoisting the Indian flag in its place. There were a total of seventeen prisoners of war, including the major and the captain (both of Pak Rangers) they had caught at the beginning. They found a deserted Sherman tank behind the post and commandeered it. There was no need to capture the Muazzam post. When the Indian soldiers had attacked Gazi, the Pakistani soldiers occupying Muazzam fled from the Indian BOP. The tricolour was rehoisted there at dawn, vindicating the defeat in the rest of the sector.

Though 15 Rajput had taken over the Gazi post, around 7.30 a.m. the Pakistan Army sent a few companies there and used their artillery to shell it till 15 Rajput withdrew from Gazi. The Pakistanis took back Gazi but did not cross the border to claim Muazzam yet again.

The post would remain with India till the unilateral ceasefire was announced after the fall of Dacca in the eastern theatre. Tikka Khan had planned a massive attack on the Fazilka sector on

13 December, which was delayed because its size was depleted by a diversion of some of its units to Sind. Gen. Tikka Khan planned to use the depleted infantry division on 15 December, but it, too, got delayed by a day, because it took longer for them to cross the Sutlej. By the time they were ready to launch, Pakistan had accepted India's offer of unilateral ceasefire.

BSF's Post Group Artillery

The BSF's firepower was limited to two- and three-inch mortars. The army officers who had joined the BSF when it was put together, had recommended the creation of a separate post group artillery (PGA) for the border force. However, due to some objections, the project was shelved.

During the 1971 liberation war, the BSF had to rely on the Indian Army for artillery support. Lt Col N.G. O'Connor had requested artillery support from the Indian Army on multiple occasions, such as when he conducted a raid on a Pakistan Army base in Jadurani in East Pakistan, as well as later, when he attacked the Pakistan Army BOP during the Bantara battle. Asstt Comdt P.K. Ghosh had asked for artillery support when disrupting Pakistan Army supplies on the Chittagong–Dacca trunk road in July 1971.

The Indian Army had witnessed the need for artillery support, and it supplied the BSF with 4.2-inch mortars and 3.7-inch howitzers to enhance the BSF's firepower. The BSF appointed Brig. R.P. Mittal as its artillery commander and tasked him with raising twenty PGA units. There were a number of Indian Army gunners who had joined the BSF. Brig. Mittal picked officers and personnel from among them to man the PGA units. There were two units of the BSF artillery deployed in Rajasthan, three each in Kashmir, West Bengal and Tripura, and four BSF artillery units were deployed in Gujarat in November 1971.

Asstt Comdt N.S. Choudhary, a former Indian Army gunner, was posted with his artillery unit in Malda. He had previously led a BSF company there, for its 71 Bn, till July 1971. During the initial phase of the liberation war, he had captured a Pakistan Army-run police station in Rohanpur, near Nawabgunj, in East Pakistan.

Dy Comdt Joginder Singh led the artillery units that were deployed in Gujarat. The BSF battalions posted to Dantiwada in Gujarat had launched attacks across the border and captured villages in Pakistan. On 17 December, they captured Virawah village and were moving further westwards. Dy Comdt Joginder Singh was asked to provide artillery support. He went for a reconnaissance mission on his jeep to assess the targets. When returning to the base in Virawah, Pakistan Army soldiers ambushed them with machine-gun and mortar fire.

A bullet from the machine-gun spray hit Dy Comdt Joginder Singh, but he jumped out of his jeep and attacked them with the few men he had taken for the mission. He fought with his bare hands till he was killed in action.

He was posthumously awarded the Vir Chakra for his gallantry.

* * *

Apart from Punjab, India's western frontier included the states of Jammu and Kashmir, Gujarat and Rajasthan. The Pakistani forces were concentrated at Punjab, and they also made forward attacks on J&K. There, too, the BSF fought alongside the Indian Army, under its operational command. All along the western front, the BSF captured several Pakistani border posts and army camps across the border from Gujarat and Rajasthan, where the IAF provided air support to some of the missions. The BSF held these posts after the war as well, till the posts were handed back following inter-governmental negotiations. Some of those battles and successes are highlighted in the following paragraphs.

Rann of Kutch

The Thar–Karachi sector in Pakistan was under its army's 18 Infantry Division, comprising a regular infantry battalion based in Naukot, eight companies of Indus Rangers and three Mujahid companies. These units were deployed opposite the Rann of Kutch in Gujarat.

When the war broke out in this area, the BSF, on its own, launched a number of set-piece attacks and captured fifteen enemy posts. The BSF's 1 Bn captured Pakistani BOPs at Kalibet, Vingur, Paneli and Jattarai. Its 2 Bn first took over the Pakistani BOP at Jaleli and moved forward to capture Nagarparkar and Virawah. And 3 Bn captured the Vingoor BOP.

After the war, the Indian and Pakistan Army officers calculated the area captured by the Indian forces as 1038 square kilometres. Most of the campaign was carried out by BSF units with support from 10 Para Commando of the Indian Army. They continued holding the area till it was returned following inter-governmental negotiations.

Rajasthan

The BSF captured several Pakistani BOPs by itself in a sector of Rajasthan. In others, they jointly captured posts with the Indian Army. At the end of the war, the BSF held twenty-three Pakistani BOPs, till the Simla Agreement.

Jammu and Kashmir

The Pakistan Army tried to sneak a lot of attacks in Jammu and Kashmir to capture territory. Some of the sectors in J&K were at a very high altitude and under a thick snow cover during the war.

The Indian Army gave the Pakistanis a tough fight, and the BSF's troops there fought shoulder to shoulder with them. There were numerous army honours for those BSF units.

The BSF's 40 Bn was deployed in a position that was 12,000 feet above sea level and covered in snow. Asstt Comdt Nafe Singh Dalal was the commander of the 'Charlie' company. On 11 December, the 6/11 Gorkha Rifles of the Indian Army were tasked with capturing a Pakistan Army post. Asstt Comdt Dalal was asked to patrol the area with a platoon from his BSF company.

The patrol was called in to aid in the capture of the post and was only 50 yards away from it when the Pakistan Army fired at them with machine guns and assault rifles. Asstt Comdt Dalal took hold of an LMG and began to move forward while firing at the MMG nest of the Pakistan Army and silenced it. That gave his platoon cover to withdraw.

But another Pakistan Army MMG section opened fire at him, and he was struck down by a spray of bullets, but his men were able to withdraw to safety. Sub-Inspector R.B. Shahi saw that his company commander had been injured. Despite the heavy fighting, SI Shahi carried Asstt Comdt Dalal's limp body off the battlefield back to their post. But Asstt Comdt Dalal had been killed in action and was posthumously awarded a Vir Chakra.

Chhamb Sector of J&K

The BSF's 57 Bn was posted in the Chhamb sector of Jammu and Kashmir during the 1971 war. The Pakistan Army made several attacks on the posts that it guarded in order to claim the territory. The Pakistan Army infantry unit advanced under the cover of heavy artillery and mortar shelling on the Indian BOPs. They held their ground till orders came to withdraw from the BOPs.

The order to withdraw from the BOPs came at the last minute, and the withdrawal took place during very heavy shelling. Close to 100 BSF personnel were missing in action for a few days, but the number of missing BSF personnel decreased to eighteen later.

At the Moel BOP, Head Constable Darbara Singh, leading a machine-gun section of 57 Bn, decided to remain at the

BOP and defend it along with soldiers of 5 Sikh. But the Pakistan Army made repeated attacks, and the Indian Army's brigade command ordered the remaining troops to withdraw. HC Darbara Singh and thirteen others were found missing in action after the final withdrawal.

Rajouri Sector of J&K

The Pakistan Army made several infiltration attempts into a part of the Rajouri sector in J&K, where four companies of the BSF's 40 Bn were independently manning the border posts. The Pakistan Army's special forces unit, Special Services Group (SSG), was active in that area. But 40 Bn thwarted every attempt of this elite commando unit of the Pakistan Army to take their posts. In one attack, the BSF personnel killed one SSG commando and took two of them prisoner.

25

A Surrender in the East

When war was declared on 3 December 1971, the Razakars near the India–Pakistan border at Cooch Behar surrendered. They washed their hands of the conflict and approached a BOP under Asstt Comdt S.K. Mitra's command. They were not carrying weapons at the time and claimed that they had worked for the Pakistan Army as informers.

In the months before the war, these Razakars had been responsible for the targeted attacks on their fellow East Pakistanis as well as attacks on the BOPs. Now that the heavy fighting had begun, they had decided to ditch their masters.

Asstt Comdt Mitra did not disguise his disgust for the deserters. 'I'm not parting with my camp's rations. If the government issues rations for POWs, you will get food,' he threatened them.

Asstt Comdt Mitra instructed his men to bind the prisoners' wrists and appointed sentries to guard them while he awaited further orders. Next, he addressed his subordinate officers and all his staff, and told them that their first objective in the war was to capture the Pakistani border post at Mogolhat. The men were ready; they wanted to set off after offering a puja to Goddess Kali. The man who officiated as a pandit for the company lived near the Gitaldaha station, and he said that they would have to perform the puja in the open. The puja began at night, as the BSF

BOP lit up with candles and lanterns, and it went on till 1.30 a.m. The lights drew some fire from the Pakistani BOP, but nobody was hurt.

Before dawn the next day, they crossed the Dharla River using boats that they had hired to patrol it. Disembarking from the boats, they headed south, crossed the border into East Pakistan and went close to the Pakistani BOP in Mogolhat. The Pakistani soldiers and bordermen remained restricted to their camps. But Maity, the constable who acted as Asstt Comdt Mitra's sahayak or buddy, had another warning.

'Sir, please walk behind me and only step where I do.'

The place was riddled with anti-personnel landmines, and Maity didn't want the company commander to get blown up. They argued for a bit, but Maity was insistent. Asstt Comdt Mitra followed this request for a brief while to keep the old man happy.

As they reached the riverbank, they saw the Pakistanis fleeing. When they crossed the Dharla River and entered the Pakistan Army camp, it became clear that the Pakistani soldiers had deserted the camp in a rush. They had not expected an infantry-like march by the BSF. They had left behind their personal items at the camps, taking only the weapons and ammunition they could carry.

Earlier, the BSF personnel had recorded from their BOP that the Pakistani camp had a large number of bunkers. Up close, Asstt Comdt Mitra saw that a few of these were dummy bunkers. The Pakistan Army soldiers wanted to give the impression that their camp at Mogolhat had a higher number of soldiers than their actual strength.

The wireless operator sent a message in morse code to the Bn HQ in Cooch Behar: 'Mogolhat, stronghold of Pak Army, has been captured by Sri S.K. Mitra and company. Send trucks to retrieve Pak weapons and ammunitions.'

The message was relayed through the BSF DIG's office to higher offices. Asstt Comdt Mitra's company collected ammunitions of the calibre that they could use. The remaining weapons and ammunitions—rifles, bullets, machine guns, mortars and shells—filled two three-tonne trucks which were sent back to the Bn HQ in Cooch Behar.

Asstt Comdt Mitra would later learn that the confiscated weapons and ammo were displayed back at the Bn HQ. While the Indian and Bangladeshi forces marched forward, the Pakistan Army was using its radio station to spread misinformation about its gains. The display of the big haul was to reassure the locals that the Indian forces were successfully moving ahead.

While the trucks were being loaded, Asstt Comdt Mitra moved ahead with a smaller unit. He saw a young man in a lungi and T-shirt, who, spotting them, became uneasy. Asstt Comdt Mitra's right hand clasped the pistol stuck in its holster on his right side.

'Sir, I am not your enemy,' the man said. 'I have deserted the Pakistan Army. I can guide you.'

A Bengali Muslim soldier, he had deserted his unit in West Pakistan and made his way across India to his native village that was close by. After a brief exchange, Asstt Comdt Mitra decided to trust him.

They trudged on to Lalmonirhat, where there was sure to be a larger camp. A few companies could be there, perhaps a battalion. While moving forward, they spotted an LMG covering the road they were using to advance. A single soldier lay prone next to the mounted machine gun. There were two men usually assigned to each LMG, but here they could see only one.

They waited a little longer, but neither did the man move nor did he shoot at them. Asstt Comdt Mitra could see the magazine sticking out of the machine gun. He wondered aloud if it was a dummy as they edged forward to take a look.

A little movement but no firing.

Getting closer, they found the Pakistani soldier lying wounded beside the LMG. One of his legs had been blown off by an anti-personnel mine planted by his own army. Instead of rescuing him for medical attention, they decided to leave him there with the LMG and two magazines, to fight alone and stop the advance of the Indian and Bangladeshi forces. Writhing in agony, the man pleaded with Asstt Comdt Mitra to kill him. One of the junior officers confiscated his weapons and ammunitions, and Asstt Comdt Mitra sent two constables to find someone from the village who could take care of him till they could send him back to a POW camp.

The Pakistani soldier told them to expect more mines along the way since the Pakistan Army had fled farther inwards. True enough, Lalmonirhat turned out to be deserted. They had walked 10 kilometres from Mogolhat to Lalmonirhat slowly and cautiously, aware of the danger of anti-personnel mines all along the road. The Pakistan Army soldiers had used that time to retreat deeper.

The two constables returned with a doctor from Lalmonirhat, who was preparing to leave the area, as the exchange of fire was getting closer to the town. Asstt Comdt Mitra requested him to make the hospital functional. They had the wounded Pakistan Army soldier to take care of right away, but, as they moved further, there might be more casualties among the BSF men. Instead of sending them all the way back to Cooch Behar, Lalmonirhat would be much closer.

It was getting dark, and the doctor invited Asstt Comdt Mitra to stay at his house. But Asstt Comdt Mitra declined since his company would camp next to a bamboo grove and he couldn't opt for luxury while the rest roughed it out. The orders were to secure and hold Lalmonirhat for the next 2–3 days.

The BSF company had approached from the north and south of the Lalmonirhat airstrip (now a commercial airport), which was used by the PAF. With the war declared and its army on the backfoot, the PAF had long withdrawn its planes from there. Yet Asstt Comdt Mitra's company wanted to be sure and were prepared to damage the tarmac to prevent the PAF aircraft from landing there. The next morning, he sent a platoon and shelled the airstrip.

When orders came to proceed the next day, the BSF company marched ahead towards Rangpur, 35 kilometres away. The journey bore testimony to how bloody and gruesome the Pakistan Army's retreat was. There were fresh and decomposing corpses of civilians, including corpses of naked women.

The first river they crossed from Gitaldaha was the Dharla. The journey to Rangpur was going to take them across another river, the mighty Teesta. They covered 15 kilometres to Kaunia and halted there for the night. There was a rail and a road bridge to cross the Teesta. It was a large bridge standing on a giant span. The Pakistan Army had blown the span away and decommissioned the bridge.

It was up to Asstt Comdt Mitra's company to liberate the entire stretch along this axis to Rangpur from the Pakistan Army. The Indian Army had used another axis to head to Rangpur.

At Kaunia, Mitra commandeered an empty government school on the eastern bank of the Teesta as the company headquarters. From there, they could spot the Pakistan Army posts on the western bank. Mitra issued orders to dig trenches, make embankments and place MMGs to cover their flanks. He sent out area domination patrols to make sure no Pakistani commandos tried to attack the temporary company base.

The arrival of an Indian force, the BSF, brought out the jubilant townsfolk in Kaunia. When the Pakistani soldiers had started their retreat to Rangpur, the villagers had run for shelter. But Asstt Comdt Mitra told his men to be careful, since they did not know who the locals really were, and there were no Mukti Bahini fighters with them to distinguish friend from foe.

On the way to Kaunia, Asstt Comdt Mitra's company had also taken the help of locals to cover the rail track with dirt to make it motorable. The efficient BSF drivers used it to send supplies down to Kaunia. This route was used to deliver a battery of Post Group Artillery (PGA) to Kaunia to fire at the Pakistani soldiers across the Teesta.

* * *

Gen. Manekshaw ordered a ceasefire from 9 a.m. to 2 p.m. on 16 December. This would give Lt Gen. Aurora and Lt Gen. Niazi time to finalize the terms of the surrender in Dacca.

Around 11 a.m., Asstt Comdt Mitra and Sub-Inspector Bhadauria got out of their bunkers and began to check the Pakistani posts across the Teesta. The flash of sunlight against the binoculars attracted several rounds from a heavy machine gun. Both men dived into the trenches, binoculars swinging from their necks. The havaldar major sent out a cry for all to be alert.

'How many rounds do you have?' Asstt Comdt Mitra asked his company's inspector in charge of artillery.

'Around two hundred, sir.'

'Start firing.'

The Pakistani soldiers had been pounded for just under an hour when a white cloth mounted on a stick appeared at their post.

Surrender!

'Don't look at that, keep hammering them,' Mitra ordered.

The shelling resumed.

Dy Comdt J. Simon, who was the officiating commandant of 78 Bn, had got wind of the heavy shelling and arrived there. 'What the hell is happening here?'

'Sir, firing is happening here. Nothing wrong with it. They violated the ceasefire.'

'Very good. Keep at it.'

'Sir, you should head inside to safety.'

Soon after, the Pakistan Army stopped its shelling. The white flag appeared again. This time, an unarmed Pakistani officer appeared, furiously waving it. The Pakistani soldiers had blown up a portion of the bridge so that the BSF could not cross over. The man with the flag came to the riverbank. He wanted to negotiate. Mitra decided to personally go and talk to the Pakistan Army soldier.

'Mitra, have you gone mad? You stay here and send someone else,' Dy Comdt Simon said when he heard of it.

'Sorry, sir. I think they want to speak with the commanding officer. Besides, if I delegate someone else, he will have to keep coming back for my reply. If something happens to me, please go to my house and inform my family,' Asstt Comdt Mitra told him and went off to the Pakistani soldier.

'Are you Mitra Sa'ab?' the Pakistani officer asked him.

'Why?' replied Mitra, taken aback.

'Why won't you let us be? You have been chasing us since Mogolhat.'

'Yes, but what do you want now?'

'Sir, we are ready to surrender. What are your conditions?'

'There is no condition—I want an unconditional surrender. Any monkey business, and you will be shot at. All weapons will be surrendered here, and you cannot carry any weapons with you. If I find even a stray pistol, the person carrying it will be shot.'

Asstt Comdt Mitra told the Pakistani soldier that each boat would be loaded with a few people, and he would watch the loading from the BSF's side. When he would give the signal, the boats could cross over to their side.

'Okay, sir, we are ready to cross now.'

'No, you can only come when the government tells us to accept your surrender.'

But the Pakistani soldiers said they didn't want to wait. Asstt Comdt Mitra walked back to Dy Comdt Simon and told him that the Pakistanis wanted to surrender right away. Dy Comdt Simon informed his bosses while Asstt Comdt Mitra got busy with the preparations to accept the surrender.

The BSF personnel fanned out along their side of the riverbank, with machine guns and other weapons, to guard the entire perimeter. Word of the surrender had leaked to the village, and the villagers started to come close to the riverbank. They told Asstt Comdt Mitra to hand the Pakistani soldiers over to them. But he refused and told them to move from the riverbanks.

The boats started loading, and, one by one, ferried the Pakistani soldiers to the other side of the riverbank. The BSF personnel frisked each Pakistani soldier after they disembarked. After the final boat had arrived, they entered the details of each Pakistan Army soldier into a register. Mitra directed the BSF men to tie the Pakistanis soldiers' hands behind their backs and cover their eyes.

There was no place to hold the surrendered soldiers, and the crowd of villagers was swelling. For them, their county was already liberated, and they wanted revenge. Asstt Comdt Mitra requested Dy Comdt Simon to take custody of the Pakistan Army soldiers and transport them to the safety of the 78 Bn HQ in India.

The company's second-in-command went over to the other side with a few men on a boat. They collected all the weapons and got them back around twilight. They were laid out on the bank of the Teesta, and all details entered into a seizure register under the lights of lanterns and lamps arranged from the village. The process went on till late in the night, by which time two trucks arrived to carry the POWs away while the weapons were carted in jeeps, under security, back to the BOP.

A pain in his abdomen and a feeling of illness had been nagging Mitra for the last few days of the war, but he had been shrugging these off, keen to see the war through till the end. But that night, the pain became severe, and before dawn, a truck ferried him to the hospital in Lalmonirhat, where he arrived unconscious. When he regained consciousness, his head was in the lap of an elderly lady, who saw him wake up and called for the doctor, '*Ei, gyan firtase* [He is conscious again].'

It was the very hospital in Lalmonirhat that he had asked the doctor to reopen for wounded soldiers. From there, he was shifted to a hospital in Cooch Behar, but neither of the two hospitals could diagnose his ailment. He travelled down to Calcutta, where a doctor diagnosed him with jaundice—he had literally been fighting through the ailment the last few days of the war.

* * *

Asstt Comdt (retired as DIG) Samir Kumar Mitra was honoured with the Director General's Commendation Roll for his contribution in the 1971 Bangladesh liberation war.

'I feel proud to have been a part of the Bangladesh liberation war. A true borderman will always remain a borderman unto death,' he said in response to the award.

* * *

In the weeks leading to the declaration of war, another colleague of Mitra's from 78 Bn displayed great valour. On the night between 19 and 20 November 1971, Dy Comdt Inderjit Singh Uppal moved with two companies into East Pakistan through the Atialdanga border post. They moved into Andharijhar and engaged with the Pakistan Army, which was camped on the banks of the Torsa River, a tributary of the Brahmaputra.

The Pakistan Army position was heavily fortified with concrete bunkers, and they were armed with three-inch mortars and 105-mm artillery guns. Despite the heavy firepower and defences, Uppal and his men managed to secure the area up to Rayganj, cutting off the Pakistan Army base in Bhurungamari.

The main attacking party that breached the Pakistan Army camp was led by Uppal, who was killed during the engagement.

The following four personnel of 78 Bn BSF were posthumously honoured for the occupation of Rayganj:

Dy Comdt Inderjit Singh Uppal, Vir Chakra
Lance Naik Mohini Ranjan Chakravorty, Vir Chakra
Const. Kharka Prasad Pandey, Sena Medal
Const. Mukund Singh Negi, Sena Medal

26

The Road to Dacca

Lt Gen. Niazi's defence of East Pakistan banked on holding Dacca till international help arrived while Yahya Khan was focused on West Pakistan. He directed his divisions to withdraw to Dacca when the fighting got heavy and defend the capital till such help arrived. But there were no Chinese People's Liberation Army build-ups on India's north-eastern front, nor were there American ships trolling the Bay of Bengal.

The Pakistan Army troops in East Pakistan held out for as long as they could, and once the losses started mounting they withdrew to Dacca. In several places, by the time the Indian forces got there, the Pakistan Amy had vacated its position. Lt Gen. Niazi anticipated that the Indian Army's attack on Dacca would come from his west, that is, through West Bengal.

The combined Indian and Bangladeshi forces were called the Mitro Bahini (allied forces) and consisted of all the Indian forces—army and the BSF—as well as the Bangladeshi Forces—Mukti Bahini and the Niyomito (Regular) Bahini. The Mitro Bahini squeezed the Pakistan Army's defences from all sides.

The attacks from the west cut off the roads up to the Brahmaputra River to stall reinforcements from north Bengal, where the Mitro Bahini pushed south. In the east, Asstt Comdt Ghosh and the rest of 92 Bn were part of Kilo Force, which moved

from south Tripura, past the Feni and into Chittagong, liberating
it on 17 December. Other joint divisions moved from central
and north Tripura into the north-eastern sector of East Pakistan.
The Mitro Bahini, marching from Meghalaya in India, drove the
Pakistani force southwards to Dacca with ease.

* * *

The Pakistan Army troops kept withdrawing as its forces
concentrated to the west of East Pakistan, continuing to assume
that that was where the final thrust would come from. But the
surprise came from above.

In his book *Bullets of '71*,[54] scholar and Bangladeshi freedom
fighter Nuran Nabi has provided a vivid account of working as
an operative of the Kader Bahini—the guerrilla fighters operating
under Kader Siddiqi's leadership in Tangail district of Bangladesh
and adjoining areas. Siddiqi had appointed Nabi to coordinate
with Indian forces for arms supply to the Kader Bahini, which was
working deep inside East Pakistan in Tangail district.

Nabi visited Tura in Meghalaya thrice. The first two times
were in June and July 1971, when he secured arms for the Kader
Bahini. In August, Kader Siddiqi had himself crossed the border
through Dalu in Meghalaya, seeking shelter in India to recover
from injuries sustained during an encounter with the Pakistan
Army. He stayed for a month and built a good rapport with the
Indian Army officers, including Lt Gen. Jagjit Singh Aurora,
commander of the Indian Army's Eastern Command, and Brig.
Sant Singh, who had charge of the Indian Army's operations in
Meghalaya.

During Nabi's third visit, Lt Gen. J.S. Aurora flew down
to meet with him on 7 November. The general briefed Nabi
about the Indian Army's secret mission to seize Dacca from the
Pakistan Army.

After the meeting, Nabi was to return to Tangail. Indian military intelligence operatives would infiltrate East Pakistan soon afterwards and meet with Nabi, validating their identities by using secret passwords which were shared with him at the meeting with the general. The military intelligence operatives would stay in Tangail and identify landing sites in Tangail, where paratroopers of the Indian Army would be air-dropped. The Kader Bahini would have to secure a 10-mile radius around the landing sites by the end of November or early December.

* * *

On 20 November, the BSF battalions in Assam and Meghalaya vacated their posts with a few guards and entered East Pakistan with the Indian Army. Meanwhile, the BSF's 82 Bn went towards Kurigram, and 83 Bn moved towards Mymensingh district.[55] Battalions 84, 85, 86 and 87 moved into Sylhet and fought till the capture of Sylhet.

In October, 82 Bn had captured the East Pakistani territories east of the Brahmaputra. It was one of the few liberated zones, and the BSF kept the Pakistan Army out of that area. When the war began, 82 Bn crossed the Dharla River and occupied Kurigram on 6 December and held it.

In Sylhet district, Dy Comdt K.V. Uthaman, of 85 Bn, was directed to capture the Handatilla post with a company, armed with a 3-inch mortar and machine guns. The Pakistan Army responded with heavy shelling. The mortar and machine-gun sections drew most of the heavy shelling and had to withdraw, leaving behind the weapons. Dy Comdt Uthaman rallied his men and reorganized the attacking party into another formation. He led the company back and personally managed to get to the weapons. Combining firepower with the attack, the BSF troops were able to capture the post. From there, they advanced to a cement factory close by, which was the site of a Pakistan Army camp, and were able to capture that as well. Their final destination was Sylhet city, which they would capture and hold till the end of the war.

Battalions 84, 86 and 87 moved on another axis into Sylhet district. Asstt Comdt Lalthawma Lushai captured three Pakistan Army camps one after the other by outflanking them.

Asstt Comdt Shivaji Singh was faced with a difficult objective. On 3 December, the Indian Army directed him to clear two Pakistan Army camps in OP Hill and Kamla Bagan. Both were on elevated ground and heavily fortified. The Pakistan Army soldiers had built effective defences of well-placed machine-gun nests and rigged all approaches to the two posts with landmines. Asstt Comdt Singh and his company cleared both the posts and moved ahead for the next objectives.

Having defended Killapara at a terrible cost in May 1971, 83 Bn from Tura was directed to liberate the axis up to Mymensingh. Once that was done, Asstt Comdt Tyagi, who had defended Dalu and Killapara, led his company under Brig. Sant Singh's command to the Tangail airdrop rendezvous and then Dacca. Dy Comdt V.K. Gaur led the BSF and Mukti Bahini troops up to Mymensingh.

'Close the companies. Keep all the small items in the Bn HQ. Tomorrow, we are going in,' Brig. Sant Singh told Dy Comdt Gaur on 3 December. It was a sign that the war was here.

Dy Comdt Gaur went to each of the companies and moved every man to their company headquarters, retaining only a section in each of the BOPs.

The company at Baghmara was to march towards Durgapur and then to Mymensingh; the Mahendraganj company was to go to Jamalpur via Bakshiganj with the company at Mankachhar; and the two companies at Purakhasia and Dalu were to go to Haluaghat with Dy Comdt Gaur.

The Indian Army was going to attack first. The brigadier told Dy Comdt Gaur that his two BSF companies should wait on the right (west) side of the road, along with 500 Mukti Bahini fighters, and maintain radio silence. Once the Indian Army began the firing on the Pakistan Army positions, they would open communications and issue instructions to the BSF.

The Pakistan Army had planted mines in the area, but Dy Comdt Gaur's men navigated past them with the help of local residents, who had marked each mine in advance. Once his two companies reached the appointed position, Dy Comdt Gaur told Inspector Zail Singh to spread out for another three kilometres and set up ambushes so that they were not overrun.

Sometime later, the firing began between the two armies. The sound of the shelling got louder and the flashes of the explosions in the night became brighter as the battle drew closer. There was a small canal close by, along which Dy Comdt Gaur positioned his troops. But they did not fire their weapons because the Indian Army brigadier had told them to maintain radio silence till the army got in touch.

A little later, they heard the sound of approaching vehicles. They could not make out whether it was reinforcements for, or a retreat by, the Pakistani soldiers. Dy Comdt Gaur listened, his troops standing by in silence. He could make out that the LMG fire had subsided. If the LMG, a weapon with a limited range, was no longer in use, it meant that the two armies were no longer fighting at close range. Dy Comdt Gaur interpreted it as a withdrawal by the Pakistan Army.

Dy Comdt Gaur told his LMG sections that as soon as he fired a red flare, it was a signal for them to open fire at the approaching vehicles, and when he shot a green flare they should stop firing.

He did this twice when the vehicles got closer. The first round led to fifteen minutes of LMG fire, and then, after an interval, there was another round. The vehicles turned back without returning fire.

Around dawn, the civilians saw the Pakistani forces fleeing and informed the BSF. Dy Comdt Gaur shot off an encrypted message saying the that 'BSF has captured Haluaghat', which was the headquarters of a battalion of the Pakistan Army's Baloch Regiment. Brig. Sant Singh arrived there with his forces at around 9 a.m.

It was a terrible sight. The Pakistanis had dug hundreds of trenches and organized three lines of defences. Dy Comdt Gaur saw women's underwear strewn all over the place—something that other BSF men had seen elsewhere in East Pakistan.

A crowd of local civilians had gathered. They, too, saw the place. The Pakistanis had withdrawn. The civilians let loose their anger on those who were known to be pro-Pakistani. There was no police, and there was a lot of resentment against the non-Bengali Muslims who had been informing the Pakistani soldiers on the Mukti Bahini and pro-Bangladeshi people. Many of them had been helping the Pakistanis to kidnap women and girls. The locals were venting their frustration, built up over decades, on the pro-Pakistani people across the entire town in a bloody scene.

Dy Comdt Gaur called Hashim, the Mukti Bahini leader, and asked him to intervene. But it was difficult for Hashim to do that. Finally, Dy Comdt Gaur asked for a megaphone and made an announcement. 'I am declaring a curfew. If you don't disperse and go indoors, you will be shot.'

He told Hashim that if they had to deal with a law-and-order situation in Haluaghat, they would never reach Mymensingh or Dacca. The Indian Army and the Bangladeshi forces were moving fast, from several directions, to converge at Dacca. Hashim grabbed the megaphone and made a passionate plea to the locals to be patient and wait for justice. For the troops, moving ahead was the priority.

The BSF and Mukti Bahini went forward and captured two more positions that the Pakistanis had moved to. The first was at the banks of the Kangsa River, for which Dy Comdt Gaur took artillery support from the Indian Army. The first round of artillery fire dispersed the Pakistani troops from there.

The next town was Phulpur, twenty kilometres from Haluaghat, where they reached on 9 December. The Pakistan Army had heard of the troops advancing from the north and had already withdrawn. At Phulpur, Dy Comdt Gaur's troops found a Food Corporation of Pakistan godown. Gaur had a sentry break open the lock, asked the Mukti Bahini guerrillas to create a record and drew supplies from there. They could later pay back for the supplies by referring to the record. It was more efficient than having to source rations by traveling all the way back to the border. Both the BSF and the Mukti Bahini drew enough rations for themselves and had good meals.

The next day, Brig. Sant Singh reached Phulpur with Indian Army soldiers and saw well-fed forces ready for the next battle. He approached Dy Comdt Gaur and told him that the army's rations had been depleted.

'How much ration do you want, sir?' Dy Comdt Gaur asked.

'What can you give me?' Brig. Sant Singh replied.

'Sugar, rice, pulses.'

'That is a lot already!'

'Take what you need, as long as you sign for it.'

The next destination was Mymensingh city. On the way, there was a twenty-foot-deep river, which the combined forces had to cross. The Pakistan Army had blown the bridge up during their withdrawal, and there were not enough boats. But there was a brick kiln and huge pipes close by. They asked local villagers for help and began to dunk bricks on to the riverbed and push the pipes into it. Almost everyone pitched in. The villagers gave up and left a few times but were motivated to return and resume when the Mukti Bahini said that this was being done for the sake of their freedom. It was 8 p.m. by the time they could see bricks near the surface of the water. After another hour of piling bricks into the river, they were able to cross over at night and advanced forwards to Mymensingh.

The road from Phulpur enters Mymensingh through a bridge across the Brahmaputra–Jamuna. On 10 December, the combined forces arrived outside Mymensingh, which was a fortress of defence for a Pakistan Army brigade. They were on the eastern bank of the Jamuna. On the other bank, a huge crowd had gathered with flowers, garlands and loud chants of 'Joy Bangla'. It was an occasion of gaiety for the entire town. Some remained confined in their houses, all doors and windows shut tight, betraying their allegiance.

The combined forces headed to the circuit house, where the divisional commander of the Indian Army was to meet them. Women welcomed them in saris; Dy Comdt Gaur was surprised to see that they were not in burqas. He couldn't help blurting out, '*Aap log pardah nahin lagate* [Don't you conceal yourselves behind burqas in front of men]?'

Pat came the reply: '*Bhaiyon se purdah kyon daalein* [We don't need to conceal ourselves behind anything before our brothers].'

While the women garlanded the soldiers and Mukti Bahini fighters, Hashim arranged for another kind of garland. The walls of the circuit house were adorned with photos of Pakistan's founder, Muhammad Ali Jinnah, Gen. Yahya Khan and other military leaders. He hung garlands of shoes on those photos.

The Indian Army had taken many prisoners of war, who often came willingly to surrender to the BSF. An old man in a beard walked right up to Dy Comdt Gaur and asked to be shot. He was afraid of the vengeance of the Mukti Bahini and the majority, pro-Bangladesh civilians in the city. On the way, Dy Comdt Gaur had seen evidence of that vengeance: the havoc that the Bangladeshis had wreaked within just a week of victorious fighting. Dead and mutilated bodies lay everywhere—a response to the genocide perpetrated by the Pakistanis.

The locals had stalled a train at the Mymensingh station; it had come from Jamalpur and was en route to Dacca. But the occupants, mostly women, had locked themselves in. In East Pakistan, the Biharis dominated jobs in the Pakistani railways and had managed to load the train with their own people when the war broke out. They were off to Dacca, fleeing the wrath of the Mukti Bahini and vindictive Bengali civilians; they intended to escape to West Pakistan from Dacca.

Dy Comdt Gaur made his way to the train and demanded that the doors be opened. But the passengers refused, claiming that they were likely to be killed. He coaxed them to come out by guaranteeing their safety and then took them to a safe location, because the railway station was full of very angry Bangladeshis demanding blood.

That evening, Asstt Comdt B.S. Tyagi also reached Mymensingh using a different axis from Meghalaya. He returned late to the circuit house, and the only empty room he found was the one previously occupied by the Pakistan Army's sector commander.

Early next morning, an armed man of Afghani origin walked in and shook Asstt Comdt Tyagi awake. 'Hey there, get up! Where is the telephone? And ask the orderly to get some tea for me,' the man said in Punjabi.

Asstt Comdt Tyagi was quick to sense that this man was a Pakistan Army officer and replied to him in Punjabi, which he spoke fluently. He said that he would call for tea and asked the man to sit down. Another Indian Army officer, Vijay Singh, was also in the room. He casually asked the Afghani to keep his weapon on the table and sit down on the chair. Since the entire conversation took place in Punjabi, the Pathan, obviously a Pakistani officer, did not smell a rat. As soon as he set his weapon down, Asstt Comdt Tyagi jumped up, snatched it and announced that the Pakistani officer was under arrest.

Unaware that Mymensingh had fallen, the Pakistani officer had sneaked into the city and gone to the sector commander's room to report. Finding Asstt Comdt Tyagi there, he had thought that Tyagi was either the batman of the Pakistan Army commander or a junior officer. They searched the Pathan and found maps and documents, establishing that he was a commando with the Pakistani Special Services Group (SSG), which is responsible for covert operations. That made them conduct a more thorough search, and they found a small .22 pistol tucked into his boots, and cyanide capsules and blades concealed in its soles.

A few hours later, a Mukti Bahini squad came to meet with Brig. Sant Singh. The 75-kilometre stretch of road from Mymensingh to Kalihati (Tangail), via Madhupur and Ghatail, had been cleared by the Kader Bahini.

Brig. Sant Singh called for Dy Comdt Gaur and told him to remain in Mymensingh and hold it. The brigadier was moving ahead with his own company and with a BSF company led by Asstt Comdt Tyagi. They were headed for Kalihati to meet with the Kader Bahini and the Indian Army's paratroopers.

On 16 December 1971, the Indian Army knocked on Dacca's door with a letter offering the Pakistan Army a chance to negotiate a surrender. And the BSF continued to hold the positions that had been secured till the Bangladeshi government took over in 1972.

Epilogue

After the War

Four days after Lt Gen. Niazi surrendered to Lt Gen. Aurora, Yahya Khan resigned as the president of Pakistan and Zulfiqar Ali Bhutto took charge. It was the defeat of Pakistani forces, surrender of East Pakistan and the liberation of Bangladesh that had forced Yahya Khan to resign. The architect of Pakistan's fate was Mujib; it was perhaps a twist of irony that his designs ultimately put Bhutto in power in Pakistan.

By the time the war got over, Mujib had been moved from Mianwali prison in Pakistan and was being held under house arrest at an ISI safe house in Rawalpindi. A week after the surrender, President Bhutto came calling to meet the man whose struggle for East Pakistan's emancipation had made him the head of his country.

The Pakistan Army had arrested Mujib on the night between 25 and 26 March. They flew him to West Pakistan a few days later and interned him there. Mujib spent close to nine months in solitary confinement at Lyallpur jail. According to Raja Anar Khan, a retired Pakistani ISI spy, the ISI planted him in a cell next to Mujib as an undertrial prisoner.

A Pakistani military court sentenced Mujib to death for treason and sedition. He remained at the Lyallpur jail till the Indo–Pak war broke out and was shifted to the Mianwali prison. The transfer, according to Raja Anar Khan,[56] was in a prison vehicle stacked with pillows and quilts, so that nobody could identify the prisoners being transferred. Mujib was moved again to the ISI safe house in Rawalpindi when Pakistan lost the war.

The day Bhutto met with Mujib in December 1971, they were equals, but Bhutto had lost the war. Bhutto narrated[57] to Mujib what Yahya Khan had said when handing over charge of Pakistan to him: 'Mr Bhutto, I've created the greatest blunder of not killing Sheikh Mujibur Rahman.'

There had been multiple opportunities for doing that. For instance, there could've been an assassination attempt before or after the election. There was a failed bid to kill Mujib on the night between 25 and 26 March, before he was arrested. There was another opportunity, after the military court in Pakistan sentenced him to death by hanging. But Yahya had somehow not been able to pull it off.

The day he handed over power to Bhutto, Yahya Khan wanted revenge and asked Bhutto's permission to kill Mujib. But Yahya Khan and the Pakistani military had lost. Waiting in the wings to assume power, Bhutto had lost a war even before taking control of the country. They had surrendered, and to kill Mujib at that time would have been a huge international scandal. Besides, India held around 1,00,000 Pakistani POWs.

All through his incarceration, Mujib's jailers made sure that he never read the news and was not updated about developments of the liberation war. After it had lost the war, there was considerable international pressure on Pakistan to release Mujib.

On 8 January, the Pakistanis suddenly whisked off Mujib in an unmarked vehicle to the airport, from where he was flown on a special Pakistan International Airlines plane to London. There, he briefed the international press for the first time. The Indian government had arranged a plane to fly him back to South Asia—a brief stop at New Delhi before landing at Dacca. The Indian government tasked a diplomat with the job of escorting

Mujib from London. They had chosen Shashanka Banerjee, a diplomat who had been posted as political officer of the Indian deputy high commission in Dacca in 1962. Back then, Banerjee had met with Mujib and the *Daily Ittefaq* editor Manik Miyan on Christmas Eve, 1962. Banerjee had couriered to Nehru their letter asking for India's assistance.

Dacca

Joint assistant director of the G-branch in the Eastern Frontier, B.N. Chaturvedi was sent to cover the arrival of Mujib in Dacca on 10 January 1972. He was put up at the circuit house and went to the airport to receive Mujib. The landing of the plane drew cheers from the large crowd that had gathered, and the gusto amplified when Mujib appeared at the plane door and stood on the gangway waving at his supporters. He stood there soaking in his first taste of a liberated Bangladesh.

Next, Dy Comdt Chaturvedi headed to the Hindu locality in Dacca to see if they required any assistance from the BSF. On his way back to the circuit house in the evening, he stopped at a restaurant for dinner. Dy Comdt Chaturvedi was not of Bengali origin but had studied in Calcutta and had served for a long time in West Bengal, so he knew and spoke Bengali quite well. But his accent was unmistakable to the ears of the Bengalis. Dy Comdt Chaturvedi ordered his dinner and was eating when he noticed that three young men were watching him. They looked at him and whispered to each other. It rang a few alarm bells in his head. He drew some money from his wallet, placed it on the table and exited the restaurant.

He boarded a cycle rickshaw waiting outside and began his journey to the safety of the circuit house. They had moved about a kilometre when three men on bicycles rushed towards them, surrounded the cycle rickshaw and made it stop. They began shouting threats.

'*Shala Punjabi, mere dao* [Bloody Punjabi, kill him]!'

'*Yeh sala Punjabi, isko mar do* [Kill this bloody Punjabi]!'

The three youngsters had mistaken the native of Uttar Pradesh as a Punjabi from Pakistan, their former oppressors. In the days after the war, more gory details of murders and rapes of Bengalis committed by the Pakistanis had emerged. So the youngsters were out for blood.

'I might resemble a Punjabi from Pakistan, but I assure you I am not. I am an Indian and have come here to cover the arrival of Bangabandhu. How will it look if you kill me or harm me on the very day he has come back?' Dy Comdt Chaturvedi said. He drew on whatever persuasive skills he had to at least create doubt in their minds, and, finally, they let him go.

'*Theek aachey, choley jaan* [Okay, you can go].'

As the boys pedalled away, an autorickshaw turned a corner and drew closer to Dy Comdt Chaturvedi. He paid more than the agreed fare to the cycle rickshaw puller, jumped into the waiting autorickshaw and reached the circuit house in Dacca safe and sound.

The Roll of Honour

A year later, Asstt Comdt Ghosh was at the hospital in Belonia, Tripura. The chief medical officer, Dr Majumdar, had invited him for dinner. Mrs Majumdar had made quite a spread, and the three ended up chatting about the war. The topic turned to how the doctors had had to cope with the number of patients that came to the hospital. Whenever they heard the sound of shelling in the distance, they would be prepared to receive the casualties.

'Many of the patients who were injured during the liberation war have been cleared for discharge. They are all on their way home,' Dr Majumdar said.

Asstt Comdt Ghosh was reminded of the girl who nearly died during the Battle of Subhapur. The pathetic scene of her trying to cry and being only able to whimper had stayed with him for a long time. He asked after her and whether she made it.

Dr Majumdar wanted a description of the girl. Asstt Comdt Ghosh tried, as best he could, to recall. He described the injury, since he remembered that quite clearly. There was only one girl who had come to the hospital with such an injury.

'Would you like to see her to see if it is the same person?' asked Dr Majumdar.

'It will be difficult to recognize her, but I would appreciate it if I could meet with her in case it jogs my memory,' Asstt Comdt Ghosh said.

They headed to the hospital. They went past the gate, into the building and towards the ward. Ghosh was filled with anticipation. As he entered a ward, the doctor called out a name, and a girl sat up in her bed. A tube light at the far end was the only source of dull light. Asstt Comdt Ghosh could not make out her face. They went closer. Hearing of the arrival of the chief medical officer, some nurses came into the ward.

Dr Majumdar spoke to the girl while Ghosh tried to make out if it was the same one. But try as he might, he could not. He moved closer, so that his own face was illuminated as well. The girl turned and stared at Asstt Comdt Ghosh.

'Do you recognize this man?' Dr Majumdar asked.

A long pause.

She burst into a huge smile. 'He is the camp sahib [commander],' she replied.

That smile was the biggest medal of honour for Asstt Comdt Ghosh. He didn't need a photograph. The smile was etched in his memory forever.

War Memorial in Tripura

By January the war had ended, and it left a vacuum after nine months of fighting, shelling, black ops and victory. There was a complete lull at the border. The BOPs were no longer in the thick of fighting. The Mukti Bahini fighters had also vacated the camps. The personnel, including the company commanders, felt an emptiness.

Asstt Comdt Ghosh decided to propose a war memorial; it would keep his troops busy. Besides, he thought, the BSF, the Indian Army and the Mukti Bahini—all had suffered casualties. So a war memorial would be a fitting tribute to all who had fought.

Asstt Comdt Ghosh called for a *sainik sammelan*, an open meeting of all ranks of soldiers. He pitched the idea to build a war memorial and asked for suggestions as to what it should be. Everyone agreed, and the discussion began.

Three people stood up—one head constable and two constables. This was the MMG section at the pond at the Srinagar (Tripura) BOP that had been subjected to an entire Pakistan Army artillery battery and had made it out alive. The MMG detachment commander, the head constable, was a Nepali Christian; one of the two constables was a Muslim, Constable Rahman, and the other was a Hindu, Constable Ban Bihari Chakraborty—both were natives of Tripura.

'Before there is a war memorial, there should be a Kali temple at this camp,' said Rahman and the Nepali Christian head constable.

'Why a temple for Goddess Kali?' Ghosh's curiosity was piqued.

They narrated their experience of the day of the shelling. They had been cooped up in the bunker by the pond and had figured out quite early that the shells were meant for the MMG nest. Asstt Comdt Ghosh had not allowed them to leave the bunker because of the danger posed by splinters from the mortar shells exploding around them. They were shaken and feeling miserable. Chakraborty started to chant the name of Goddess Kali and advised the other two to do the same. Some pray to Goddess Kali as 'Rana Kali' (literally, Kali the goddess of war/battlefield). The three of them chanted together, and it kept them sane through the one hour of shelling that they endured.

The shells landed in the pond, on its marshy bank, on trees and were swallowed up by elephant grass, but none landed in their machine-gun nest. They believed that they had made it out alive because of their prayers to Rana Kali. Now, after the war had ended, they pitched the idea of a Rana Kali temple at the Srinagar BOP.

Asstt Comdt Ghosh smiled but stayed quiet. He had watched the scene that the gunners recounted at the Srinagar BOP unfold with his own eyes. The bunker was protected from small arms and machine-gun fire from the front with sandbags and bricks. But every time he had heard a shell whistling down on that position, his heart sank, as if it, too, was taking a swan dive from the sky towards the fortified machine gun nest. The corrugated iron sheets on the bunker would have yielded to the shelling. He looked again in the direction of the bunker and wondered how they were saved from the shells blowing away the flat, thin metal sheets that acted as a roof.

There had been a storm the previous night. The rain and wind had lashed against a bamboo grove that was next to the pond. The bamboo stems swayed in the wind, and then the rain had lashed against the bamboo trees, bending them at an angle till they formed a natural overhead cover to the bunkers.

The observation officer had probably corrected the mortar fire. There were close to fifteen shells that could have hit the tin roof. But the bamboo-grove roof had blocked them; the shells hit the bamboo trees and exploded there, keeping the three bordermen safe in their bunker.

Asstt Comdt Ghosh smiled to himself when others in the company got up and said that the goddess had truly saved these men and that a temple must be built to honour the goddess.

But there weren't enough funds in the company to build a temple. There was some material in the 'defence store' of the company—corrugated iron sheets and material from the dismantled bunkers used in wartime by the BSF and Indian Army.

Both Indian and Bangladeshi villagers learnt about this project. They offered their services to help with the construction. But there were neither bricks nor cement. The company commander spoke with the public works department, which supplied some spare material.

The Bangladeshi villagers were adept at building houses. They designed and built the temple with the help of Indian villagers in Srinagar.

On the day of the inauguration, in early 1972, villagers—Hindu and Muslim, Indian and Bangladeshi—thronged the BOP. A priest came from a nearby town to conduct the first official puja. Traders and artisans from both countries set up a festival on the border.

By that time, the Bangladeshi government was in power and had raised the Bangladesh Rifles—predecessor to the Border Guards Bangladesh (BGB)—to guard its borders. They were invited to the inauguration of the temple. A year later, they celebrated the first anniversary of the founding of the war memorial temple.

'People came and prayed, regardless of caste, creed and religion. I didn't realize its import at the time, but I know now that it was an important step for communal harmony. The temple still stands tall at the Srinagar BOP,' DIG (retd) P.K. Ghosh told the author fifty years after the temple was inaugurated.

The story of the war memorial's inauguration didn't end there. The Srinagar BOP in Tripura had become the fulcrum of the BSF and Mukti Bahini operations in the months leading up to the war.

Before the war, there was a thin strip of elephant grass separating the camp from the paddy fields in East Pakistan. Late on the evening of 31 March 1971, Asstt Comdt Ghosh's company had built a road that connected the BOP to the Dacca–Chittagong trunk road through the patch of elephant grass and paddy fields. It was used in the BSF's first black op to blow up the Subhapur road bridge. In the months to come, both the Mukti Bahini and the BSF would use it several times. Mukti Bahini guerrillas would refer to the patch of road as 'Captain Ali's Road', which was about half a kilometre long.

The last clandestine operation from Tripura, before the war, was Operation Winter Frost, in which the combined forces of the Indian Army, the Mukti Bahini and the BSF had claimed the Belonia Bulge. 'Captain Ali's Road' had proved useful then too to outflank the Pakistan Army's position.

Bangladeshi politicians were invited and went to the Srinagar BOP for the inauguration of the Rana Kali Mandir. They used 'Captain Ali's Road' to access the war memorial from Bangladesh and recognised it as a symbol of friendship between the BSF and Mukti Bahini, India and Bangladesh. Among the visiting Bangladesh politicians was Dr Amir Hussain, and he said that the patch of road should be officially given a name.

Ghosh pointed out that the patch of road would probably not survive. It wasn't an official passage between India and Bangladesh. Besides, it was fertile land, and farmers would claim it for the next season of paddy cultivation.

But Amir Hussain was adamant. 'We will name it Captain P.K. Ghosh Road,' he said.

Ghosh was amused. He burst into peals of laughter when he heard that the Awami League leaders wanted to name the road after him.

'If you, at all, have to name the road, then it must stand for something that has a connect with Indo–Bangladeshi friendship.

It must symbolize a deep connection with this liberation war that we have fought, for the creation of Bangladesh. If there is something or someone to remember, we must remember something that will make people think of these past nine months,' said Ghosh and suggested a name.

The Awami League leaders agreed as soon as they heard it. Another inauguration followed, and a sign was put up there bearing the legend:

'Captain Ali (Captain P.K. Ghosh) Road.'

Acknowledgements

In early November 1971, Rustamji sent a signal to one of his battalion commandants: 'BSF is making history.' This book is the first draft of that history, based on the archives of the BSF and extensive interviews with surviving BSF veterans of the 1971 Bangladesh liberation war.

I thank all of the personnel across the BSF's ranks who have contributed to this book. It is not possible to name each and every one, but I have mentioned the officers I interacted with as a reflection of the entire departments under them.

Director General (retd) Pankaj Singh (now deputy national security adviser) was on board with this project from day one, and gave me access to the BSF's records and retired officers and personnel. He wanted that the stories of the BSF's role in the liberation war should be told, and independently.

Krishna Rao, second-in-command, PRO, BSF, was the key resource behind the research for this book. It is easier to write about bravado and commitment during conflict, but Rao showed me what a soldier is off the battlefield. His discipline and commitment to his duty helped me attribute the same qualities to many of the BSF officers I was writing about. He has a razor-sharp memory, incisive analytical skills, and if he doesn't have an answer, he will find the person who does.

Both Rao and Dy Comdt Pathak have an infectious smile and constant enthusiasm, and I have not seen them buckle under pressure. Pathak works quietly, in the background, and I experienced the fruits of that labour several times.

DIG S.S. Guleria was a key resource person from the minute we met while he was in Kolkata. He reminded me of the editor I never had and was helpful in the most surprising ways, connecting me to his network of veterans and sharing his knowledge, which is deep. I met him again at the BSF Academy in Tekanpur, where he gave me great insights into the BSF.

Vizesh Rana, second-in-command, BSF, shared time, put me up and fed me while I interviewed his father, Leela Ram Rana, and arranged border visits near Siliguri. His family was extremely warm and even fed me one of the best Hilsa meals I have had outside of my parents' home.

Anil Rawat, second-in-command, BSF, runs a smooth ship at the Faculty of Studies of the BSF Academy in Tekanpur and was very helpful with sharing material from the archives there. He pored over every available file to make my job easier.

Tripura is one of the two Indian states that I had never visited before writing this book. DIG Saroj Kumar Singh was an excellent host and a great storyteller. Both he and Dy Comdt Sanjay Singhania facilitated my visits to the BOPs and Bn HQs across the state.

In one of those HQs, I was pleasantly surprised to bump into Mukesh Kumar, second-in-command, who authored the chapter on the liberation war in the BSF's official history book. A great writer and researcher within the BSF, he was able to fill in many blanks and provide leads.

The company commanders of Belonia and Srinagar located former constables who had served as commandos, so that I could interview them and also visit the border camps and checkposts that I have written about.

A number of retired officers shared their valuable time to me and invited me into their homes. They put up with long hours of grilling, which can be exhausting. That includes IG V.K. Gaur and IG B.N. Chaturvedi, both of whom are wonderful storytellers. A humble person, Gaur played down his own role while telling me of the bravado of other officers. He is an encyclopedia of the BSF's role in the 1971 war. Chaturvedi is a natural storyteller and made things easy for me.

Comdt P.K. Ghosh spent several hours over many days humouring my questions and travelling back in time, despite personal crises.

DIG S.K. Mitra is a stickler for facts and accuracy, and is blunt about it. He has served with many BSF officers and remembered the tiniest details about them which came in handy.

Khusro F. Rustamji's son, Cyrus Rustamji, and his biographer, P.V. Rajgopal (IPS), both took time to go through the manuscript and sent across helpful suggestions.

A big thanks to everyone at Penguin Random House India for getting me through the process. Milee Ashwarya has been there for me anytime I have reached out, and Elizabeth Kuruvilla was interested in commissioning this book the first time we sat down to discuss it. A special thanks to Vineet Gill for his most professional work and keen eye in editing the manuscript. A big thanks to Vijesh Kumar for the grunt work he puts in behind moving the titles.

Jayanti Ghosh, the daughter of former BSF IG, Eastern Frontier, Golak Bihari Majumdar, was most gracious with her time and memories from 1971. She recounted important facts that she learnt from her father, some of them during the liberation war and later, when she helped with his notes. She was also able to provide a glimpse into the reality of Bengal and India in 1971. Sadly, she passed away while this book was being prepared for publication.

Veteran journalist Manash Ghosh was kind in sharing insights from his reporting on the liberation movement and is one of the few civilians to have written about the BSF's role in Calcutta and West Bengal. He had a great bond with Golak Bihari Majumdar, which gave him exclusive access to information.

Nihar Ranjan Chakraborty was ninety-nine when I met him and could remember the approximate time of day along with the events he was recounting.

I am grateful that one of Bangladesh's foremost media consultants and fellow press freedom workers, Miraj Chowdhury, introduced me to documentary film-maker and mediaperson Kawser Mahmud. We shared geeky moments from our research on the Swadhin Bangla Betaar Kendra. He was kind enough to share transcripts of his interviews with Belal Mohammad for a documentary he is filming.

The writer and historian Sudeep Chakravarti has always been a great motivator for all my endeavours. For this book, he pointed me to some of the better books written on the 1971 war.

Ashima Sharma is a fantastic researcher and provided invaluable support to this book. Every time we have collaborated, she has amazed me with her depth and rigour.

Thanks to Saloni for adjusting our life around logistical challenges and helping with the manuscript.

My parents, Ashoke and Uma, took off much of the load from my personal life as I camped at their home to write this book. A double thanks to my mother, Uma Majumdar, who acted as a research assistant, helping me with translations and transcriptions of audio interviews.

A big thank you to Abhyuday and Ashavari, who have run several covert operations to get me where I am.

A number of friends have been extremely supportive while I worked on this book. Praveen Donthi put me up and put up with me during research trips. Satadru Mitra went beyond the regular tenets of friendship to support me. Dr Rajeev Dhavan and Aniruddha Bahal have always been a constant source of support and encouragement. Shantanu Guha Roy, Suman Chattopadhyay and Mohammad Ali are some of the journalist friends who always rush in to help when I ask for support.

Faith, Pattie, Tarun and Pavithra are my personal pillars of support. In Kolkata, my friends Gautam and Priyanka, Vicky and DP, Raja Sinha Roy, Soumik, Ronny Sen, Tanya Sen and Ayan Mitra made sure I was not always alone during the isolating process of writing. A big thank you to Seema Sondhi, who is a source of personal inspiration.

Frontier-Wise Details of BSF Casualties in the 1971 War

Frontier	Killed	Wounded	Missing	Total
Rajasthan & Gujarat	8	46	7	61
Punjab	50	156	105	311
Jammu	6	17	20	43
Kashmir	6	12	0	18
West Bengal	28	78	1	107
North-Eastern Frontier	27	83	0	110
Total	125	392	133	650

List of BSF Honours for the Liberation War

Padma Bhushan

1. Khusro Faramurz Rustamji, IP
2. Ashwini Kumar, IP

Param Vishisht Seva Medal

Golak Bihari Majumdar (first civilian to be awarded the PVSM)

Mahavir Chakra

Asstt Comdt Ram Krishna Wadhwa (posthumous)

Padma Shri

1. Brig. Bhuvan Chand Pande, IG, BSF Academy
2. P.R. Rajgopal, IG, G-branch

Ati Vishisht Seva Medal

Brig. Joginder Singh Sindhu, DIG, Bandipur

Vir Chakra

1. Lt Col Noel Gregory O'Connor
2. Dy Comdt Joginder Singh
3. Dy Comdt Inderjit Singh Uppal (posthumous)
4. Asstt Comdt Chandan Singh Chandel
5. Asstt Comdt Nafe Singh Dalal (posthumous)
6. Asstt Comdt Lalthawma Lushai
7. Sub-Inspector Ajit Singh
8. Head Constable Hari Singh
9. Head Constable Mohinder Singh (posthumous)
10. Naik Chanan Singh
11. Naik Umed Singh (posthumous)

In addition to these there were forty-six Sena Medals; forty-four mentions in dispatches; five Vishisht Seva Medals; forty-one Fire Services Medals for Gallantry; nine President's Police and Fire Services Medals for Distinguished Services; thirteen Police Medals for Meritorious Service; and 184 DG's commendations.

List of Interviewees

IG (retd) Dr G.P. Bhatnagar
IG (retd) B.N. Chaturvedi
IG (retd) Virendra Kumar Gaur
DIG (retd) Samir Kumar Mitra
DIG (retd) Leela Rama Rana
DIG (retd) H.C.S. Rawat
DIG (retd) Dharamveer Singh Dahiya
Comdt (retd) Parimal Kumar Ghosh
Comdt (retd) P.K. Chatterjee
Comdt (retd) Prithwish Kumar Halder
Comdt (retd) Roopak Ranjan Mitra
Comdt (retd) Sukhdev Choudhuri
Comdt (retd) Laxmi Narayan Saini
Dy Comdt (retd) NS Chaudhury
Head Constable (retd) Dulal Chandra Dey
Head Constable (retd) Nikhil Ghosh
Head Constable (retd) Kshetra Mohan Majumder
Head Constable (retd) Tapan Dey
Head Constable (retd) A.R. Rai
Head Constable (retd) Bimal Chandra Dutta
Jayanti Ghosh
Manash Ghosh
Nihar Ranjan Chakravarty

Notes

Prologue

1. Gary Jonathan Bass, *The Blood Telegram: Nixon, Kissinger, and a Forgotten Genocide* (New York: Alfred A. Knopf, 2013).
2. Ibid., p. 98.
3. Guru Saday Batabyal, *Politico Military Strategy of the Bangladesh Liberation War, 1971* (Oxfordshire: Routledge, 2021), pp. 153–54.
4. A.A.K. Niazi, *The Betrayal of East Pakistan* (New Delhi: Manohar,1998), pp. 53–54.
5. P.V. Rajgopal, *The British, the Bandits and the Bordermen: From the Diaries and Articles of K.F. Rustamji* (New Delhi: Wisdom Tree, 2009), p. 334.

Chapter 1: The Bloody Road to Bangladesh

6. Sashanka S. Banerjee, *India, Mujibur Rahman, Bangladesh Liberation and Pakistan* (California, USA: Createspace Independent Pub), 2011.
7. Muntassir Mamoon, *Bangabandhu Ki Bhabe Amader Swadhinota* (Bangladesh: Mowla Bros, 2014).
8. Chandrashekhar Dasgupta, *India and the Bangladesh Liberation War* (New Delhi: Juggernaut, 2021), pp. 40–2.
9. Ibid.

10. Lynn E. Smith, 'Oral History', audio interview of Michael Nicholson, Imperial War Museum, 2002, https://www.iwm.org.uk/collections/item/object/80022448

11. https://www.forbes.com/sites/worldviews/2012/05/21/1971-rapes-bangladesh-cannot-hide-history/?sh=46f18ea016df

Chapter 2: The First Plan

12. The speech and descriptions of events in Tripura are based on the author's interviews with DIG (retd) P.K. Ghosh.

13. Maj. M. Rafiqul Islam, *A Tale of Millions* (Bangladesh: Adeylebros, 1974).

14. A section, of ten or eleven soldiers, is the smallest unit of an army.

Chapter 4: Mission Sanction

15. P.V. Rajgopal, *The British, the Bandits and the Bordermen: From the Diaries and Articles of K.F. Rustamji* (New Delhi: Wisdom Tree, 2009).

16. Ibid.

Chapter 5: A Helpful Neighbour

17. Rajgopal, *The British, The Bandits and the Bordermen*, p. 302.

18. Ibid., p. 298.

19. Ibid., pp. 305–06.

20. Ibid., p. 306.

21. Sheelendra Kumar Singh, *Bangla Desh Documents, Vol. 1* (India: South Asia Books, 1999), p. 284.

Chapter 6: Mujibnagar

22. Brig. R.P. Singh, 'An Eyewitness Account of the Mujibnagar Government's Swearing-in Ceremony', *Daily Star*, 17 April 1971, https://www.thedailystar.net/opinion/news/eyewitness-account-the-mujibnagar-governments-swearing-ceremony-2078617

23. Rajgopal, P.V., *The British, the Bandits and the Bordermen* (Wisdom Tree, India) 2009, p 308

24. Rajgopal, *The British, the Bandits, the Bordermen*, p. 308.

25. Sheelendra Kumar Singh, *Bangla Desh Documents, Vol. 1* (India: South Asia Books, 1999), p. 281.

Chapter 7: The Diplomatic Switch

26. Rajgopal, p. 309.

27. Author's interview with Nihar Ranjan Chakravarty.

28. Rajgopal, p. 310.

Chapter 9: Prisoner of Covert War

29. The ECOs were commissioned to join the Indian Army during the 1962 Indo–China war and served during the 1965 Indo–Pakistan war.

Chapter 11: The Fall of the Subhapur Bridge

30. Maj. M. Rafiqul Islam, *A Tale of Millions* (Bangladesh: Adeylebros, 1974).

31. Ibid.

Chapter 13: Radio Revolution

32. Kawser Mahmud, video interview of Belal Mohammad.

Chapter 15: When Is Winter Coming?

33. Reginald Prentice, House of Commons Debate, 5 August 1971, vol.822,column1929,availableat:https://hansard.parliament.uk/Commons/1971-08-05/debates/f2911c59-381f-433d-8334-ac1e36f32a88/Adjournment(Summer)?highlight=east%20pakistan%20refugee#contribution-c8f39a88-b52d-4419-99a1-aafcbff13b1c; and at: https://api.parliament.uk/historic-hansard/commons/1971/aug/05/adjournment-summer-1

34. Ibid., column 1925.

35. Clare Hollingworth, 'War Spirit Grows on Trigger-Happy Pakistan Border', *Daily Telegraph* (London), 9 July 1971.

36. Clare Hollingworth, 'Indian State Swamped by Refugees', *Daily Telegraph* (London), 9 July 1971.

37. Rajgopal, p. 322.

38. Col Batabyal, p. 219.

Chapter 16: 'The BSF Is Making History'

39. Notes taken by Michael Barnes, MP, during 'War-on-Want Mission' to India and West Bengal in May 1971.

40. A.A.K. Niazi, *The Betrayal of East Pakistan* (New Delhi: Manohar, 1998), pp. 53–4.

41. *After Action Report-1971* (declassified), 20 Mountain Division, Indian Army, 'Preliminary Operations in East Pakistan', p. 10.

42. Noel Gregory O'Connor, *The Soldier Is Not Afraid: An Account of Operation Sikander, Bangladesh War 1971* (Bhopal: Allied Publishers, 1980).

Chapter 17: Capture of Bantara and Bee Stings in Khanpur

43. Major Agha H. Amin, *Interview with a Mujahid: Maj Gen Tajammal Hussain Malik* (Pakistan Defence Journal,

2001), available at https://www.academia.edu/42712544/
Major_General_tajammul_hussain_malik_Hero_of_Battle_
of_Hilli_and_twice_Coup_maker and https://defence.pk/
pdf/threads/interview-with-a-mujahid-maj-gen-tajammal-
hussain-malik-from-2001.663265/

44. 'After Action Report', 20 Mountain Division, p. 10.
45. Anirudh Deshpande (ed.), *Border Security Force: India's First
     Line of Defence* (New Delhi: Shipra Publications, 2015).

Chapter 19: Sabotaging Chengiz Khan

46. B. Raman, *The Kaoboys of R&AW: Down Memory Lane* (US:
     Lancer, 2013).
47. Nitin A. Gokhale, *R.N. Kao: Gentleman Spymaster* (New
     Delhi: Bloomsbury India, 2019).
48. P.V. Rajgopal, *The British, the Bandits and the Bordermen*
     (New Delhi: Wisdom Tree, 2009).
49. Virendra Kumar Gaur, *Yun Janma Bangladesh* (Hindi),
     (New Delhi: Samayik Prakashan, 2013).
50. Rajgopal, p. 332.

Chapter 22: G-Men

51. Author's interview with IG (retd) B.N. Chaturvedi.

Chapter 23: Home-Made Rockets

52. P.V. Rajgopal, *The British, the Bandits and the Bordermen*.

Chapter 24: Nothing's Quiet on the Western Frontier

53. Maj. Gen. Sukhwant Singh, *India's Wars Since Independence*
     (India: Lance, 2009).

Chapter 26: The Road to Dacca

54. Nuran Nabi, *Bullets of '71: A Freedom Fighter's Story* (Dhaka: Shahitya Prakash, 2012).

55. Details regarding the advance from Tura to Mymensingh are based on the author's interview with IG (retd) V.K. Gaur and the intelligence report of Asstt Comdt S.R. Ghosh (sector HQ in Shillong), p. 59 of file: BSF Archive/002.

Epilogue

56. Source: https://en.dailypakistan.com.pk/16-Dec-2022/raja-anar-khan-a-police-officer-who-spent-months-with-sheikh-mujib-ur-rahman-in-pakistani-jails-in-1971; https://www.youtube.com/watch?v=NoINiarhCS4&t=590s

57. Source: https://www.thedailystar.net/sites/default/files/upload-2014/gallery/pdf/bangabandhus-interview-full-version.pdf